The National Council for Cr _____
Sweden

Everyday Violence in Contemporary Sweden

Situational and Ecological Aspects

Per-Olof H Wikström

Research Division
Stockholm, January 1985

Report No 15

The National Swedish Council for Crime Prevention (Brottsförebyggande rådet) established 1974, is a government agency under the Ministry of Justice. The Council headed by a board of 20 persons appointed by the government and representing a wide range of important functions in the community. The Council has an office with a permanent staff.

The address is:
Brottsförebyggande rådet
Atlasmuren 1
S-113 21 STOCKHOLM, Sweden
Telephone: (Stockholm) 08-22 97 80

The Council publishes reports in Swedish and English. The Council also issues abstracts on crime and correction in Sweden.
This report can be ordered from
Liber Förlag
Kundtjänst
S-162 89 STOCKHOLM, Sweden

ISBN 91-38-08580-5
Omslag Förlagsateljén
Produktion AB Allmänna Förlaget
Tryck Gotab, Stockholm 1985

Contents

4

Foreword

This dissertation is a result of several years of research into the topic of crimes of violence. During that period several persons have made contributions through their encouragement, practical assistance and valuable comments. Some acknowledgements will be made here, while some will appear in the introduction (Chapter 1).

My supervisor has been Professor Knut Sveri, to whom I especially wish to express my thanks for the way in which he supported my research efforts from the very beginning.

At the university I also, in particular, wish to acknowledge Professor Carl-Gunnar Janson, from whom, among other things, I have learned much about methodology, and my colleague Marie Torstensson, with whom I have had many stimulating conversations over the years.

At the National Swedish Crime Prevention Council, where this dissertation was completed, I wish to thank the Director of the Council, Bo Svensson, and the head of the Research Division, Professor Torbjörn Thedéen, for affording me the opportunity to complete this work under as good financial and working conditions as possible. I am also grateful to the latter for valuable comments on parts of the dissertation.

At the Council I wish to thank too, all my colleagues, and, in particular my long-time friend Jan Andersson, for the pleasant and stimulating milieu in which I have worked.

Two persons have made significant contributions with regard to coding work. Johan Gåsste coded most of the data in the Big City Crime Study (see Introduction) and Kerstin Öhrnell, at the Council, measured distances and coded data of ward characteristics in the 21 Police Districts Study (see Introduction). To these two may be added Lars Dolmén, who helped me with some compilation of statistics in the final stage of this report.

Eva Anderson, at the Council, did a tremendous job transcribing the report. Without her professional and enthusiastic support this report would probably still not have been completed.

If I had chosen to dedicate this dissertation to anyone, it would surely have been to the girls in may family: Karin, Erika and Ellen. Partly because they are so significant a part of my life, partly because of their, so far, everlasting patience with all my late night and weekend work.

Several funds have sponsored the different research projects on which this dissertation is based. These projects are presented in the introduction (Chapter 1). Here I shall list them and the funds sponsoring each. When more than one fund is shown, they are listed in order of financial contribution.

Research Project	Funds
The Gävle Study	The Swedish Research Council for the Humanities and the Social Sciences
The 21 Police Districts Study	The National Council for Crime Prevention. The Scandinavian Research Council for Criminology
The Big City Crime Study	The National Police Board. The National Council for Crime Prevention
The Stockholm Violent Crime Study	The National Police Board

In addition to this it should be mentioned that the Project Metropolitan, from which the data of **the Cohort Study** is taken, operates on grants from **the Bank of Sweden Tercentenary Foundation**.

1   Introduction

Who beats who, where and when, and under what circumstances? This is what this dissertation is all about. Its subject is the phenomenon of violent crimes in contemporary Sweden from a situational and an ecological perspective. By violent crimes are meant unless otherwise stated, murder, manslaughter (including attempted) and assault (simple and aggravated).

The ecology of crime may simply be viewed as the branch of social ecology that studies criminal motivation and criminal events from a socio-ecological frame of reference. Situational analysis may in this context be regarded as a form of micro-ecology.

Social ecology – the study of man's relationship to his social and physical milieu – has been characterized by analysis carried out on the areal level in urban settings (see e.g. Janson, 1980; Timms, 1971). The ecologically oriented research into crime has followed the same lines. Of prime concern has been possible neighbourhood and situational effects on criminal motivation and crime occurrence.

Some researchers have remarked that ecology and epidemiology, regarded as methods, are barely distinguishable (Carlsson in SOU 1972:76 p. 16). Others have labelled social ecology as areal epidemiology – the geographical version of epidemiology (Baldwin & Bottoms, 1976:16). Epidemiology as research strategy focuses upon the distribution of phenomena in terms of time, place and persons, and its correlates (Lilienfeld & Lilienfeld, 1980).

Theoretically ecological research focuses upon cultural and structural influences on crime. Ecological analysis may be carried out at various levels (e.g. national, regional), but it seems to be in studies of local environments (e.g. cities and neighbourhoods) that structural and cultural influences on behaviour are best explored. It is often very difficult to find empirically adequate models of direct links between, for example, structural and cultural properties of regions and behaviour. As an example see the debate on the existence of a regional subculture of violence in the southern USA (Doerner, 1978a; Doerner, 1978b; Erlanger, 1976; Gastil, 1971; Hackney, 1979; Loftin & Hill, 1974; Smith & Parker, 1980).

One merit of the ecological and situational approach to the study of crime has been its empirical fruitfulness in generating theories of the social causes of crime. The early studies by the Chicagoans of the ecology of crime (e.g. Shaw & McKay, 1969) was very important for the development of social theories of criminal motivation. Many of the theories still of current interest, such as subcultural theories, or the form of social disorganization theory emphasizing social control, grow out from the early research into the ecology of crime (Kornhauser, 1978). Today the main theoretical and research interests within the ecological research tradition (or environmental criminology, as it has been called) are in the study, and explanation of environmental influences on crime occurrences (e.g. Brantingham & Brantinghamn, 1981).

Another merit of the ecological and situational approach is the comparatively high relevance for crime prevention measures this kind of research has had. One classical example, as recently described by Schlossman & Sedak (1983), is the efforts of Shaw and his associates in the Chicago-Area Project to influence the social milieu of so called Delinquency Areas in the direction of prevention. Other examples are the present strong interest in situationally directed crime prevention (e.g. Clarke & Mayhew, 1980) and the in many respects similar approach that stresses crime prevention through manipulation of the physical environment (e.g. Newman, 1972; Jeffery, 1977).

Situational aspects of violent crimes have been treated in a vast number of studies (e.g. Wolfgang, 1958; McClintock, 1963). More sparse are studies of the ecology of violent criminality, although there are some good examples of major research taking into consideration ecological aspects of violent crimes (e.g. Curtis, 1974). Efforts to jointly analyse situational and ecological aspects of violent crimes seem to be rare (e.g. Dunn, 1976).

In Sweden there have been only a few studies on the ecology of crime or that have encompassed ecological aspects of crime (e.g. Janson, 1953, 1971; SOU 1972:76 ch 2; Werner, 1964; Nilsson, 1984). None of these studies has focused upon the ecology of violent criminality.

1.1 An Overview of the Research Project, Its Parts and Data

The dissertation consists of several studies that I have made during the years 1978–1984. Their common feature is that they deal with violent criminality either from a situational and/or an ecological aspect. The exception is the cohort study described in Section 1.1.4 below.

In all but two of the studies I have used my own empirical material.

The exceptions are the already mentioned cohort study in which I was privileged to be allowed to use the data base of the Project Metropolitan (Dept. of Sociology, University of Stockholm) for my purposes, and a study of regional variations in violent crimes in which I used material collected by the National Health and Social Welfare Board and the Dept. of Sociology, University of Stockholm, in co-operation. In addition it should be acknowledged that in one of my studies I was enabled to add data from Nils Bejerot's needle-marks study (see Section 1.1.3).

Besides my own studies I have used some data on violent criminality that I have analysed while working as the secretary of an expert group and a working group evaluating, respectively, the experimental (Ds S 1982:2) and the permanent closing down on Saturdays of the state-owned liquor stores (Ds S 1984:8).

Some of the results and discussions appearing in the dissertation have been published in research reports and articles (Wikström, 1980; 1981a; 1981b; 1982; 1983a; 1983b; 1983c; 1984a), while some material is presented for the first time.

In schedule 1 I give an overview of the different studies and introduce the headings that I have attached to them. I shall refer to these headings later in the text when data from the respective studies are used. Thereafter I present the studies in greater detail in Sections 1.1.1 to 1.1.6.

In many ways the different researches that I have undertaken have grown out of each other. This is true, at least, of my three main studies, as will be evident from their presentation.

1.1.1 The Gävle Study

My first real study in the field of violent criminality was the Gävle Study. It was a study of all violent crimes reported to the police during the years 1968–1970 and 1973–1975 (N=989) in a medium-sized Swedish municipality with about 80,000 inhabitants – 60,000 living in the urban area.

The purpose of the study was to investigate victim-offender characteristics and the circumstances of the violent event. In the course of my work I became interested in ecological aspects of violence and made some preliminary efforts to include these aspects.

Gävle is a diversified city. It has a large harbour and military camp, many industries and schools of different kinds, several public service and administrative institutions. Many of its population and other characteristics closely resemble those of the whole of Sweden. Some authors have remarked that, although it would be wrong to describe any single place as typical of Swedish conditions, Gävle is at least well

13

Schedule 1

Name of study	Area and period of study. Number of studied crimes	Main subject of study	Main data used
The Gävle Study	Municipality of Gävle. 1968–1970 and 1973–1975 N = 989	Crime situation, Victim–offender relationship and characteristics	Police reports/investigation records, General Criminal Register, Social Files, Municipality and areal population and other statistics
The 21 Police Districts Study	21 police districts (56 municipalities) N = 5 889	Interurban variations, Intraurban variations, Urban-rural differences	Police reports/investigation records, Municipality and areal population and other data
The Big City Crime Study	The municipality of Stockholm. January–July 1982 N = 940	Intraurban variations, Victim-offender relationship and characteristics	Police reports/investigation records, Police Register, Local register of intravenous narcotic users, Data of scenes of illegal / antisocial activities, Municipality and areal population and other data
The Cohort Study	The Greater Stockholm Area. Cohort data 1953 – July 1979	Age at onset, distribution, persistence and specialization	Data about cohort members criminality and social background from the Project Metropolitan (University of Stockholm) data base
The Stockholm Violent Crime Study	The municipality of Stockholm 1978–1979	Preliminary effort to study violent crimes in a big city. Forerunner to the Big City Crime Study	Police reports (data stored on tapes)
The Regional Variations Study	The 70 A-regions of Sweden. 1978	Regional correlates of violent criminality with other social problems, unemployment, alcohol consumption and alcohol abuse	Official statistics for A-regions from a data base created by the National Health and Social Welfare Board and Dept. of Sociology, University of Stockholm

qualified to be characterized as not atypical (Trost & Lewin, 1978).

The data collected in the Gävle Study was taken from four sources. The **police reports** and **investigation records** of the 989 studied cases were carefully read and coded (see Appendix 1). A short summary of the violent event and the preceding circumstances was compiled. The addresses of the scenes of crime, victims resident and, if known, suspects resident were also tabulated.

Extracts from the **General Criminal Register** were made for all known offenders with a full and correct ID number. This register contains

14

essentially information regarding previous convictions with the major exception of those leading only to fines. No convictions before 1945 are included. The register comprises only persons aged 15–80 years. Further, those entered in the register who have not been recorded in the ten-year period following their last record are excluded from the register. A check of data concerning the whole of Sweden in 1975 and 1976 showed that about half of the convictions for crimes of assault and theft did not appear in the General Criminal Register (Wikström, 1980:13).

A better source of information on previous criminality was the Police Register containing the same information as the General Criminal Register but also, and most important, convictions leading only to fines. Information on previous criminality in the Big City Crime study has been taken from the Police Register (see Section 1.1.3). In the cohort study the data about criminality are taken from the Police Register (see Section 1.1.4).

For all known offenders a search through the **files of the local social authorities** was made. If the offender appeared in the files his or her file was picked out and coded. The information in the files contains primarily social security received, known alcohol and drug problems and known child welfare problems. Regarding the two latter items, measures taken by the social authorities are also recorded in the files. Only offenders who lived, or had lived, in the municipality of Gävle could appear in the Social Files since these are local, contrary to the General Criminal Register that is nationwide. This means that some offenders residing outside the municipality of Gävle may appear in the Social Files of other municipalities, but are coded in the study as not appearing. Of the 530 offenders searched for in the Social Files 15 % had a home address outside the municipality of Gävle. Yet one in seven (14 %) of these offenders was recorded in the local Social Files, indicating that some of the non-residents of Gävle had previously lived in the municipality of Gävle.

Population and other data on the areal level for the city of Gävle were collected from the statistical unit of the municipality.

The relationship between the first three of the four materials used is illustrated in Figure 1.

1.1.2 The 21 Police Districts Study

A natural next step in my research, as it occurred to me after completing the Gävle Study, was to make a comparative study of violent criminality in Swedish cities. One reason for such a study was that the official statistics show that the rates of reported violent crimes may vary markedly between municipalities of about the same size. Further, these differences in many instances have a stability over time. This is illustrated in Table 1 for medium-sized Swedish

15

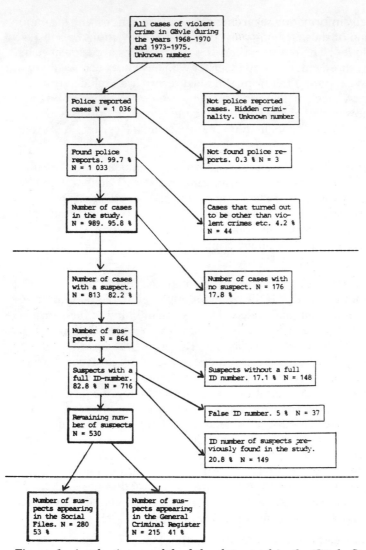

Figure 1. A selection model of the data used in the Gävle Study

municipalities. The rate differences are especially remarkable in the group of municipalities with 75,000–100,000 inhabitants.

A problem with the municipal statistics in judging intercity variations is that they encompass a varying degree of small places and rural areas. The concept of city has unfortunately been abolished officially in Sweden. Hence there are no official statistics of violent crime rates in cities for recent years. In the official statistics the concept of urban area (locality) is used, but no crime statistics are published for such units. Despite these inadequacies I decided that the differences between municipalities were large enough to justify a study of intercity variations.

Table 1. Reported violent crimes per 10,000 inhabitants in Swedish municipalities with a population between 75,000–140,000 in 1975. Figures for the years 1975–1979

Municipality	1975	1976	1977	1978	1979
100,000—140,000					
Uppsala*	34	34	42	44	37
Norrköping	30	25	32	29	26
Västerås	33	33	41	36	33
Örebro*	26	28	31	34	36
Linköping	27	27	27	29	23
Jönköping*	26	28	33	27	29
Borås*	35	35	38	33	29
Helsingborg	33	31	34	33	35
75,000—100,000					
Sundsvall	22	24	23	20	23
Eskilstuna*	42	33	35	35	33
Gävle*	20	23	27	27	20
Södertälje*	51	60	64	58	56
Umeå	46	41	38	41	28
Lund	30	32	35	35	31
Average for Sweden	27	26	29	28	28

Source: Statistiska meddelanden; R 1979: 7.1, R 1980: 5, and R 1980: 8.
*Figures for police districts marked with an asterisk may be affected by a change in the procedure for referring cases to municipalities that took place in 1978 (see SMR 1980: 8). However, this change has no great impact on the figures.

As a consequence of the official nonexistence of the concept of city in Sweden I had to make my own boundaries for the cities included. This was done by taking as starting point the old boundaries of the cities. These were then adjusted with regard to areas built after the abolishing of the city concept and decided upon in discussions with local people regarding what they felt were the "natural" bounds of the city.

Another aim of the 21 Police Districts Study was to extend the preliminary efforts to study intracity areal variations of violent criminality as was done in the Gävle Study. The unit of analysis chosen was the wards of the cities. The general strategy for this analysis was to treat all studied cities as one and find out general patterns of violent crime structure and its correlates.

Finally, I was interested in studying differences in the structure of violent criminality between urban and rural areas. There are reasons to assume that urban-rural differences in the violent crime structure would appear and that this would be of some importance for understanding the urban dimension of violent criminality.

To sum up, the 21 Police Districts Study had three purposes; to study A/ interurban variations, B/ intraurban variations, and C/ urban-rural differences in violent criminality.

Twenty-one police districts were chosen for the study. In 9 cases the police district boundaries coincided with those of a municipality and in the rest the police district covered more than one municipality. In all, 56 municipalities with altogether about 2,200,000 inhabitants corresponding to 27 % of the Swedish population were studied (see Table 2).

Table 2. Names of police districts and municipalities included in the 21 Police Districts Study. Numbers of inhabitants of the municipalities and police districts in 1978

Police districts	Municipalities	Inhabitants 1978	
Boden	Boden	28,752	36,076
	Jokkmokk	7,324	
Luleå	Luleå	67,180	67,180
Umeå	Umeå	78,827	
	Nordmaling	7,852	
	Vännäs	11,397	112,728
	Robertsfors	7,530	
	Vindeln	7,122	
Östersund	Östersund	55,403	
	Berg	8,916	
	Bräcke	9,276	111,976
	Krokom	13,231	
	Ragunda	7,645	
	Strömsund	17,505	
Sundsvall	Sundsvall	94,375	
	Timrå	18,904	126,782
	Ånge	13,503	
Gävle	Gävle	87,491	87,491
Uppsala	Uppsala	143,386	143,386
Västerås	Västerås	117,599	
	Hallstahammar	18,437	147,463
	Surahammar	11,427	
Södertälje	Södertälje	78,568	78,568
Eskilstuna	Eskilstuna	91,097	91,097
Falun	Falun	49,585	49,585
Sandviken	Sandviken	43,078	
	Hofors	13,797	63,387
	Ockelbo	6,512	
Karlstad	Karlstad	73,619	
	Forshaga	12,012	
	Grums	10,985	118,961
	Hammarö	11,460	
	Kil	10,885	
Örebro	Örebro	116,817	116,817

18

Police districts	Municipalities	Inhabitants 1978	
Norrköping	Norrköping	120,251	
	Finspång	25,044	165,321
	Söderköping	10,916	
	Valdemarsvik	9,110	
Linköping	Linköping	111,424	
	Kinda	10,608	139,195
	Ydre	4,282	
	Åtvidaberg	12,881	
Jönköping	Jönköping	108,179	108,179
Borås	Borås	103,387	103,387
Halmstad	Halmstad	75,290	
	Hylte	11,219	107,289
	Laholm	20,780	
Helsingborg	Helsingborg	101,046	
	Bjuv	14,662	137,768
	Höganäs	22,060	
Kalmar	Kalmar	52,751	
	Borgholm	10,944	
	Emmaboda	11,362	116,785
	Mörbylånga	12,297	
	Nybro	21,584	
	Torsås	7,847	

Total number of inhabitants in studied police districts: 2,229,421.

The investigation records of the crimes are filed in each police district, so police district became for practical reasons the sampling unit. The criteria for the choice of police districts are presented below.

The number of police districts to be included was determined by resources in time and money and by a somewhat arbitrary decision I made, that 20 police districts would be enough for a meaningful analysis of intercity variations. The combination of these two demands resulted in the exclusion of Sweden's three biggest cities. The reason was that the data collection for one such city would require too great resources to make it possible to cover 20 cities. However, I planned for and hoped to get future resources to study violent criminality in one of the big cities. This was also achieved (see Section 1.1.3 below).

After the decision to exclude the three big cities the selection procedure followed a stepwise pattern[1]. First I decided to include the police districts with the next ten biggest urban areas after those of the three big cities. The population of these urban areas varied between

[1]It should be stressed that the purpose of the selection was not to get a representative sample of violent crimes in Sweden, but essentially to include the vast majority of medium-sized cities.

19

65,000–100,000. The next ten police districts were chosen with two purposes in mind; first, to get a geographical spread over Sweden of the cities studied, and then to include at least five small cities (population of urban area below 40,000). Finally, I added one city (Södertälje) to the 20 already chosen for the special reason that it was a high-immigrant city located near Stockholm with a high violent crime rate (see Table 1) and was in the focus of interest at the time in the general debate concerning social problems and consequences of high immigration. Map 1 shows the location of the main urban areas of the studied police districts. The concentration of studied police districts to some parts of Sweden is a consequence of a higher population density and greater number of large urban areas in those parts.

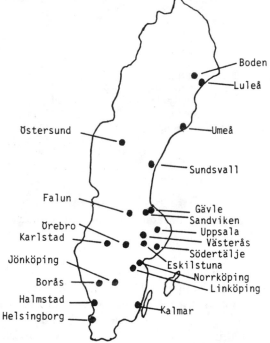

Map 1. Map showing the location of the main urban area of the studied police districts

The number of reported violent crimes in the studied police districts in the research year 1978[2] varied from 105 up to 626 (Table 3). In all, about 6,000 cases, or one fourth of all reported violent crimes in Sweden in 1978 were studied.

As shown in Table 3, not all of the violent crime reports were included in the study. The prime reason for the exclusion of some cases was that they turned out to be other than violent crimes when picked out

---

[2]Data from Södertälje were taken from the year 1979, but this is judged to be of no great importance for the results obtained.

Table 3. Number of reported violent crimes, of which coded crimes in the 21 studied police districts

Police district	Number of reported* violent crimes	Number of coded crimes
Boden	105	104
Luleå	160	156
Umeå	347	341
Östersund	160	159
Sundsvall	253	233
Gävle	213	208
Uppsala	626	574
Västerås	492	492
Södertälje	386	350
Eskilstuna	320	320
Falun	106	106
Sandviken	129	122
Karlstad	213	204
Örebro	392	392
Norrköping	384	367
Linköping	355	348
Jönköping	288	287
Borås	349	333
Halmstad	225	208
Helsingborg	377	364
Kalmar	226	221
Total	6,110	5,889

*Cases reported according to a data list obtained from the Data Unit of the National Police Board.

for coding. Other reasons were that it became clear during the investigation that no crime had been committed or that the file was missing or hade been borrowed by another police district at the time of the coding. It also happened that one violent event appeared in several reports. In these cases only one report was coded. Further, some reported crimes had occurred outside the police district, in some cases even outside Sweden.

The data of the 21 Police Districts Study were A/ **the police reports and the investigation records**, and B/ **statistics of population and other characteristics of municipalities and wards** collected from the statistical units of the local municipal authorities (Appendix 2). The code sheet used in the 21 Police District Study was largely the same as in the Gävle Study (Appendix 1). However, I excluded some of the more difficult-to-code variables, e.g. preceding actions and alcoholic intoxication. Variables like these require, for reasons of reliability, that the investigation records are intensely studied and that statements of offenders, victims and witnesses are carefully weighed against each other, which is a very time-consuming procedure. The average time taken by me to code one investigation record was for economical reasons shorter than in the Gävle Study, so I had to assign some priorities among the more difficult-to-code variables[3].

Besides coding the reports to the police and investigation records, I compiled the addresses of the offender, the victim and the scene of the crime, to make an ecological analysis possible. At a later stage, when data were collected, the distances between the offender's residence, victim's residence and scene of the crime for the addresses in the cities were measured on maps of the cities to enable studies of criminal mobility.

1.1.3   The Big City Crime Study

In the Big City Crime Study my trilogy of studies of violent criminality in Swedish cities was completed. To the data of violent criminality in medium-sized and smaller cities were thereby added data for Sweden's biggest city – Stockholm, perhaps the only Swedish city that in an international perspective would qualify as big city.

The Big City Crime Study was not only an investigation of violent crimes, but also included crimes of robbery, vandalism and residential burglary. Only data that are of relevance for the analysis of violent crimes will be reported here.

As opposed to the 21 Police Districts Study, in which all reported violent crimes during a single year were included, a sample of violent crimes reported during the first seven months of 1982 was taken in the Big City Crime Study[4]. Every third reported simple assault (N=799) and all reported cases of aggravated assault, murder and manslaughter, including attempted, (N=156) was sampled. Three cases of simple assault and eight of aggravated assault and murder/ manslaughter were excluded since, when coded, they turned out to be other crimes. Four cases in the category of aggravated assault and murder/manslaughter were missing. Hence 796 cases of simple assault and 144 of aggravated assault and murder/manslaughter were studied. In the analysis of all studied violent crimes simple assaults are weighted by three, giving a total of 2,532 violent crimes[4].

The sample of simple assaults was systematic, i.e. every third reported case was included. As a check on the adequacy of the sample a comparison was made with some data available for all reported cases of simple assault in the first seven months of 1982. These data were taken from a run I made of a data tape supplied by the Data Unit

---

[3] I spent between one and one and a half weeks in each police district working on the coding. In some districts this time was not enough and I had to assign more time to coding work.

[4] The reason for taking a sample were economical. Since parts both of the winter and summer period were included, the seasonal variations that occur between summer and winter are assumed not to significantly affect the result compared with a sample from a full year.

of the National Police Board. The compared variables were month, weekday and hour of the crime. 95 % confidence intervals were computed but in no instances were the differences significant (Table 4).

Table 4. A comparison of month, weekday and hour of simple assault in the first seven months of 1982 according to sample data and data for all reported cases. Per cent

	All cases %	Sample %
MONTH		
January	15	15
February	12	12
March	14	15
April	12	13
May	16	15
June	17	16
July	14	14
Total	100	100
WEEKDAY		
Monday	10	10
Tuesday	11	12
Wednesday	12	12
Thursday	12	14
Friday	21	21
Saturday	23	21
Sunday	12	10
Total	101	100
TIME		
24.00—03.59	26	26
04.00—07-59	3	3
08.00—11.59	5	6
12.00—15.59	12	10
16.00—19.59	21	23
20.00—23.59	33	33
Total	100	101

The Stockholm police district covers the municipality of Stockholm and that was the research district. The population of the municipality of Stockholm is about 650,000, that of the Greater Stockholm area about 1.4 millions. Some parts of the municipality of Stockholm have no "natural" demarcations from other parts of the Greater Stockholm Area, which causes some problems in the ecological analysis.

Several sources of data were used in the Big City Crime study. The **police reports** and **investigation records** were carefully read and coded. Addresses of the scenes of crime, the victims and the offenders were compiled. The distances between the addresses located in the municipality of Stockholm were measured on a map. The code sheet used was largely the same as in the 21 Police Districts Study (Appendix 1).

Contrary to my previous studies, most of the coding was done by another person than myself. I issued careful instructions and made some checks of the coding to ensure that it was done in the same way as by me.

From the **Police Register** (Section 1.1.1 above) information was gathered both about the offenders' and the victims' previous criminality. The recorded crimes were coded in nine categories (Table 5).

Table 5. Classifications of previous criminality according to chapters and paragraphs in the Swedish Penal Code and other Laws

Crime category	Definition*
Theft	Ch 8 § 1—4 and 7—9
Fraud	Ch 9 § 1—5 and 8—10
	Ch 10
	Ch 11
	Ch 14
	Ch 15 § 8—13
Vandalism	Ch 12
Robbery	Ch 8 § 5—6
Violent crimes	Ch 3 § 1—3 and 5—6
	Ch 6 § 1—2
	Ch 17 § 1
	Ch 21 § 7
Molestation, unlawful threats, intrusion etc	Ch 4 § 5—7
Traffic crimes	The Road Traffic Act**
Narcotic crimes	The Narcotic Drugs Ordinance
	The Narcotic Drugs Act
Other crimes	Other chapters and paragraphs in the Penal Code and other laws

*Chapters and paragraphs in the Penal Code unless otherwise stated.
**Offences against the Road Traffic Ordinance, such as speeding, are not included here or elsewhere.

Since violent crimes in this study have been defined as murder, manslaughter and assault, it should be pointed out that the definition of previous violent criminality is somewhat broader. The latter includes violence against officials, rape, and violence and threats to members of the armed services by other members of the armed services.

Professor Nils Bejerot kindly permitted me to use his **register of intravenous narcotic users** in order to see how many of the offenders and victims appeared in that register. Two types of information were collected from the register; a) if the offender/victim had a record during the year 1981 or first half of 1982, and b) if the offender/victim had a record at any time in the years 1979 – June 1982.

24

Bejerot's register consists of all arrestees in Stockholm. Needle-marks are used as indication of intravenous drug use. The method has been described by Bejerot (1975:59–72) and judged by him to be reliable for diagnosing intravenous drug use.

The purpose of including these data was a wish to see how many of the offenders and victims were or recently had been hard drug users and, especially, their involvement in cases of violent crime in the central parts of Stockholm.

To try to create an index of the occurence of **illegal and some other antisocial activities** in the wards of Stockholm, addresses of places known by the police where the following activities occurred with some regularity in the first half of 1982 were gathered through the local police authorities:

- Receiving of stolen goods
- Meeting place for alcoholics (outdoors)
- Place of illegal sale of alcohol
- Meeting place for drug addicts (outdoors)
- Place of illegal sale of narcotics
- Pad rooms
- Illegal gambling club
- Club for illegal alcohol sales
- Prostitution (apartments)

The information asked for was to be of the kind that the police knew of, or had grounded reasons to suspect, the occurrence of the activity. Of course the reliability of this information depends on the police's present knowledge of such activities and is likely to vary from one activity to another. As basis for creating a crude index of illegal and other antisocial activities in the wards, such information seemed fairly good or, at least, the best available.

Data about **population and other characteristics** for the wards of Stockholm was gathered mainly from the statistics bureau of the municipal authorities (USK) and the planning office of the regional authorities (Stockholms Läns Landstings Regionplanekontor) (see Appendix 2).

In figure 2 an outline of the structure of the Big City Crime Study is shown.

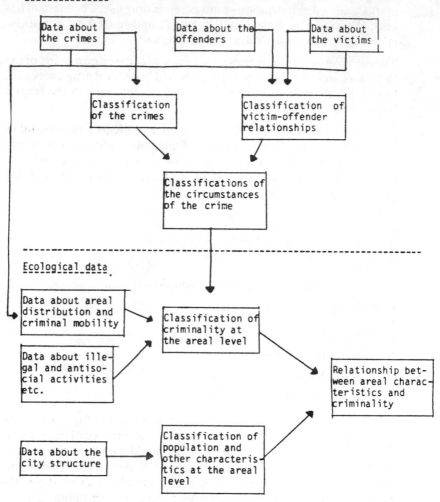

Figure 2. *An outline of the structure of the Big City Crime Study*

1.1.4 The Cohort Study

The Project Metropolitan is a longitudinal study of a 1953 birth cohort from the Greater Stockholm Area. The project and its data are described in "Project Metropolitan. A Presentation and Progress Report" by the director of the project, Professor Carl-Gunnar Janson (1984).

The Project Metropolitan birth cohort consists of all those born in the Greater Stockholm Area in 1953 who, resided in that area in 1963. In all, it comprises 15,117 individuals, both boys and girls. The data I have used cover the ages up to 25–26 years (July 1979).

26

When I first approached Project Metropolitan and asked for permission to work with the project's database I had in mind to make a study confined to the violent offenders of the birth cohort. However, as I worked with the material, I expanded my ambition to make a study of the patterns of criminality in a birth cohort. The focus was on age at onset, crime distribution, persistence and specialization. Here only results of relevance for violent criminality will be reported.

The data about the cohort members' criminality is taken mainly from the Police Register (Section 1.1.1 above). The Project Metropolitan crime classification consists of seven categories.

The contents of these categories are largely the same as in the classification of previous criminality that I used in the Big City Crime Study (Table 5). This is no coincidence, since I made that classification so that it would be comparable with the crime data from the Project Metropolitan. However, there is one important difference. In The Big City Crime Study classification of previous criminality I broke up the violent crime category of the Project Metropolitan crime classification into three; A) violent crimes, B) robbery and C) molestation, unlawful threats, intrusion, etc. Combined these three categories are equivalent to the Project Metropolitan violent crime category. This means also that the violent crime category of the Project Metropolitan crime classification is much broader than the definition of violent criminality given in the beginning of this chapter. However, crimes of assault will most likely be the dominating crimes in the category for the ages studied.

1.1.5   The Regional Variations Study

The Regional Variations Study of violent crime is based on data collected by the National Health and Social Welfare Board and the Dept. of Sociology, University of Stockholm, with the main purpose of studying alcohol related problems. The data are on the levels of provinces and A-regions. A-regions are units in the official statistics created to cover functional areas of major urban areas and their surroundings. Sweden is divided into 70 A-regions. Only data for A-regions was used.

The purpose of the Regional Variations Study was to explore the regional correlates of violent criminality with social problems, alcohol consumption, alcohol abuse and unemployment. All data are taken from various sources of official statistics and concern the year 1978 (the same year as was studied in the 21 Police Districts Study).

1.1.6 The Stockholm Violent Crime Study

The Stockholm Violent Crime Study may in some respects be regarded as a forerunner to the Big City Crime Study. It was an investigation of all reported cases of murder, manslaughter, assault, robbery, rape, molestation and bag-snatchings in 1978 and 1979 in the Stockholm police district (municipality).

The data used were those available on tapes at the Data Unit of the National Police Board. These data are taken from the information on the report sheet filled out when a crime is reported. The main information used was age, sex and nationality of the offender, general type of crime circumstances such as occurring indoors or outdoors, between acquaintances or strangers, time of crime commission and police areal code for area where the crime took place. The police areal codes were adjusted to the municipality's areal statistics to make some comparisons possible.

1.2 Plan of Parts and Chapters

The dissertation is organized in four main parts. In **Part 1** (Chapters 2 and 3) the focus will be on the problems caused by hidden criminality, since the results presented are based on police-recorded criminality.

In Chapter 2 factors thought to be of importance for a varying dark figure of different types of violent events, such as visibility, social distance of victim-offender and severity of the crime, are discussed. Clearance and offender representativity are other treated topics. The possibility of a spatially differing dark figure and clearance rate totally and for specific types of violent crimes is discussed in Chapter 3.

The **second part** (Chapters 4, 5 and 6) is concerned mainly with the questions; who beats who and under what circumstances? In Chapter 4 classifications of violent crimes, among other things, are discussed and criticized. A classification based on the participants' acts previous to the violent event is proposed, applied empirically and related to victim-offender characteristics.

In Chapter 5 the concern with the violent event continues. Some non-exclusive types of assault circumstances are discussed; e.g. foreigners' fights, assaults among addicts and criminals, and female victimizations.

Chapter 6 deviates from the previous two. Here results concerning violent criminality from a study of patterns of criminality – age at onset, crime distribution, persistence, specificity – in a birth cohort up to young adulthood are presented. A question raised is whether there are any "violent offenders".

In the **third part** (Chapters 7, 8, 9, 10, and 11) the ecological aspects – where and when – will be considered. Situational and ecological patterns are interrelated.

In Chapter 7 the focus is on temporal patterns of violent criminality. Chapter 8 presents a regional study of violent criminality in Sweden in relation to variations in other social problems, alcohol consumption, alcohol abuse and unemployment.

Urban-rural differences in rate and structure of violent criminality are the subject of Chapter 9. Interurban and intraurban variations in crime rate and structure in relation to city and ward characteristics are the theme of Chapter 10. This is followed by a special analysis of intraurban variations in Stockholm (Chapter 11). Altogether the violent criminality of 22 Swedish cities of varying size has been investigated.

The final and **fourth part** is devoted to a summary and discussion of some of the results presented.

Part 1

Recorded and Actual Crimes of Violence

The results presented in this dissertation are based on recorded crimes of violence. The problems of using police records for conclusions about actual crimes of violence are discussed in this Part.

Its main contents are as follows. First, the problems that may be caused by hidden criminality when using police records are defined in relation to the research objects. Second, a review is presented of Swedish research of relevance to the topic and an analysis of police records to throw some light on the problem. Third, on this basis two examples of hypothetical differential dark figures are formulated. Fourth, these examples are used in calculations to have some rough assessment of the effect of differential dark figures on crime, victim and offender descriptions. Finally, similar calculations are made with reference to areal variations in frequency and structure of crimes of violence.

Not all violent crimes are reported to the police and hence there is a dark figure[1] that is probably quite high as indicated by Swedish victim surveys (Lenke, 1978; Persson, 1977; SCB, 1981). However, this fact does not necessarily constitute a problem in research of this kind since no efforts are made to assess the actual number of violent crimes. Instead, it is differences in the structure of hidden and reported crimes that may cause problems. For example;

- if the dark figure varies for different categories of a variable, or

- if the dark figure for the category of one variable varies with the categories of another.

A constructed example of the latter case is shown in Table 6. Table 6A shows the fictitious actual frequencies of a cross-table of two variables. Table 6B shows the dark figures for the cell and marginal frequencies where the marginal frequencies have the same dark figure but the dark figures of the cell frequencies vary considerably. The resulting frequencies of recorded crimes are shown in Table 6C. Comparison of the actual and the recorded frequencies shows that, while there is no actual correlation of the variables (6A), the data of recorded crimes (6C) show a rather strong correlation.

There are good reasons to believe that there are differences in the numbers of hidden violent crimes of different sorts. I begin Chapter 2 by a discussion of the importance of a) severity of the crimes, b) social distance between victim-offender, and c) visibility of the crime, for variations in reporting violent crimes.

Differences in the structure of hidden and reported violent crimes may also, but not necessarily, affect the representativity of the

---

[1] I.e. the figure by which the recorded crimes should be multiplied to get the actual number of crimes.

Table 6. Constructed example of how combinations of variables with equal dark figures for all categories may cause biased relative frequencies of cells when the variables are combined

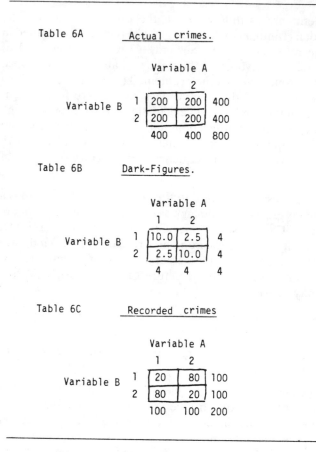

Table 6A   Actual crimes.

		Variable A		
		1	2	
Variable B	1	200	200	400
	2	200	200	400
		400	400	800

Table 6B   Dark-Figures.

		Variable A		
		1	2	
Variable B	1	10.0	2.5	4
	2	2.5	10.0	4
		4	4	4

Table 6C   Recorded crimes

		Variable A		
		1	2	
Variable B	1	20	80	100
	2	80	20	100
		100	100	200

recorded offenders. If offender characteristics of the studied variables vary between types of violent crimes with differing dark figures, this will be a source of error in the offender descriptions. For example, if the dark figure of assault in homes is greater than for crimes committed elsewhere, and females commit most of their violent acts in homes, this may contribute to an underestimation of the number of female violent offenders. (The same line of reasoning applies also to the victim descriptions.)

There is a proportion of the crimes where no suspect is found. If there is any selection as regards which offenders get caught and which don't, there will be another source of error in the description of the offenders. However, it should be stressed that only offender selections that affect values of studied variables produce a bias in the

34

results, an obvious but perhaps sometimes overlooked fact. The clearance of violent crimes (when an individual has been connected with the crime) will be discussed in Chapter 2.

Finally, in Chapter 3, I shall penetrate a topic of special relevance for the ecological parts of the dissertation, namely the possibility of a spatially varying dark figure and clearance rate and possible consequences of that for the results.

2 Variations in Dark Figure and Clearance of Different Types of Violent Events – a Discussion

2.1 The Structure of Hidden and Recorded Crimes of Violence

In discussing how violent crimes get recorded by the police it is the reporting behaviour of two kinds of actors that is of relevance; a) the victim, and b) the witness. In general, but not always, it might be assumed that the reporting propensity of the victim is greater than that of a witness. Further, in many cases there are no witnesses.

As mentioned in the introduction to this Part, there are three main factors that are often thought to be of importance for the reporting of a violent crime. The first of these factors – severity of crime – is likely to affect both the victim's and the witness's propensity to report the crime. The second factor – social distance between victim-offender – may at first sight appear to be of concern only for the victim's reporting propensity. But witnesses may be sensitive to a perceived social relationship between the participants in the violent event. Further, social distance may have a more direct relevance when the witness is a friend or relative of one or both of the victim and the offender. Finally, the third factor – visibility – is by definition only of importance for the witness's role in the reporting of violent crimes.

The discussion in this Chapter will take as main point of departure the results of Swedish victim surveys. In addition I have tried to get some information of relevance for the problem through the coding of who brought the recorded crimes to the attention of the police (21 Police Districts Study) and, which was possible before 1982 in cases of violent crimes on private premises, the percentages of victims who withdrew their charges (The Gävle Study).

The persons notifying the police of the crime have been classified in five categories; 1) the victim, 2) the police (cases when the police themselves detected the crime), 3) watchman/doorkeeper, 4) other official or person at work (e.g. doctor, restaurant employee, taxi-driver, etc), and 5) private persons. I have used few and broad categories to gain reliability instead of abundance of detail. However, it should be stated that this was a difficult variable to code. It was primarily through careful readings of the victims' and the witnesses' statements in the police investigations that this information was obtained.

The coding of who brought the crime to the attention of the police requires some comments. First, if the crime was reported at the police station, the person reporting the crime was coded. In cases when the police arrived at the scene of the crime, the person who called for the police was coded unless the violence was detected by the police during their patrolling. In cases when the victim specifically asked another person to call the police on his behalf, the victim was coded as the one notifying the police. In cases when the victim and another person independently contacted the police shortly after the event, preference is given to the victim in the coding.

Second, unreported violent crimes that came to the knowledge of the police during their investigation of another crime were coded in the police category. The reason for this was to include all cases of violent crimes reported as a result of police work (patrolling, investigation) in one category.

As expected, in most cases (two thirds) it was the victim who brought the crime to the attention of the police (Table 7). Of greater interest is to relate this to different characteristics of violent events, as will be done in Section 2.1.3.

Table 7. Who notified the police of the crime? Data from the 21 Police Districts Study

Notifier	N	%
The victim	3 795	67
The police	256	5
Watchman/doorkeeper	167	3
Other official/ person at work	414	7
Private person	1 024	18
Total	5 657	100
Missing data: 232		

2.1.1 Severity of Crime

The probably most important factor determining whether a violent crime will be reported is the severity of the crime. A safe assumption is that nearly all violent crimes in which a person is killed by another are recorded. For example, in cases of so called sudden death the police generally make investigations even if there is nothing initially pointing to commission of a crime.

In cases of severe injury not causing death of the victim there are several conditions that determine whether they come to the notice of the police even against the will of the victim (which happens); for example, when an ambulance is called to a place with a badly hurt person and there is a suspicion that a crime has been committed, the police are often informed by the organization which issued the alarm. However, far from all severe crimes are known by the police. In a study of 192 persons treated at a Stockholm hospital for knife wounds the authors (Blomqvist et al., 1980) report that 42 % of these cases were not known by the police[2].

Generally the victim's propensity to report a violent crime is greater in more severe than less severe cases, as shown in Swedish victim surveys (Persson, 1977:66; SCB, 1981:85)[3]. Respondents were asked whether they had been the victim of a violent crime during the last year and, if so, whether they had reported it to or contacted the police. In one of these studies (SCB, 1981) it is shown that 15 % of the victims subjected to violence not leading to any visible marks, and 27 % of the victims in cases resulting in visible marks, stated that they had contacted the police.

Excluding killings, the presented results indicate a monotone relationship between reporting propensity and severity of crime. This is also the conclusion drawn in the other mentioned victim survey (Persson, 1977). However, inclusion of killings makes it likely that the relationship between severity and cases known by the police has a curvilinear fashion[4].

2.1.2 Social Distance

A common hypothesis is that the better the victim and the offender know each other, the less is the victim's propensity to report a violent crime, or as it has been put: the propensity to report crime increases with the social distance between victim-offender (Persson, 1972:140).

It is, however, difficult to get any direct support for the social distance factor in Swedish victim surveys (Persson, 1977; Lenke, 1978; SCB,

---

[2] In a study from 1970 of 143 victims of violent crimes visiting casualty departments at Stockholm hospitals (Lenke, 1973), no relationship between reporting to the police and victims' injuries was found. However, the smallness of the sample and the fact that only 34 persons in the study had minor fractures or worse injuries make comparison of the percentage of reported cases of all categories of victim's injuries somewhat unreliable. Of all the 143 victims 42 (29 %) reported the crime to the police.

[3] It seems reasonable to assume that the same type of relationship also holds for witnesses of violent crimes, although their threshold for reporting is probably higher.

[4] This is of course related to the fact that other factors than reporting propensity come into play, i.e. the much greater efforts of the police to clear up the case when the victim is killed.

1981). But this is not to be expected, since victim surveys have proved to be of limited value for the study of violence among intimates (Persson, 1980:21).

If one is willing to accept that severity of crime is a crucial factor in the selection of what violent crimes come to the attention of the police, some indirect evidence of the social distance factor might be taken from data of recorded violent crimes.

It has been argued (Persson, 1972) that, since the proportion of crimes between acquaintances is higher in more severe than in less severe cases, this would indicate a lower propensity to report in cases between people who know each other. To be true, such a conclusion requires that there is no close relationship between injury to the victim and social distance between victim-offender.

In a study of convictions for violent crimes in Sweden 1975 (Kühlhorn, 1984) it is shown that there is a positive correlation between injury to victim and whether or not the crime was committed in an apartment. Since crimes between acquaintances dominate among crimes committed in apartments[5], and the opposite is true of crimes committed elsewhere, this might cast doubt on the assumption that there is no relationship between social distance and victim's injury. The author (p. 133) draws the conclusion that there is less possibility for others to intervene in a violent act that causes generally more severe injury to the victim in cases in apartments. However, another possible explanation is that it is a consequence of a lower propensity to report in cases of violence occurring among intimates; the threshold for reporting in relation to severity of crime may be higher. Another factor when using data of convictions which might also contribute to a correlation between injury to victim and crime occurring in apartments is the legal rule (before 1982) that it was required, in cases of assault on private premises, that the victim should report the crime before legal action could be taken. Exceptions from that rule were if the crime was aggravated or if the prosecutor judged it to be of "public concern" to prosecute. The latter was seldom done, as shown in some studies (Gerle-Holmström, 1968:16–17; Brodin, 1978:26). In a vast number of cases between intimates (see below) there was no report of the crime by the victim or the report was withdrawn. This means that these cases do not appear in data of convictions.

To further complicate the issue, however, it has been shown, not only in studies of reported crimes (convictions), that the victims in cases in apartments tend to be more severly injured, but also in one of the victim surveys (SCB, 1981). The authors of the latter study find this alarming since, as they say, the dark figure is higher in these than in

---

[5]Consequently also a positive correlation between acquaintanceship and severity of injury to victim is reported in the study.

other cases (p. 79). But at the same time they show that a much larger proportion of those victimized in apartments state that they have contacted the police than those victimized elsewhere. For example, of those subjected to violence leading to visible marks 55 % of those victimized in their own apartments as against 16 % of those victimized in streets and public places say they had contacted the police about the crime (p. 85). In cases with no marks the corresponding figures were 13 and 2 per cent respectively.

Consideration of other information in the victim survey indicates that it might be a highly selective sample of those victimized in apartments who have told the interviewer about it. Hence these data do not necessarily invalidate the hypothesis of the significance of social distance in reporting violent crimes.

Of those victimized in apartments about 90 % were women and the authors notes that a remarkably large number of them were singles with children (p. 68). This might be taken as an indication that it is mainly those who have separated from the person assaulting them who are willing to tell about it. This might also explain the high percentage of those victimized in apartments who say they have contacted the police about the violence. Of special interest in this connection is that the interviews in families with two adults were carried out with both parties (p. 35), which of course may have inhibited victims from telling about violent episodes if the other party is the offender and is present at the interview.

One may further speculate whether the assumed highly selective sample of persons victimized in apartments is not part of the explanation of the more severe injuries in these cases? It does not seem unlikely that it is in the group of those most badly injured that the greatest number of persons who have broken up their relationship with the assaulter is to be found.

A way to gain some information about the victims' reporting propensity in relation to social distance is to look at the percentage of cases in which the report of the crime was withdrawn by the victim or a charge by the victim was missing (in most cases the former). Such data from the Gävle Study are presented in Table 8.

Table 8. Percentage of cases in which the victims withdrew their report or a charge by the victim was missing, by victim-offender relationship. Data from the Gävle Study

Victim—offender relationship	%
Family*	50
Other acquaintance	23
Strangers	3

*Including fiancés and recently separated.

40

As is evident, the greater the social distance between victim-offender, the lower the percentage of cases with missing charge or withdrawn report. But these figures may be misleading since, as previously mentioned, it is only in cases on private premises that the victims have the option to withdraw their report[6]. Since most cases of violence between strangers occur in public places, many of these victims are unable to withdraw their report, as has been done by half of the victims in cases between acquaintances (mainly occurring on private premises). The question is, however, whether victims assaulted by strangers would withdraw their report if they had the same possibilities to do so as victims with an intimate relationship to the offender?

Although it is difficult to find any direct empirical proof for the social distance factor, it nevertheless seems to be a reasonable assumption from a common sense point of view. In some cases it is clearly so, e.g. violence of parents against small children. Where adults are concerned, psychological factors such as dependency, feelings of shame, etc, make it likely that it is generally harder to report a close acquaintance than a stranger for a violent crime. In relation to the severity of crime factor, it seems likely that the social distance factor has the greatest importance in less severe cases.

The evidence we finally end up with, maintaining the assumption that social distance is positively correlated to victim's reporting propensity, is partly based on common sense and partly on recognition of a possible bias in empirical data, showing in some instances that rather the opposite is true. From a scientific point of view this is hardly a satisfactory situation.

2.1.3   Visibility and the Role of Witnesses

There are to my knowledge no Swedish empirical data concerning witnesses' propensity to report crimes to the police. In the Swedish National Central Bureau of Statistics' victim survey from 1978 (SCB, 1981) respondents were asked whether they had witnessed a violent crime, but unfortunately not whether they had contacted the police about it.

International studies of spectators' willingness to intervene (e.g. contact the police) when confronted with crime show this propensity to be generally low (Clarke & Mayhew, 1980:9). It might be assumed that the propensity is somewhat higher for violent crimes, and especially for aggravated violent crimes, than for crime in general.

Although witnesses' propensity to report violent crimes to the police cannot be expected to be very high, their reporting behaviour might

---

[6]This legal option was abolished in 1982.

still be worthy of consideration since (as shown in Table 7) as many as one third of the crimes studied in the 21 Police Districts Study were brought to the attention of the police by another person than the victim or detected by the police themselves.

Concerning the witness's role in notifying the police, visibility of crime is one key factor. The place of occurrence may be regarded as a major indicator of visibility. Crimes taking place in apartments are for obvious reasons generally less visible than crimes occurring in most other places. This is reflected in data from the Big City Crime Study, showing that eyewitnesses were recorded in the police investigations in 30 % of the cases in apartments but in as many as 69 % of those occurring elsewhere. Probably these figures are an underestimate of the actual difference in the proportion of witnesses. There are often special circumstances where witnesses are present in violent crimes in apartments, as discussed below.

As mentioned in the previous section, there is a close relationship between place of crime and social distance between victim-offender. Hence there is a relationship between visibility of crime and social distance between victim-offender which makes it difficult to separate the effects of these two factors.

Just as social distance between victim-offender may be of importance for the victim's propensity to report a violent crime, the social distance between the witness, the victim and the offender may affect the witness's decision whether to report a violent crime. Evaluation of the importance of social distance for witnesses' reporting behaviour is a more complicated task than in the case of victims. There are many possible combinations of witnesses relationships with the victim and the offender, as illustrated in Figure 3.

It might be hypothesized that the witness's propensity to report is generally highest in case B and lowest in case C. Case A represents an ambivalent situation for the witness, while case D is a situation where the witness may have no feeling of involvement, but at the same time no emotional or other bonds to the participants restrain him from reporting the crime.

Visibility of crime (place of occurrence) interacts with different types of social distance relationships of the witness to the victim and the offender. In cases occurring in apartments it may be taken for granted that witnesses are generally acquainted with one or both of the victim and the offender.

According to police investigations, cases with witnesses of violence in apartments generally occur during parties, often heavy drinking parties. As further indicated by reading of the police investigations, the presence of a witness in these cases does not always increase the possibility of reporting of the crime. In a number of cases in which the victim has reported the crime, information given in the interrogations

42

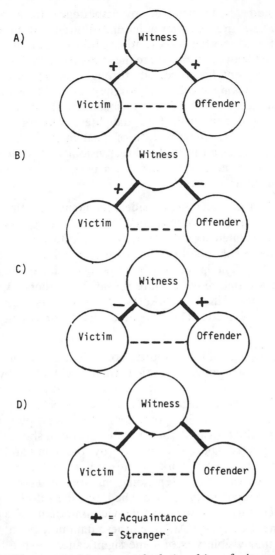

A)

B)

C)

D)

+ = Acquaintance
− = Stranger

Figure 3. Different combinations of relationships of witnesses to victim and offender in cases of violent crime

shows that witnesses have tried to talk the victim out of reporting the crime.

Although one should be careful in making statements not based on systematically analysed information, it may be of some interest to mention that it was apparent from reading the police investigations that, in most cases in which an eyewitness contacted the police, he was a friend or relative of the victim but not, or only a casual acquaintance, of the offender. These cases largely outnumbered the other social distance combinations.

43

Further, and also based on my experience from reading the investigations, there was an apparent difference between cases in apartments and at other places with regard to the number of cases in which persons not eyewitnesses to the crime contacted the police. For example a parent has revealed, through noticing injuries to her daughter and asking questions about the cause, that her daughter had been assaulted by the daughter's husband and the mother contacted the police against the will of her daughter. Another example, and probably the most common case of what might be referred to as crimes reported as a result of indirect visibility, is when neighbours hear screams or note other signs of a person being assaulted and therefore contact the police.

In violent crimes occurring outside apartments and their proximity there is a greater possibility that a witness is present and that witnesses unrelated to the victim and the offender see the crime. Further, the likelihood of persons witnessing violent crimes while at work is higher. The latter may be important, since persons at work witnessing a crime may be more prone than others to contact the police, e.g. watchmen, doorkeepers, taxi-drivers, restaurant and shop employees, etc. The policemen have, of course, a special position in this context[7].

Table 9 shows data of the proportion of violent crimes brought to the attention of the police by other than the victim by place of occurrence. As might be expected by reason of the previous discussion, this percentage is highest in cases occurring on streets. Despite cases occuring in appartments the lowest percentage is in crimes on public transport (bus, taxi, etc.) and in shops. This might seem unexpected, but is explained by the comparatively large proportion of persons at work victimized in these places. In as many as 80–90 % of the cases, depending on work category, it was the victim who contacted the police when assaulted during work. The lowest percentage of others than the victim notifying the police is in the apartment category. Although these data may be interpreted in the sense that visibility is of some significance for the bringing of crimes to the attention of the police, the results are far from being proof of that. For example, we do not know in how many cases, among those brought to the attention of the police by others than the victim, the victim at a later stage would anyway have contacted the police.

---

[7] It may be mentioned here that, while 30 % of the crimes in apartments reported by others than the victim were brought to the attention of the police by a person at work or the police detected the case themselves, this proportion was much higher (54 %) in cases occurring outside apartments (21 Police Districts Study).

Table 9. Percentage cases in which the crime was brought to the attention of the police by others than the victim, by place of occurrence. Number of cases in brackets. Data from 21 Police Districts Study

Place of occurrence	% cases in which other than victim contacted the police*	Order of ranking
Apartment/ proximity**	28 (2,194)	6
Street, square, park	40 (1,400)	1
Public transport	29 (180)	4—5
Restaurants etc	34 (1,163)	2
Shops, service institutions	29 (201)	4—5
Other places	32 (484)	3

*Including cases detected by the police.
**By proximity is meant cellar, staircase or garden.

In Table 10 the proportion of cases in which others than the victim notified the police is shown by severity of crime (presence of weapons[8]), visibility (place of occurrence) and victim-offender relationship.

The results show that other persons than the victim have a much greater role in bringing severe crimes to the attention of the police. This is true regardless of the place of occurrence and the victim-offender relationship, but the difference is greater in cases between acquaintances than strangers and in cases occurring in apartments than elsewhere. Note that the difference is greatest in the category of crimes between acquaintances in apartments.

This may partly be interpreted as a consequence of the fact that badly injured persons may be incapacitated from reporting due to their injury. Further, persons confronted with badly injured victims are likely to have a comparatively high propensity to report the crime or at least to call for medical assistance, e.g. an ambulance. In the latter case the police may be contacted by the medical personnel or the organization issuing the alarm.

With reference to visibility (place of occurrence), Table 10 shows that others than the victim have a greater role in notifying the police in cases occurring outside the apartments. This is true regardless of the victim-offender relationship, and severity of the crime.

Finally, others than the victim seem to have a slightly greater role in bringing violent crimes between acquaintances to the attention of the police but the difference is small.

[8] Presence of weapons was used as indicator of severity of crime, since types of injury to victims were not coded in the 21 Police Districts Study. The indicator has some inadequacies since victims may be badly injured without any use of weapons.

Table 10. Percentage of cases in which others than the victim contacted the police or the crime was detected by the police, by victim-offender relationship, place of occurrence and presence of weapons. Number of cases in brackets. Data from the 21 Police Districts Study

	Acquaintance		Strangers		
	No weapons	Weapons	No weapons	Weapons	
Apartments[1]/ Proximity area	25 % (1617)	49 % (331)	23 % (178)	– (36)	28 % (2162)
Other Place	37 % (1027)	58 % (157)	31 % (1898)	48 % (257)	35 % (3339)
	29 % (2644)	52 % (488)	26 % (2369)	43 % (293)	
	32 % (3132)		31 % (2369)		

[1] With proximity area is meant cellar, staircase or garden.

The results presented in Table 10 may, with due caution, be interpreted as indicating that visibility of crime, is a factor affecting the dark figure of violent crimes.

2.1.4 A Summary of Main Factors Causing a Differential Dark Figure of Violent Crimes

In Figure 4 I have, in a simplified model, summarized the discussion of factors thought to cause a differential dark figure of violent crimes.

According to the model, severity of crime is the most important factor affecting the dark figure. In aggravated cases, social distance between victim-offender and visibility of crime are hypothesized to have only a minor role in differentiating among these crimes as regards which are brought to the attention of the police.

In less severe cases, social distance between victim-offender is assumed to be the next important factor in causing a differential dark figure. Visibility of crime is hypothesized to be less important in the selection of which crimes between strangers will be known by the

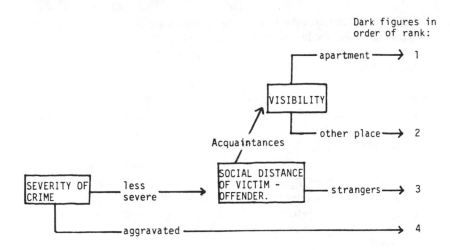

Figure 4. A summary model of the main factors causing a differential dark figure of violent crimes. Hypothetical order of ranking of dark figures

police, but to have a role in crimes between acquaintances; the combination of short social distance and low visibility produces the highest dark figure for violent crimes between acquaintances in apartments.

When describing the structure of violent crimes with police records by the variables severity of crime, victim-offender relationship and place of occurrence, there is, according to the previous discussion, an obvious need for correction for differential dark figures.

Had it been possible, with any precision, to assign values to the differential dark figures discussed, these might have been used throughout the study as correctives in the calculations based on the recorded crimes. Given the present state of knowledge, however, it would be somewhat hazardous to generally include such a correction in the results presented.

What can be done, besides acknowledging the deficiencies and trying to use the knowledge that exists in the interpretation of the results, is to give some not too unrealistic examples of the possible consequences of the existence of differential dark figures for the description of the structure of violent crimes.

The data available, excluding cases between acquaintances, suggests that the dark figure of less severe crimes is about twice as high as for aggravated crimes if a dichotomy is drawn between cases in which the violence resulted in no marks and, respectively, marks on the victim. If the term aggravated is restricted to crimes with severe wounds to the victim the sparse data that exist indicates a three-four times higher dark figure for the less severe crimes (see Section 2.1.1. above). I will use three times as a rough estimate of the difference in the number of hidden crimes between aggravated and other crimes in cases between strangers. In the data from the Big City Crime Study to be used as starting point for the calculations, cases in which the victim had minor fractures, bleeding or worse injury are counted as aggravated, while cases in which the victim had bruises or less injury are counted as less severe[9].

Taking cases between acquaintances into consideration the estimation of relative dark figures becomes an even more difficult task. The best thing to do seems to be to use different estimates. In the table below two examples to be used in the calculations are given. Needless to say, the assigned dark figures are arbitrary and, of course, most uncertain.

Table 11. Arbitrary set of dark figures for selected types of violent crimes to be used in calculations of the importance of differential dark figures. Two examples

| | Dark figures | |
	Example 1	Example 2
Aggravated crimes*	1	1
Less severe crimes, strangers	3	3
Less severe crimes, acquaintances, other places	4	6
Less severe crimes, acquaintances, apartments	5	10

*Note that it is differences in dark figures not absolute dark figures, that is the concern, which explains why aggravated cases have a dark figure of one.

The results from the calculations of the examples are shown together with the data of recorded crimes from the Big City Crime Study in Table 12.

---

[9] Note the rather low demands placed on a crime to qualify as aggravated compared to what is legally required.

Table 12. Distribution of violent crimes by severity of crime, victim-offender relationship and place of occurrence according to recorded crime (the Big City Crime Study) and two examples of calculations involving estimated differences in number of hidden crimes (see Table 11). Per cent. Orders of ranking in brackets

Crime characteristics	Police records		Calculations involving estimated differential dark figures			
			Example 1		Example 2	
Less severe, strangers, other place	29 %	(1)	39 %	(1)	23 %	(2)
Aggravated, strangers, other place	21 %	(2—3)	7 %	(4)	6 %	(4)
Less severe, acquaintances, apartments	21 %	(2—3)	36 %	(2)	54 %	(1)
Aggravated, acquaintances, apartments	14 %	(4)	5 %	(5)	4 %	(5)
Less severe, acquaintances, other place	6 %	(5)	8 %	(3)	10 %	(3)
Aggravated, acquaintances, other place	5 %	(6)	2 %	(7)	1 %	(7)
Less severe, strangers, apartments	3 %	(7)	3 %	(6)	2 %	(6)
Aggravated, strangers, apartments	1 %	(8)	0 %	(8)	0 %	(8)
	100 %		100 %		100 %	
	(N = 2 372)		(N = 6 895)		(N = 9 059)	

Note: Rather low demands compared to what is legally required have been placed on a crime to qualify as aggravated, i.e. minor fractures, bleeding or worse injury to the victim. Further, acquaintances here include all from family relationship to casual acquaintances.

The main conclusion from the discussion of differential dark figures is that description of the violent crime structure will be somewhat misleading if based on recorded crimes. The errors are likely to be in the direction of what has been shown in Table 12.

2.2 Offender and Victim Representativity. Clearance

In this section the representativity of the offenders and the victims will be discussed. The term clearance will be used for cases in which a suspect is identified, although the term clearance normally has a wider connotation for the police, e.g. includes cases in which the reported crime turned out not to be a crime.

There are several sources that might produce a selection of the recorded offenders. First, offender representativity (as victim representativity) may be affected if there are different offender (victim) characteristics in cases of violent crimes with differential dark figures. To get some ideas on this problem I will compare selected offender (victim) characteristics in recorded cases with the outcome if the presence of differential dark figures (according to examples 1 and 2 in Table 11) is considered.

Second, among the recorded violent crimes there might be a difference in offender characteristics between cleared and uncleared cases. Two ways to get information on this problem will be used: a) the estimation by victim and witnesses of selected offender characteristics in uncleared cases will be compared with the offender characteristics in cleared cases, b) a victim and crime characteristics of cleared and uncleared cases will be compared.

2.2.1 Differential Dark Figures and Offender Representativity

If offender characteristics of studied variables differ among violent crimes with differential dark figures, this will be a source of error in the overall description of the offenders based on police records.

To get some information about this possible bias, I have calculated selected offender characteristics when data have been weighted with hypothetical differential dark figures. If changes in offender characteristics appear compared to the original data of recorded offenders, this might be taken as an indication of the presence of bias due to differential dark figures. I have used the differential dark figures of the two examples given in Table 11 above in the calculations. The result is shown in Table 13.

No dramatic changes in offender characteristics appear when the possibility of differential dark figures is considered. What happens is that the proportion of young offenders and offenders committing crimes while part of a youth gang decreases. Further, there is some decrease in offenders committing crimes while at work. But the proportions of, female offenders, offenders of foreign nationality, unemployed offenders and offenders recorded for previous criminality are hardly affected by accounting for differential dark figures.

The conclusion most ready to hand seems to be that differential dark figures as a source of error in the offender description is no great problem. It will mainly produce some overestimation of young offenders in data of recorded offenders.

This conclusion rests, of course, on the assumption that the hypothetical differential dark figures are not too far from the actual differential dark figures and, most important, that they have the same direction as the actual ones.

Table 13. Data of selected characteristics of recorded offenders and two examples of the outcome when these data have been weighted by differential dark figures according to severity of crime, victim-offender relationship and place of occurrence (see Table 11 above). Data from the Big City Crime Study

Selected offender characteristics (%)	Recorded offenders	Calculations involving estimated differential dark figures	
		Example 1	Example 2
Female offenders	6	7	7
Offenders aged below 25 years	27	21	18
Offenders of foreign nationality	29	28	28
Unemployed offenders	21	19	20
Offenders recorded for previous criminality	57	57	57
Offenders in youth gang	9	7	5
Offenders at work	12	11	8

2.2.2 Differential Dark Figures and Victim Representativity

The same calculations as were made for offenders concerning the possible importance of differential dark figures have also been made for victims. The results are shown in Table 14.

Table 14. Data of selected victim characteristics in recorded crimes compared with two examples of the same data weighted by differential dark figures (see Table 11 above). Data from the Big City Crime Study

Selected victim characteristics (%)	Recorded victims	Calculations involving estimated differential dark figures	
		Example 1	Example 2
Female victims	36	47	55
Victims aged below 25 years	27	25	23
Victims of foreign nationality	20	21	22
Victims recorded for previous criminality	38	34	32
Victims in youth gang	3	2	2
Victims at work	9	9	7

Note: No data about victims' employment status were gathered in the Big City Crime Study.

The most notable change that occurs when considering differential dark figures is the increasing proportion of female victims. Data of recorded victims are then likely to underestimate the proportion of female victims. Further, as was also the case for the offenders, there is some overestimation of the number of young victims. The analysis indicates also some overestimation of victims previously recorded for crimes.

2.2.3 Clearance

The data of offenders concerns suspected offenders. Some of these may have been suspected on false grounds and then we have to account for a proportion of falsely accused offenders in the data. If there is any systematic selection with regard to offender characteristics, some offenders being suspected on less adequate grounds, this might be a source of error in the offender descriptions.

In a study of violent criminality in Stockholm in 1969 (Lenke, 1974) the author tried to explore this possibility through comparisons of the proportion of offenders with selected characteristics (previously punished, foreigners, aged 20–30 years) among those suspected and among those charged for the crimes. The comparisons were made separately for a group of crimes defined as peace-of-the-streets crimes and for other crimes (for definitions see Lenke, 1974:12). The result lends no support to the hypothesis that some types of offenders were suspected on less adequate grounds.

There is a proportion of reported violent crimes in which no suspect is identified. This proportion is, however, not as large for violent crimes as for many other types of crime, e.g. in the Big City Crime Study a suspect was missing in 25 % of the cases. In the Gävle Study the corresponding figure was 18 %.

If there is any selection with reference to offender characteristics concerning which offenders get caught and which don't, there will be a source of error in the offender descriptions.

One way to study this possible source of error is to compare recorded offender characteristics with offender characteristics estimated by victim and witness in uncleared cases. Three such offender characteristics were considered: sex, age and nationality of offender.

Nationality of offender was dropped, since further penetration of the data indicated that there was a marked selection of cases in which estimations of offender nationality were given: in the vast majority of the recorded cases the offender was of Swedish nationality, but in the uncleared cases only a small minority were estimated to be Swedish. The probable reason is that no estimates of nationality have been given in most cases when the offender was judged by victim and witness to be Swedish. But it would be risky to assume that all the offenders in uncleared cases with no estimation of nationality were Swedish. Therefore nationality of offender was not used in the comparisons.

The comparisons of sex of offender[10] showed that there were less female offenders in the uncleared (3 %) than in the cleared (7 %) cases. Sex may be regarded as a most reliable attribute to estimate and the result also seems reasonable from the point of view that it is crimes outside apartments that heavily dominate among the uncleared cases. A much higher proportion of female than male offenders commit their crimes in apartments. The conclusion will be that there is some overestimation of female offenders in data of recorded offenders.

More important differences occurred when comparing the offenders' ages (Table 15). There is a much higher proportion of young offenders in uncleared cases, which somewhat counteracts the previously indicated overestimation of young offenders due to more young offenders in cases with lower relative dark figures (see Section 2.2.1). Other Swedish research has also shown that offenders in uncleared cases have been estimated to be younger than in cleared cases (Lenke, 1974).

Table 15. Age of offender in cleared cases of violent crimes compared to age of offender estimated by victims and witnesses in uncleared cases. Data from the Big City Crime Study and the Gävle Study. Per cent

| The Big City Crime Study | | | The Gävle Study* | | |
Age	Cleared (%)	Uncleared (%)	Age	Cleared (%)	Uncleared (%)
0—10	0	0	0—19	17	31
11—20	13	30	20—29	39	33
21—30	34	39	30—	44	36
31—40	30	23			
41—	23	8		100	100
	100	100			
	N=1846	N=270		N=836	N=112

*Differences in age classes due to differential coding of victim/witness estimate of offender's age in the two studies. Number of cases refers to number of offenders and not to number of crimes as in the data from the Big City Crime Study.

---

[10] Data from the Big City Crime Study.

53

Comparisons of crime and victim characteristics in cleared and uncleared cases of violent crimes may give some information of relevance for the problem of possible differential clearance. Such a comparison is shown in Table 16.

Table 16. A comparison of victim and crime characteristics in cleared and uncleared cases of violent crimes. Data from the Big City Crime Study

Selected crime and victim characteristics (%)	Cleared	Uncleared
Friday–Saturday	39	49
20.00—03.59	55	67
In apartments	45	22
In street, square	17	29
Female victims	44	18
Victims below the age of 25	26	29
Victims of foreign nationality	21	15
Victims badly injured or killed*	6	7
Eyewitnesses	55	50

*All cases of killing were cleared; by badly injured is meant broken limbs or worse injury to the victim.

The main difference between the cleared and uncleared cases is that the latter tend to occur more often on Fridays-Saturdays and at nighttime, less often in apartments, and to involve female victims. This result is of course related to the fact that when a case between acquaintances is reported – which more often than other cases occurs in apartments and involves female victims – the victim will know who the offender is. These crimes may be regarded as cleared as soon as they are reported.

Further, the noted differences between cleared and uncleared cases with regard to the proportion of young and female offenders is consistent with the differences shown in crime and victim characteristics between cleared and uncleared cases. Young persons are less, and females more, involved as offenders in violent crimes in apartments than elsewhere, which then, at least partly, explains the higher proportion of young and lower proportion of female offenders in uncleared cases.

So far the bias in the overall offender descriptions has been discussed. A more complicated problem is the possible bias in comparisons of offender characteristics according to crime characteristics due to differential clearance. However, bias in the overall offender description need not necessarily mean that bias is present in descriptions of offender characteristics according to crime characteristics and vice versa.

54

First, it may be said that this problem is probably not too serious since the proportion of cases with missing offenders is relatively small. Second, if there is any bias, it is not generally likely to be of great magnitude because that would require both rather big differences in crime characteristics between cleared and uncleared cases and that such differences are accompanied by rather big differences in differential clearance by offender characteristics.

2.3 Differential Dark Figures and Differential Clearance as Sources of Error – a Summary of the Discussion

In Chapter 2 differential dark figures and differential clearance as sources of error when describing, for example, crime situations from police records have been discussed. The results presented and the conclusions drawn are far from definite. They should be looked upon as tentative.

In Table 17 the outcome of the discussions in the preceding sections is summarized. On the whole the problem of differential dark figures and differential clearance appears not to be a very serious one.

Table 17. A summary of the discussion of main sources of error and bias indicated in studied variables

Source of error	May produce bias in	Main bias indicated
Differential dark figures	a) Crime characteristics	See Table 12
	b) Overall offender description	Some overestimation of young offenders
	c) Overall victim description	Underestimation of female victims. Some overestimation of young victims and previously recorded victims
Differential clearance	a) Overall offender description	Some underestimation of young offenders
	b) Description of offender characteristics by crime characteristics	

55

3 Spatially Differing Dark Figures and Clearance

In the previous chapter differential dark figures and clearance were discussed from the point of view of possible errors in crime and offender (victim) descriptions based on recorded violent crimes. In this Chapter I shall direct attention to the reliability of data of spatial variations of recorded crimes of violence criminality because of their special importance for the ecological parts of this dissertation.

Several critics have pointed out that ecological research may be biased due to areal variations in clearance and hidden criminality. One early critic was Robison (1936) in her work "Can Delinquency be Measured?".

However, despite the long history of ecological studies not much research has been done in this field. The few studies that have been made indicate that data of recorded crimes generally give a fairly good picture of areal variations of criminality (Mawby, 1981).

When studying the ecology of crimes of violence there are three distributions to consider: a) crime distribution, b) victim distribution, and c) offender distribution.

3.1 Reliability of Areal Distribution of Recorded Violent Crimes

The problem that confronts us may be split up into two: First, errors in the areal variations of the frequency of violent crimes. Second, errors in areal variations of crime characteristics. The main source of these possible errors is areal variations in crime characteristics related to differential dark figures.

In the Stockholm Violent Crime Study (Wikström, 1981a) it was shown that the structure of violent crimes differed between inner- and outer-city areas. Not surprisingly, inner-city areas have a far greater proportion of violent crimes outside apartments than outer-city areas, and hence the reverse is true with regard to crimes in apartments.

On the basis of this result one would expect that the number of hidden violent crimes would be at least somewhat higher in outer- than in inner-city areas (see Section 2.1.4).

To test this hypothesis (using data from the Big City Crime Study), the proportion of violent crimes in inner- as compared to outer-city areas was calculated for data of recorded crimes and for these crimes weighted according to the two examples of differential dark figures previously used (see Table 11 in Chapter 2).

The result was as expected. While the proportion of violent crimes in inner-city areas using police records was 57 %, this proportion decreased when the calculations included the two examples of differential dark figures (52 % example 1, and 46 % example 2).

To further explore this source of error and to get some clearer indication of its magnitude, correlations were computed for the 130 areal units of the municipality of Stockholm using as variables a) the recorded violent crimes, b) two variables created where each areal observation of the original frequency-of-violence variable was weighted with hypothetical differential dark figures. For example, wards with only aggravated violent crimes would have the same frequency of the original variable and of the two variables involving estimated differential dark figures, while wards with a high frequency of less severe violent crimes between acquaintances in apartments would have much higher frequencies of the differential dark figure variables than of the original variable. The result is shown in Table 18.

Table 18. *Zero-order correlations of the areal frequency crimes of violence. Original recorded crimes and two examples weighted according to hypothetical differential dark figures (see Table 11 in Chapter 2). Data from the Big City Crime Study*

	Data series weighted with hypothetical differential dark figures	
	Example 1	Example 2
Recorded violent crimes	98	90

Note: Coefficients have been multiplied by 100.
N=130.

There is a very high correlation between the original data series and those weighted with differential dark figures. This may be taken as an encouragement for the use of data of recorded violent crimes to describe actual areal variations in crimes of violence. However, since there is some decrease in the magnitude of the correlation in the more extreme of the two examples (example 2), allowing for more extreme differential dark figures would probably lead to a further decrease in the correlation coefficient.

Inspection of the residuals for the 130 wards, predicting the original series from the series weighted with differential dark figures, showed for both equations that all of the highest negative residuals were found among the inner-city areas and especially those having the highest frequencies of the original variable, while the highest positive residuals were all found among the outer-city areas and especially those having the highest frequency of the original variable.

This means that the frequency of violent crimes in high frequency outer-city areas tends to be somewhat underestimated, while that in high frequency inner-city areas tends to be somewhat overestimated when comparisons are made between wards on the basis of police records. However, the overall errors are not large, as shown by the high correlation coefficients.

The next question to be considered is how large errors there will be when comparing crime characteristics of different wards? A simple indication of this may be the comparison of inner- and outer-city areas for the cases when differential dark figures are considered and when they are not (Table 19).

Table 19. A comparison of selected crime characteristics for inner- and outer-city areas. Data of recorded crimes and two examples when these data have been weighted with hypothetical differential dark figures. Data from the Big City Crime Study

| Crime characteristics | Order of ranking. Percentages in brackets | | | | | |
| | Inner–city areas | | | Outer–city areas | | |
	Rec.	Ex. 1	Ex. 2	Rec.	Ex. 1	Ex. 2
Less severe, strangers, other place	1 (40)	1 (49)	1 (38)	3 (14)	2 (15)	2 (9)
Aggravated, strangers, other place	2 (29)	3 (12)	4 (9)	4 (11)	5–6 (4)	5–6 (2)
Less severe, acquaintances, apartments	3 (11)	2 (22)	2 (35)	1 (35)	1 (59)	1 (73)
Aggravated, acquaintances, apartments	4 (7)	5 (3)	5–7 (2)	2 (23)	3–4 (8)	4 (5)
Less severe, acquaintances, other place	5 (6)	4 (10)	3 (12)	5 (6)	3–4 (8)	3 (7)
Aggravated, acquaintances, other place	6 (5)	6–7 (2)	5–7 (2)	6–7 (4)	7–8 (1)	7–8 (1)
Less severe, strangers, apartments	7 (2)	6–7 (2)	5–7 (2)	6–7 (4)	5–6 (4)	5–6 (2)
Aggravated, strangers, apartments	8 (0)	8 (0)	8 (0)	8 (3)	7–8 (1)	7–8 (1)
	(100)	(100)	(100)	(100)	(100)	(100)

Note: For definitions of crime characteristics see Table 12.

58

The results show that there will probably be some bias in a comparison of crime characteristics between wards of different types. For example, while the proportion of the dominating type of crime in outer-city areas – less severe cases between acquaintances in apartments – is likely to be markedly underestimated in police records, the same is not true for the dominating type of crime in inner-city areas – less severe cases between strangers outside apartments. Despite errors of this type, it is important to note that no radical change in terms of the order of ranking of crime characteristics is likely.

3.2 Reliability of Areal Distribution of Victims of Recorded Violent Crimes

Although the areal distribution of crimes and victims will differ, the reliability of the victim distribution may be regarded as dependent upon the same source of error as the crime distribution, since with a few exceptions a reported crime is accompanied by a recorded victim.

Table 20 shows the correlations between the victim distribution in the recorded cases correlated to the same data series weighted according to the two dark figure examples. As in the case of the crime distribution there are very high positive correlations.

Table 20. Zero-order correlations of the areal frequency of victims of violent crimes. Original recorded victims and two examples weighted according to hypothetical differential dark figures (see Table 11 in Chapter 2). Data from the Big City Crime Study

	Data series weighted with hypothetical differential dark figures	
	Example 1	Example 2
Recorded victims of violent crimes	96	92

Note: Coefficients have been multiplied by 100.
N= 130.

The Statistics Bureau of the Municipal Authorities of Stockholm has, for a division of the municipality into 16 areas, published victim survey data collected in the years 1978–1981 by the National Bureau of Statistics (USK, Utredningsrapport 1984:3). There is then some opportunity to compare areal variations of victims of violent crimes from victim survey data and data of victims of recorded crimes (Big City Crime Study).

However, there are several complications. First, the victim survey data are based on the years 1978–1981, while the data of victims of recorded crimes are from the first seven months of 1982. Second, the victim survey data cover both violence and threats of violence, while the data of recorded crimes include only the former. Third, as stated in Section 2.1.2, victim surveys are likely to miss most of the violence among intimates.

The first problem may not be too serious. The second may be. But there was not much I could do about it. The third problem I have tried to avoid to some degree by comparing the victim survey data only with the areal distribution of victims of recorded violent crimes between strangers.

To these problems may be added that the victim survey data are based on about 2,000 interviews[11], so there will be, on average, about 125 interviews in each of the 16 areas. This means that we have to expect quite high random variations in the percentages. Further, the data of recorded victimizations cover only victimizations that have occurred within the municipality of Stockholm.

The result of the comparison is shown in Table 21. Calculation of Spearman's rank correlation coefficient showed that the ranks were positively correlated ($r_{rang}=0.43$) but did not reach statistical significance at the 5 per cent level.

3.3   Reliability of the Areal Distribution of Offenders in Cases of Recorded Violent Crime

When considering the offender areal distribution, not only may the differential dark figures be a major source of error but also the differential clearance among areas.

Considering first the differential dark figures, using the same practice as in the case of the crime and the victim distribution (Table 22), it is found that the correlation of the original data series with the two weighted with differential dark figures is somewhat lower in comparison with the coefficients that resulted when the same calculations were made for the crime and the victim areal distribution. But still the correlations are to be regarded as high.

Errors in the recorded data of offender areal distribution will result if the areal distribution of the offenders in the uncleared cases differs a lot from that of the cleared cases. We have no specific information

---

[11] The number of cases used in the calculations was not given in the USK report, but it is stated that 500–600 interviews per year have been conducted in the municipality of Stockholm, which means about 2,000–2,400 interviews in four years.

60

Table 21. A comparison of the relative frequency of victims of violent crimes between victim survey data 1978–1981 and data from recorded crimes in the first seven months of 1982. Municipality of Stockholm

Area of Stockholm	Per cent of population victimized	Recorded victims of violent crimes between strangers per 1,000 inhabitants
Norrmalm, Gamla Stan	15	1.1
Östermalm	9	0.9
Kungsholmen	16	1.1
Södermalm	15	1.7
Brännkyrka	10	0.9
Enskede	5	0.6
Farsta	10	1.4
Hägersten	9	1.1
Skarpnäck	8	1.5
Skärholmen	16	1.4
Vantör	10	1.4
Bromma	16	1.1
Hässelby Spånga,	7	0.5
Kista	10	1.0
Vällingby	13	1.6
Västerled	10	0.0

Source: Victim survey data: Table 56, USK Utrednings-rapport 1984:3. Recorded crimes: The Big City Crime Study.
Note: It is only meaningful to compare the ranks and not the values of the figures, since victim survey data and data from recorded crimes cover different periods.

Table 22. Zero-order correlations of the areal frequency of offenders in cases of violent crime. Original recorded offenders and two examples weighted according to hypothetical differential dark figures (see Table 11 Chapter 2). Data from the Big City Crime Study

	Data series weighted with hypothetical differential dark figures	
	Example 1	Example 2
Recorded offenders in cases of violent crime	92	87

Note: Coefficients have been multiplied by 100.
N = 130.

about that. Some facts about clearance and areal distribution in general may, however, throw some light on the problem.

We know that when a case between acquaintances is reported, there is nearly always a known suspect. Further, many of these cases tend to be local, i.e. the offenders live in close proximity to the victim. We know also that crimes between acquaintances are much more common in outer-city areas. As a rule, in uncleared cases the victim and the offender are strangers, and these crimes more often occur in inner-city areas where it is likely that the offender has travelled a distance from his home address when committing the crime. So there might be, but not necessarily, some scope for differences in areal distribution of offenders in cleared and uncleared cases. But as stated before, in most cases there is a suspect. There have to be quite marked differences in areal distribution of offenders in cleared and uncleared cases before the overall areal distribution will be seriously affected by this source of error.

3.4   Conclusion

The efforts in Chapter 3 to make an analysis of possible bias in the areal distribution of recorded crimes of violence, victims of and offenders in cases crimes of violence, indicate that we might get a fairly good picture of the overall areal variations from data of recorded crimes. However, allowing for greater differential dark figures, or bringing in sources of errors not discussed here, might mean that other conclusions can be reached. The analysis is far from conclusive.

Part 2

Situational Aspects

Victim and Offender Characteristics

Violent Offenders in a Birth Cohort

The object of study in this dissertation was defined in the introduction as crimes of violence. But, of course, the interest is not primarily on why people break the law. It is rather on why people turn to violent actions.

Fortunately most violent actions are legally prohibited and hence there is a close overlap between the concepts of violent crimes and violent actions. It is only in case of self-defence, or as a part of their work, notably the police, that some people may under special circumstances legally use violence[1].

Some authors have stressed the importance of distinguishing between **legal** and **criminal** violence in the analysis of violence (McClintock, 1974; Kühlhorn, 1984). There is obviously a different background for the actors who use violence in these cases, but if one is to attempt to give a full picture of the use of violent actions it may be regarded as a shortcoming if cases of legal use of violence are not included. It is only in cases when persons think that a "legitimate user" of violence has exceeded the rules that the case might appear in studies of recorded crimes of violence.

It is not all types of violent criminal actions that will be the concern here. The focus is on what might be called **everyday violence**, a term used somewhat loosely to cover confrontations between people in their daily living excluding such violent acts as are carried out as part of stealing (robbery) or to commit a sexual offence (rape), although, as should be pointed out in this context, some crimes legally classified as assault, and included in the study, may essentially share many characteristics of rape and robbery, e.g. cases legally defined as assault and stealing instead of robbery. Further, it should be made explicit that the legal crime category "violence or threats against officials" is omitted, signifying that there will be an underestimation of assaults directed against officials in the data used.

Violent actions may be regarded as a special class of **aggressive response**. Aggression has been defined in a variety of ways. Authors have pointed out the great confusion that exists concerning the meaning of aggression (Fromm, 1976:12). Study of a selection of definitions of aggression used certainly confirms this view (e.g. Hilgard et al., 1975:337; Davies, 1970:613; Fromm, 1976:209; Dollard et al., 1939:11; Baron, 1977:7; Buss, 1961:1; van den Berghe, 1974:779; May, 1974:134; Lorenz, 1974:5; Cahoon, 1972:466).

To simplify the matter, definitions of aggression can be divided into two major classes according to whether aggression is mainly viewed as a drive or as a behaviour. An example of the former may be taken from Brenner's discussion of the concept of aggression in psychoanalysis, where he says that aggression is "... *an instinctual drive in man's*

---

[1]The handling of violent actions as part of a sport, e.g. boxing, presents a special problem in this context and will not be treated here.

mental life." and that there is conformity of opinion that *"... the aim of aggressive drive is 'destruction of the object'"* (Brenner, 1971, page 137 and 140).

Outside the psychoanalytical and ethological research traditions (see Lorenz, 1974) the most common definitions of aggression are behavioural. Restricting our attention to this type, there are still important differences between definitions. One major issue appears to be whether to exclude the subjects' intentions from or include them into the definition (Cahoon, 1972, is an example of the former position, and Davies, 1970, of the latter). Other issues concern the objects of aggression; whether to include animals (e.g. Buss, 1961), or both animals and property (e.g. Dollard et al., 1939), or restrict them, to human beings (e.g. Baron, 1977). Some authors even advocate the inclusion of the objects intentions into the definition of aggression (Baron, 1977). What all these authors, with one exception (Cahoon, 1972), agree upon is that aggression is to be defined as harmful to its object. So, minimally, there is agreement that aggression is a behaviour that is harmful to its object[2]. Further, it seems difficult to omit the subjects' intentions since then accidents will fall into the class of aggressive behaviour or, for example, attempted killing, where the killer fired at the victim and missed would fall outside the class of aggressive behaviour.

Some authors equate the concepts of aggression and violence (e.g. Davies, 1970), but here violence will be viewed as aggressive responses by physical means as distinguished from verbal attacks.

A problem when defining aggression in behavioural terms is how to treat the emotions often involved in aggressive acts. The concept of anger may be used for these emotions.

Since this is no study of psychological factors affecting the occurrence of violent actions, I shall not penetrate the issue further by, for example, discussing relationships between anger, aggression and violent actions. But some conceptual clarity seemed to be the minimum required before proceeding to discuss a major task of Part 2– exploring the situations in which violent actions occur.

There is no easy way to define a situation. The actors and the proximity milieu may be regarded as components of a situation. But since human perception is selective, each actor may have his own definition of the situation. This subjective **definition of a situation**, although an interesting aspect of the occurence of violence (e.g. Athens, 1974; Prus, 1978), is not possible to study with the kind of data we possess. Instead, some more objective description has to be used for exploring the circumstances in which the violent event occurred.

---

[2]In this context it may be mentioned that, e.g., for those having a view of aggression like Lorenz (1974), or May (1974), aggression is not always harmful.

One aspect of the circumstances is what might be referred to as a **structural aspect**. Exploration of victim-offender relationships in terms of sex, age, nationality, etc, might be regarded as an example of that. Such a description leaves out the actions of the victim and the offender preceding the violent event, so there will be a need to complement it with a study of **preceding actions**, e.g. verbal arguments, intervention, etc.

Some authors have tried to describe the violent event "action by action" (Shoham et al., 1975; Felson & Steadman, 1983), but such a description was judged to be too unreliable with regard to the data used here. Instead I shall describe the actions of the victim-offender confined to previous actions in broad categories in order to gain reliability rather than abundance of detail.

Structural descriptions of the violent event are static and cause no problem with regard to the point in time which should be described (i.e. the time of the violent event). Descriptions of preceding actions are of a sequential nature, there being a natural point in time to end the description (the violent act) but no such point in time when to start.

An aspect treated by Goldstein (1975) under the heading "The Role of Situational Factors in Violence" is **the motive of the offender**. Although interesting, just as is the actor's definition of the situation, the motive for the crime is a difficult aspect to study from police records since motives are of a private nature. Only the offender knows his motive and, if stated in the police investigations, it might not always be the true motive[3]. In cases of missing offender there is no source of information concerning the offender's motive, while victim and witnesses may give reliable information on victim-offender characteristics and relationships and actions preceding the violent event.

One of the best known studies in the field of crimes of violence is Wolfgang's research into criminal homicide in Philadelphia (Wolfgang, 1958). Wolfgang's strategy of analysis may be described as mainly structural. Different chapters are devoted to, e.g., race and sex differences, age differences, interpersonal relationships, etc. But there is also a special chapter on motives.

Wolfgang's analysis of the motives for criminal homicide well illustrates the great difficulties in exploring motives on the basis of data of recorded crimes. Wolfgang himself states that the motive"... refers to the ostensible and police record motive" and that "... several motives may be involved in the same homicidal act" (Wolfgang, 1958:187).

---

[3]Even greater difficulties appear if one is willing to accept the existence of subconscious motives.

A look at Wolfgang's classification of motives (Table 23) shows that there is likely to be some overlap; also that some classes rather describe circumstances than motives, e.g. domestic quarrels. The Wolfgang motive classification has also, with minor changes, been applied in another major US study of criminal homicide and aggravated assault (Curtis, 1974:66).

Table 23. Wolfgang's classification of motives of criminal homicides in Philadelphia. Per cent

	%
1. Altercation of relatively trivial origin; insult, curse, jostling etc.	35.0
2. Domestic quarrel	14.1
3. Jealousy	11.6
4. Altercation over money	10.5
5. Robbery	6.8
6. Revenge	5.3
7. Accidential	3.9
8. Self–defence	1.4
9. Halting of felon	1.2
10. Escaping arrest	1.0
11. Concealing birth	1.0
12. Other	3.4
13. Unknown	4.8

Source: Wolfgang (1958:191).

In Sweden, for example, Roes & Nordström (no year given), in a study of murders in 1957 and 1965, and Koch (no year given), in a study of assaults in Stockholm in 1966, have treated the motive aspect. In both these studies the motive classification has very little informational value since the principles of classification are very obscure, e.g. in Koch's study classes like "quarrel at youth club" and "severe alcohol damage" are given as motives.

In this dissertation no effort will be made to explore the motives for the violent action. Instead, I shall focus upon the circumstances of the violent event in terms of structural characteristics and preceding actions.

A well-known study of the circumstances of the violent event is that of McClintock (1963). The general strategy of McClintock's analysis, as it appears, was to start with a classification of the circumstances of the violent event and then to relate this to crime, victim and offender characteristics.

McClintock (1963:27-28) points to several problems of classification: the heterogeneous and complicated nature of the violent event, the difficulties in getting precise information concerning the circumstances and discrepancies between the offenders and their victims describing these circumstances, and, as for Wolfgang, the problem of getting information on the reason or the motive for the violence.

The six main classes of the McClintock classification are shown in Table 24. McClintock himself states that classes I and II are motive-based and given priority over the remainder that are said to be based on circumstances.

Just as in the case of Wolfgang's motive classification, there again appears to be some overlap, even if one takes into account that classes I and II are given priority over the rest. It seems possible, although perhaps not so common, that cases described in class III may occur, e.g., in public houses (class IV) or at public places (class V). Further, class II may equally well be characterized as based on circumstances (preceding actions) as on motives. It may finally be noted that class III appears to have victim-offender interpersonal relationship as a major defining variable, while classes IV and V obviously are defined according to place of occurrence. In this connection it may be mentioned that McClintock, in a later work, referred to the classification as primarily based "... on the overall situation in which the incident occurred and on the previous relationship of the parties involved" (McClintock, 1974:141).

Table 24. McClintock's classification of the circumstances of violent events in London. Per cent for the year 1960

		%
I.	Attacks in order to perpetrate a sexual offence	6.0
II.	Attacks on police officers or on civilians intervening to prevent crime or to apprehend a person who has committed a crime, or who is suspected of possessing an offensive weapon	12.1
III.	Attacks resulting from family disputes, quarrels between neighbours or between persons working together.	30.8
IV.	Attacks in or around public houses, cafés and other places of entertainment	19.7
V.	Attacks in thoroughfares and other public places	29.7
VI.	Attacks in special circumstances, including attacks on prison officers, injury resulting from criminal negligence, and attacks by persons of unsound mind	1.7

Source: McClintock (1963:33).

Focusing on Swedish research, excluding my own, two major empirical studies of violent events have been published to date. Lenke (1974) analysed violent crimes in Stockholm in 1969 in two broad categories mainly based on place of occurrence; peace-of-the-street crimes and other crimes. In a recently published study of convictions for violent crimes in Sweden in 1975 one major aim was to analyse the "... sequence of actions of the victim and the offender, i.e. the conflict situation" (Kühlhorn, 1984:53, my translation). After a detailed discussion of various conflict situations these are summarized in seven main classes of fundamental conflicts with subgroups (Table 25).

Table 25. Kühlhorn's classification of fundamental conflicts in cases of violent crime in Sweden. Only the seven main classes given. Data of convictions for violent crimes in Sweden in 1975. Per cent

Type of conflict	%
Partner crimes	13
Defamation	19
Personal territory	7
Conflicts of interest	8
Conflicts of authority	26
Not identified conflicts	21
Other	6

Source: Kühlhorn (1984:111).
Note: My translation. Wider definition of crimes of violence than in the present study.

According to Kühlhorn (1984:79) the classification was developed inductively. A priority scheme seems to have been applied in the classification. It is stated, for example, that conflicts thought to arise from strong emotions – partner crimes and defamation – were first considered. A look, e.g., at the special analysis made of partner crimes (p. 80–96) shows that some of the types of conflict mentioned may be regarded as equally well qualified, e.g., for the category conflicts of interest. The author points also to the fact that the demarcation between categories in some instances may be vague (p. 100).

There are several problems in drawing up a classification scheme that can be applied to data of recorded violent crimes, as illustrated by the review of selected classifications. I think the main issue is one of having a classification consisting of a small number of substantial classes, i.e. classes that grasp the essential variations in the circumstances of the violent event, and at the same time to have non-overlapping principles of classification.

Ideally, when exploring the relationship between types of circumstances and violent actions, we should start by collecting a sample of situations (which is, of course, hardly an easy task). Then, we should study with what frequency violent actions occur in different types of situations. Most research on this topic, including the present one, starts, so to speak, at the wrong end, with a sample of violent crimes where the frequency of different types of situations is calculated.

The obvious implication is that it is not valid to draw direct conclusions about the importance of different situations generating

70

violent actions from data based on a sample of violent crimes. Another way to put the problem is that, although our ultimate interest is in **situational determinants** of violent actions, what we actually are studying is the **phenomenology of violent events**.

Considering the present research orientation in the study of violent events, there seems to be a preoccupation with specialized problem areas, e.g. family violence, sports violence, youth violence, child abuse, street violence, etc. Further more, notably in the field of family violence, there is also a tendency to develop specific explanations of violent actions. Even within such a limited area of research as family violence there are authors who claim the advantage of explaining wife-assaults separately from other forms of violence in the family (Dobash & Dobash, 1981).

Although specialization has its benefits, the risk seems to be to get lost in a too narrow perspective of violent actions, ignoring the similarities and differences that might exist between different types of violent action. Along with the specialized studies, there seems to be a need for a more general perspective on violent actions, in its own right, but also to serve as a frame of reference, in which findings from specialized studies can be placed. In this context I believe that the development of classifications of violent events that are empirically relevant and exploration of the dimensions of the violent event are major tasks.

In Chapter 4 of Part 2 I shall analyse the circumstances of the violent event from the point of view of a classification of the parties' actions preceding the violence. I have tried to develop a classification that is both substantial and non-overlapping. The main strategy has been to classify the cases on the basis of general circumstances that might be thought to be more reliable than information on details of the violent event. It also seemed easier to reach the goal of an exclusive classification if broad and simple principles of classification were used. The risk was to have a less substantial classification but I believe that a fairly good compromise between the, not of necessity but often for practical reasons, somewhat conflicting demands of substantiality and exclusiveness of classes has been achieved. Further, through the analysis of the preceding actions in relation to other crime and to victim and offender characteristics the classes will, so to speak, be filled with more substance than they initially had.

In Chapter 5 another strategy for analysing the circumstances of violent events will be adopted. Instead of making a classification of violent events based on selected defining characteristics of the event I shall try to see whether it is possible empirically, by means of factor analysis, to derive meaningful clusters of victim-offender characteristics to be used as starting point for analysis. It is then dimensions of victim-offender characteristics that will be the subject for exploration in Chapter 5.

A special reason for making this analysis on the bases of the data from the Big City Crime Study was that in that study data that, in studies of crimes of violence are "normally" collected only for the offenders were also collected for the victims. It appears that most studies of violent crimes focus upon collecting data about the offenders. In fact it is quite difficult to get information about, e.g., the previous criminality of victims of violent crimes. In Sweden few such studies have been published. For example, one concerned patients in casualty departments in Stockholm (Lenke, 1973) and another, also conducted in Stockholm, people admitted to casualty departments for treatment of knife wounds (Blomqvist et al., 1980). Both these studies show that a rather large proportion of the victims of violent crimes are known for previous criminality, so there is obviously some interest in seeing whether this also holds in a more general sample of victims of violent crimes.

In Chapter 6 there will be a shift in focus. An analysis of the violent offenders in a birth cohort is presented. The subject of research is a study of age at onset, distribution, persistence and specialization in crimes of violence.

4 Actions Preceding the Violent Event

Chapter 4 consists of an analysis of the violent event with the point of departure in a classification of the violent crimes based on the victim's and the offender's actions preceding it.

First, the classification of the preceding actions will be presented and discussed. Second, the preceding actions will be related to demographic characteristics of the victim and the offender, i.e. age, sex and nationality, and to victim-offender interpersonal relationship. Third, offender characteristics in different classes of preceding actions will be analysed in some greater detail using, for example, data about their previous recorded criminality and social problems. Finally, preceding actions will be analysed in relation to selected crime characteristics, e.g place and time of occurrence, victim's injury, etc.

Two samples from the Gävle Study will be used: The **crime sample** (N=989) and the **offender sample** (N=530) (see Figure 1 in Section 1.1.1). The latter differs from the first in that it only contains cases with a known offender, and further that multiple offenders during the studied periods will only be included once.

4.1 Actions Preceding Violent Events in Gävle 1968–1970 and 1973–1975 – a Classification

The classification used may be regarded as hierarchical and exclusive and is illustrated in Figure 5. First, cases were sorted according to whether any intervention on the part of the victim or the offender preceded the violent act. Second, the intervention cases were classified according to whether the intervention was made by officials/person at work or by civilians. Note in this connection that since cases of violence or threats to officials are not included in the study, there will be an underestimation of intervention cases.

The non-intervention cases were classified according to whether a verbal argument preceded the violent act or not. The verbal arguments were then classified into cases in which the cause of the argument was situational, i.e. here and now, or whether it concerned a more longstanding relationship between the victim-offender or events further back in time. The latter cases were classified with regard to whether the conflict was of an economic or a social nature, e.g. business relationship or family relationship.

The cases referred to as non-intervention cases with no verbal argument preceding the violent act were divided into cases in which the victim or the offender molested the other and those in which the violence was a result of a sudden attack with no previous interaction.

Finally, there was a group of cases that could not be referred to any of these classes.

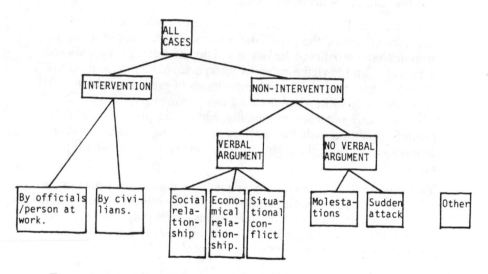

Figure 5. Principles of classification of actions preceding the violent act illustrated

Table 26 shows the distribution of cases in the various classes. The table will be used for some further comments on the contents of each class.

By **intervention** is here understood verbal instructions or physical action to prevent or stop a course of behaviour, take charge of a person, get rid of a person or refuse entrance to a person. Note that either the offender or the victim may have been the intervening party.

In many cases intervention takes the form of physical force. In most other cases a threat of physical force if the person does not obey the verbal instructions is latent. There is in most cases an obvious conflict of authority.

74

Table 26. Actions preceding the violent act. Data from the Gävle Study. The crime sample

Preceding actions	N	%
INTERVENTION		
By officials or other person at work	84	8
By civilians	62	7
NON—INTERVENTION		
VERBAL ARGUMENTS		
Social relationships	219	23
Economic relationships	44	5
Situational	262	28
NON—INTERVENTION		
NO VERBAL ARGUMENT		
Molestation	146	16
Sudden attack	81	8
OTHER		
Other	44	5
Total	942	100

Missing cases: 47

In cases of intervention no split in the classification has been made between cases involving verbal argument or not. The reason for that is that such a split would not add much information, since generally intervention is accompanied by verbal argument concerning the intervention or the grounds for it. There are too few cases in which intervention is unaccompanied by verbal argument to make it meaningful to refer these cases to a special class.

Examples of common types of cases of intervention are when the police take persons into charge or when restaurant employees refuse people entrance or request people to leave the restaurant. Example of intervention by civilians are cases when a person interferes to stop a fight or tells a gang of youths sitting smoking and drinking in a staircase to leave the place.

Cases of **non-intervention** have been divided into those in which the violent action developed from a verbal argument and those in which it did not. Violent actions classified as resulting from a **verbal argument** were further subdivided according to whether the conflict concerned the immediate situation or had to do with relationships or events further back in time. One may object here that all cases in which violence resulted from a verbal argument should be regarded as situationally induced. But I believe that information whether the conflict can be traced back in time or not is essential. In this connection it should be pointed out that any errors of classification in this respect are likely to go in the direction of underestimating conflicts related to previous relationships or events.

75

In general it may be said that the conflicts classified as situational were of a trivial origin. Examples of such conflicts may be who first ordered a taxi, who stood first in a queue, or conflicts emerging from one of the parties accidentally pushing the other while dancing or when comments on something from one of the parties did not get the approval of the other.

There were two distinct types of conflict with a previous background. The main group was those concerned with or related to the social relationship of the victim and the offender. This group includes almost all cases of so-called family violence. The other group was those cases where the conflict was related to some aspect of economic relationship between the victim and the offender, e.g. debts, quarrels about ownership and business deals. In some cases these economic relationships concerned illegal activities.

Cases in which **no verbal argument** preceded the violent action were classified either as molestation or sudden attack. What mainly separates cases classified as verbal argument and as molestation is that, in the former, both parties were highly active in the argument, while in the latter one of the parties did not respond or responded only to a minimum extent, as by saying "leave me alone". Note that either the offender or the victim may have been the one molesting the other. In cases when information given in a police interrogation conflicted as regards whether both parties had been active in a verbal argument or not, the case was classified as missing.

As sudden attack were classified those cases in which no information in the police report or the interrogation showed that any interaction between the victim and the offender had preceded the violence. It should be mentioned here that cases in which, mostly, young persons fired at others from a long distance with air-guns are counted as sudden attack, although they differ a lot from the rest of the sudden attacks in which the offender directly attacked the victim by physical means or with weapons. Although meeting the criteria for the class, it was perhaps not so wise to include the air-gun cases among those of sudden attack.

To be complete, most classifications have an "other" category. Our classification is no exception from that rule. An example of a case classified as "other" is when two friends started to wrestle for fun but the wrestle developed into a real fight. Here we have a case not preceded by intervention, nor developing from a verbal argument, nor a case of molestation or sudden attack.

4.2 Sex, Age, Nationality and Interpersonal Relationship

In Section 4.2 action preceding the violent event is related to demographic characteristics (sex, age, nationality) and interpersonal relationship of victim-offender. Sex, age and nationality of the victim and offender by type of preceding action are shown in Table 27.

Table 27. Preceding actions by sex, age and nationality of victim and offender. Per cent. The crime sample

	Intervention By officials, etc	By civilians	Non–intervention– verbal arguments Soc. Rel.	Econ. Rel.	Situational	Non–intervention– no verbal argument Molestation	Sudden Attack
OFFENDER'S SEX							
Male	98	97	92	100	99	100	100
Female	2	3	8	0	1	0	0
VICTIM'S SEX							
Male	91	89	31	94	88	86	77
Female	9	11	69	6	12	14	23
OFFENDER'S AGE							
0—19	10	28	5	9	24	42	61
20—29	52	55	28	36	45	41	24
30—39	22	9	33	29	16	9	7
40—	15	8	33	25	14	7	7
VICTIM'S AGE							
0—19	7	14	13	6	17	27	28
20—29	39	33	28	25	44	39	35
30—39	31	19	29	25	18	12	9
40—	22	33	30	43	20	23	28
OFFENDER'S NATIONALITY							
Swedish	87	89	87	94	89	90	88
Other Scandinavian*	2	5	5	2	5	5	9
Outside Scandinavia	11	6	7	4	6	4	3
VICTIM'S NATIONALITY							
Swedish	94	94	93	96	91	95	98
Other Scandinavian*	3	5	3	0	4	2	2
Outside Scandinavia	3	1	4	4	5	3	0

*Including Finland.

4.2.1 Sex

It is consistently reported in research throughout the world (Ferracuti & Newman, 1974:80; Curtis, 1974:32–34) that offenders in cases of violent crime are predominantly male. A look at the different classes of preceding action (Table 27) shows that the percentage of female offenders is between zero and 3 per cent in all but one class: verbal arguments with background in the victim-offender social relationship. The great majority of crimes of females belonged to this class. This is in close accordance with findings from other research.

For example, Rosenblatt & Greenland report that the vast majority of cases in which a female was suspected of committing a murder occurred in a domestic setting (1974:177). McClintock (1963:48) shows that the majority of female crimes of violence were to be classified as "Domestic disputes etc". A Swedish study (Somander, 1979:33) of convictions in 1976 for violence that caused the death of the victim also shows the same kind of circumstances of the crime to dominate for female offenders.

While females constitute a low proportion of offenders, they are as much as one fourth of the victims (Table 28). Probably this is an underestimation, as the analysis in Section 2.2.2 indicated. Just as in the case of offenders, female victimization is great in the class of verbal arguments concerned with the social relationship of the victim-offender. In fact, this is the only category in which there are more females than males. For the sake of clarity it should be mentioned in this context that the comparatively high proportion of female victims in the category sudden attack is "explained" by the air-gun cases, in which almost exclusively females were those fired at. Excluding the air-gun cases the female percentage is the lowest of all categories.

Table 28. Relationship between sex of the victim and the offender. The crime sample. Per cent

| | The victim | | |
	Male	Female	
THE OFFENDER			
Male	73	24	97
Female	1	2	3
Total	74	26	100

N=989

4.2.2 Age

Age is a factor strongly related to both incidence and type of criminality (e.g. Sveri, 1960). It is often claimed that the age factor should be accounted for in explanations of crime, but this proposition has recently been challenged (Hirschi & Gottfredson, 1983), a matter that I will not go into here.

78

Considering crimes of violence, Ferracuti & Newman (1974:180) write: "That assaultive crimes, such as homicide, are predominatly crimes of young males from their late teens to their early 30s, is now well established…". There is no point in arguing this generalization on the basis of our data (Table 27). But there are marked age differences between offenders according to the circumstances (preceding actions) of the violent event.

The offenders are markedly younger in non-intervention cases in which the violence did not result from a verbal argument than in other cases. The mean age of offenders in molestation cases was 24 years and in sudden attack 21 years, which can be compared with the mean age of offenders in crimes of violence resulting from a verbal argument concerned with the victim-offender social relationship, which was the highest, 36 years. There is obviously a difference in the general circumstances of the violent event for young and for older offenders.

The age distribution of victims of violence in different circumstances tends to be similar to that of the offenders (Table 27). The overall correlation (r.) between the victims' and the offenders' age is 0.32. In Table 29 the victim-offender age correlations are shown separately according to action preceding the violence.

Table 29. Zero-order correlation of victim-offender age by preceding actions. The crime sample

	Victim—offender age (r.)
INTERVENTION	
By officials etc	19
By civilians	−6
NON—INTERVENTION— VERBAL ARGUMENTS	
Social relationship	49
Economic relationship	50
Situational	27
NON—INTERVENTION— NO VERBAL ARGUMENT	
Molestation	7
Sudden attack	11

Note: Coefficients have been multiplied by 100.

The strongest relationship between the age of the offender and victim is found in cases classified as resulting from verbal argument not concerned with intervention. It should be mentioned that the age similarity of victim and offender will be somewhat stronger in the group of cases referred to as verbal argument concerned with the social relationship of victim-offender if cases of assault between parent and child, or vice versa, are excluded.

4.2.3 Nationality

The nationality, or ethnicity, of the victim and offender will be a subject treated in Chapter 5. Here I will only comment upon differences between circumstances of the violent event according to nationality of offender-victim. As shown in Table 27, there is no great differences in this respect, with some exception for conflicts concerned with economical relationships, sudden attack and situational conflicts. In this context it should be pointed out that Gävle is a city with a small foreign population. About 3 % the years studied.

4.2.4 The Association of Victim-Offender Demographic Characteristics with Actions Preceding Violent Crimes

As shown, there are differences in the demographic characteristics (sex, age and nationality) of the offender and victim between different types of circumstances (preceding actions) of the violent event. The question to be raised here is how well we predict the circumstances of the violent event from a knowledge of the offender's and the victim's sex, age and nationality.

To answer this question, I have used a method described by Overall & Klett (1972:400–410) called the Pattern-Probability Model[4]. In a simplified way it may be described as follows: The starting point for the calculations is the relative frequencies of classes of variables included (Table 27). For each combination of classes of victim and offender – sex, age and nationality – it is calculated which is the most probable class of preceding actions. Then all cases with this combination of victim-offender demographic characteristics is referred to that class of preceding actions. Finally, the original classification of preceding actions is compared with that based on victim-offender demographic characteristics.[4]

Using the Pattern-Probability Model, as many as 32 % of the cases were referred to the correct class of preceding actions solely from a knowledge of the offender's and the victim's sex, age and nationality. There were, however, marked differences in the success of the demographic classification for different types of preceding actions, as shown in Table 30. There is obviously a stronger relationship of victim-offender demographic characteristics to some types of preceding action than to others.

---

[4]I wish here to acknowledge the help given me by Jan Ahlberg in drawing up a Fortran programme on the basis of that presented by Overall & Klett (1972:412), which facilitate making these computations.

Table 30. Demographic and original classification of actions preceding the violent event

Demographic classification	Interventions		Original classification					
			Non-intervention-Verbal arguments			Non-intervention-No verbal argument		
	By officials etc	By civilians	Soc. rel.	Econ. rel.	Situational	Molestation	Sudden attack	Total
By officials etc	**19**	19	6	9	29	15	3	100
By civilians	9	**14**	10	4	44	18	2	101
Soc. rel.	3	2	**75**	1	12	5	2	100
Econ. rel.	5	11	19	**18**	40	6	1	100
Situational	3	0	18	3	**49**	18	9	100
Molestation	4	11	15	12	38	**16**	4	100
Sudden attack	10	2	8	1	42	25	**12**	100

The most common combination of victim-offender demographic characteristics is that of males in the ages 20–29 when both are of Swedish nationality. Of all cases 15 % were of this kind. Table 31 shows the most common combinations for each of the categories of preceding actions.

Table 31. The most common demographic characteristics of victim-offender according to preceding actions. Only combinations with more than 5 % of the cases given. The crime sample

```
INTERVENTION BY OFFICIALS*
SEX                 NATIONALITY               AGE                        %
Male    Male    Swede       Swede     20—29      20—29       16
Male    Male    Swede       Swede     20—29      40—         13
Male    Male    Swede       Swede     0—19       40—         10
Male    Male    Swede       Swede     0—19       0—19         8
Total                                                        47
INTERVENTION BY CIVILIANS
Male    Male    Swede            Swede    20—29   20—29      18
Male    Male    Swede            Swede    20—29   40—        14
Male    Male    Outside Scan Swede        30—39   30—39       8
Total                                                        40
VERBAL ARGUMENTS    SOCIAL RELATIONSHIP
Male    Female  Swede       Swede     40—        40—         13
Male    Female  Swede       Swede     30—39      30—39        9
Male    Female  Swede       Swede     40—        30—39        7
Male    Female  Swede       Swede     30—39      20—29        6
Male    Female  Swede       Swede     20—29      20—29        5
Male    Male    Swede       Swede     20—29      20—29        5
Total                                                        45
```

VERBAL ARGUMENTS	ECONOMICAL RELATIONSHIP					
Male	Male	Swede	Swede	40—	40—	14
Male	Male	Swede	Swede	30—39	40—	12
Male	Male	Swede	Swede	30—39	30—39	9
Male	Male	Swede	Swede	20—29	40—	9
Male	Male	Swede	Swede	20—29	20—29	9
Male	Male	Swede	Swede	0—19	30—39	7
Male	Male	Swede	Swede	0—19	20—29	7
Total						67
VERBAL ARGUMENTS	SITUATIONAL CONFLICTS					
Male	Male	Swede	Swede	20—29	20—29	22
Male	Male	Swede	Swede	0—19	20—29	9
Male	Male	Swede	Swede	20—29	40—	9
Male	Male	Swede	Swede	0—19	0—19	6
Total						46
MOLESTATION						
Male	Male	Swede	Swede	20—29	20—29	17
Male	Male	Swede	Swede	0—19	0—19	13
Male	Male	Swede	Swede	0—19	20—29	9
Male	Male	Swede	Swede	20—29	40—	7
Total						54
SUDDEN ATTACK						
Male	Male	Swede	Swede	0—19	0—19	19
Male	Male	Swede	Swede	0—19	20—29	9
Male	Male	Swede	Swede	20—29	0—19	9
Male	Female	Swede	Swede	0—19	20—29	9
Male	Male	Swede	Swede	20—29	40—	6
Male	Male	Swede	Swede	40—	0—19	6
Male	Female	Swede	Swede	20—29	20—29	6
Total						64

*Characteristics for offender given first.

4.2.5 Interpersonal Relationships

Perhaps the most common ground both, in the general debate and in research, for differentiating between types of violent crimes is that of interpersonal relationships, e.g. family violence, violence between strangers, etc.

The distribution of victim-offender relationships is shown in nine classes in Table 32. A little less than half of the cases occurred between strangers, while in remainder the victim and offender have some sort of acquaintance. By casual acquaintances is meant those in which the persons got to know each other on the same day or, in a minor number of cases, on the day before the violence occurred, and in which, as far as can be judged from the police records, the acquaintance was broken off after the violent action. By acquaintance by recognition is meant persons who recognize each other but are not acquainted in the way this term is normally used, e.g. neighbours who recognize each other but have no close relationship. Among the acquaintance categories "other close acquaintances" is the dominating category. It should be pointed out in this context, as discussed in Chapter 2, that the dark figure of violent crimes is likely to be related to the social distance of the victim-offender, implying the probability that the proportion of cases between strangers is overestimated.

Table 32. Interpersonal relationship between victim-offender. The crime sample. Per cent

Interpersonal relationship	N	%
Married, cohabiting	81	9
Parent–child or vice versa	21	2
Formerly married/cohabiting	34	4
Other relatives	7	1
Work or school mates	25	3
Other close acquaintance	197	22
Casual acquaintance	57	6
Acquainted by recognition	65	7
Strangers	402	45
Total	889	99

Missing cases: 100

The distribution of categories of interpersonal relationships according to preceding actions is shown in Table 33. As might be expected, there are quite marked differences between different circumstances of the violent event. Intervention by officials, molestation and sudden attack are types of crimes generally occurring between strangers, while the reverse is true of verbal arguments concerned with social relationship[5] or economic relationship conflicts. In cases of intervention by civilians and situational conflicts about half of the cases occur between strangers.

What separates the interpersonal relationships of victim-offender in cases of verbal argument in economic and in social relationships is that the latter are predominantly among family, or formerly family members, while the former are predominantly between acquaintances or casual acquaintances. The cases between strangers in the category "economic relationships" refer, e.g., to those in which a person who has bought a second-hand car and feels cheated visits the seller to try to annul the contract but they get into a quarrel that results in violent action.

---

[5] A natural consequence of the definition of the category.

Table 33. Interpersonal relationship of victim-offender by actions preceding the violence. The crime sample. Per cent

	Intervention		Non–intervention– verbal arguments			Non–intervention– no verbal argument	
	By offi– cials etc	By civi– lians	Soc. rel.	Econ. rel.	Situa– tional	Moles– tation	Sudden attack
Married, coha– biting	0	2	39	0	0	0	0
Parent–child or vice versa	0	3	7	0	0	0	0
Formerly mar– ried/cohabiting	0	0	15	4	0	1	0
Other relati– ves	0	0	3	0	0	0	0
Work or school mates	1	2	4	2	5	2	0
Other close acquaintances	2	29	27	48	26	11	10
Casual acquain– tances	0	6	0	27	9	6	0
Acquainted by recognition	18	4	5	2	9	6	10
Strangers	79	54	0	17	51	74	80
Total	100	100	100	100	100	100	100

4.3 Recorded Previous Criminality and Other Social Problems of the Offender

In this section the focus will be on the offender's recorded criminality and social problems previous to the studied violent crime. The 530 offenders with a correct ID number, appearing once or more as offender during the years studied, will be the unit of analysis in this section instead of the 989 crimes as in the previous section (see Figure 1 in Chapter 1).

As many as 19 % of the offenders were recorded for more than one violent crime in the municipality of Gävle during the six years studied (1968–1970, 1973–1975). Together these 99 individuals were reported for 262 violent crimes or a mean of 2.6 crimes (range 2–8) per person.

It is worth to note that 12 % of the offenders also appeared as victims of violent crimes in the municipality of Gävle during those years. Of the offenders victimized, as many as 38 % were reported more than once for committing a violent crime during the six years. Clearly we have a group among the offenders which might be said to be active in crimes of violence both as offenders and victims.

In this section the intervention cases will appear as a single category, and conflicts with an economic background are lumped together with those having a background in a social relationship. The reason is simply that, when using data of the offenders, these categories would have been too small to make comparisons justified. The only class of circumstances in which the number of offenders will be below 50 with this new subdivision is that of sudden attack.

Of offenders known for more than one violent crime in Gävle during the years studied more than half (55 %) had been involved only in crimes of the same type of circumstances. Notably, about one fifth of the multiple violence offenders had been engaged only in relationship conflicts, and another fifth only in situational conflicts.

The multiple offenders involved in different types of circumstances of the violent event during the years studied will be excluded when comparison is made between the classes of circumstances.

4.3.1 Previous Recorded Criminality

Excluding recordings of the violent crimes included in this study, it turned out that 28 % (150) of the offenders appeared in The General Criminal Register before the (first) studied violent crime. Whether this is to be regarded as a high figure or not is not so easy to say. One point of reference may be a result from a study of a nationwide representative sample of males aged 15–75 years, which shows that 8 % of them appeared in the General Criminal Register (Tham, 1979:110). In this connection it should be noted that there are not many of the violent offenders who belong to the oldest age categories. The mean age is 29 with a standard deviation of 12 years. Further, of some interest may be that when the percentage recorded for criminality at a later date (June 1979) was checked, the proportion of the violent offenders recorded had risen to 43 %. Yet the violent crimes included in the study were excluded.

Considering recordings for previous crimes of violence, 15 % of all offenders, and 52 % of those appearing in the General Criminal Register, had a record of previous violent crimes. Nearly all of these offenders were also recorded for other types of criminality as well. This shows that, in terms of previous career, it is hardly adequate to refer to the offenders, or some of them, as violent criminals if by that is understood offenders predominantly engaged in crimes of violence. However, among those highly active in previous criminality it might be possible to differentiate between those also highly active in crimes of violence and those who are not. This topic will be further treated in Chapter 6. It is of interest to note that the multiple violence offenders during the years studied and those violent offenders who were also victimized for crimes of violence during the same years were to a higher degree recorded for previous criminality than the other offenders.

4.3.2 Previously Recorded Social Problems

Of the 530 offenders 38 % were recorded in the local Social Files in Gävle before the occurrence of the (first) violent crime in the study. It was as common to be recorded for receiving social security (22 %) or being known for alcoholic problems (21 %) as to be recorded by the child welfare authorities (20 %). Note that an offender may be known for several of these problems.

4.3.2.1 Social Security

For most of the offenders receiving social security this happened on several occasions. Less than 10 % received social security only once as against more than half on more than 20 occasions. Note the comparatively low mean age (29) of the offenders.

There are clear indications that many of the offenders receiving social security also had alcoholic problems. As many as 70 % of those receiving social security were also known by the local social authorities for alcoholic problems.

4.3.2.2 Alcoholic Problems

A fairly large proportion of the offenders may be regarded as alcoholics according to the information in the local Social Files. The great majority of the 21 % of the offenders recorded for alcoholic problems were known for repeated drunkenness offences, and as many as half of them had been treated at an institution for alcoholics (10 % of all violent offenders). There was a clearly greater proportion of the older offenders, i.e. 40 years and above, who had been treated for alcoholic problems (21 %) compared to younger (9 %). Of those 40 years and above who were recorded in the General Criminal Register 40 % had also been treated for alcoholic problems, while the corresponding figure for those 40 years and above not known in the General Criminal Register was 16 %.

4.3.2.3 Child Welfare Problems

One fifth (20 %) of the offenders were known by the child welfare authorities. In most cases (61 %) the reason for the Child Welfare Committee making an investigation was criminality on the part of the offender. Other reasons were, e.g., drunkenness (14 %) or drug-abusing parents (7 %). Most of the offenders known by the child welfare authorities had been a concern for the authorities during a long period. Nearly half (45 %) had some time been taken into charge by the authorities.

4.3.3 Association between Previous Recorded Criminality and Social Problems

As already indicated, there is an association between offenders with recorded criminality and various types of other social problems. The zero-order correlations are given in Table 34.

Table 34. Zero-order correlations of previous recorded criminality, received social security, alcoholic problems and child welfare problems. The offender sample

	Criminality	Social security	Alcoholic problems
Social security	36		
Alcoholic problems	35	60	
Child welfare	36	43	49

Note: Coefficients have been multiplied by 100.
N = 530

4.3.4 Recorded Criminality and Social Problems by Preceding Actions

After this general background of recorded criminality and social problems of the offenders[6] I shall turn to the exploration of any differences in previous criminality and social problems according to the circumstances (preceding actions) of the violent event (Table 35).

Table 35. Recorded previous criminality and other social problems by preceding actions. The offender sample. Per cent

Previous records	Intervention By official or civilian	Non–intervention– verbal arguments		Non–intervention– no verbal argument	
		Relation– ship	Situa– tional	Moles– tation	Sudden attack
Criminality	23	32	31	22	23
Social security	23	29	20	18	4
Alcoholic problems	23	31	28	18	12
Child welfare	16	11	23	33	38
No record	53	46	47	47	42

Note that the same individual may be known for several different previous social problems. Hence the percentages do not total 100.

---

[6]More detailed information is given in Wikström (1980).

What is striking in Table 35 is the rather small variations in the proportion of offenders with previous records. The offenders with least previous records appear in the intervention category, which is "explained" by a number of cases in which officials (who as a rule have no previous record) are the suspects. Despite this, it is only offenders in sudden attack cases who have a somewhat more frequent previous record.

Consideration of types of previous record shows variations among the categories of circumstances. Records of previous criminality are more common in relationship and situational conflicts than in other circumstances. Social security records are more common in relationship conflicts and less common in sudden attack cases. Recorded alcoholic problems are more common in relationship and situational conflicts and less so in sudden attack cases. Finally, child welfare records are more common in sudden attack and molestation cases but less common in relationship conflicts. These differences may partly be attributed to age differences between the offenders in different categories of circumstances.

4.4 Characteristics of the Crime

So far in this chapter victim and offender characteristics in different types of circumstances (preceding actions) have been the point of focus. In this section some other characteristics of the crimes will be dealt with; alcoholic intoxication, weapons and injuries, place and time of occurrence.

4.4.1 Alcoholic Intoxication

In studies of violent crimes it is generally reported that a high proportion of the offenders are intoxicated. In studies of homicides, for example, the following proportion of intoxicated offenders has been given: 54 % (Wolfgang, 1958), 74 %, 87 %, 89 % (three Soviet studies reported by Connor, 1973), 50 % and 55 % (no year given, Roes & Nordström).

In a study of aggravated assault (Pittman & Handy, 1964) the authors find that only 23 % of the offenders were intoxicated. Pittman & Handy, however, regard the result as a likely underestimate (1964:467). In Swedish studies Koch (no year given) reports that 60 % of the offenders were intoxicated, while the corresponding figure in Lenke's study (1974) is 30 % in cases of simple assault and "a majority" in aggravated assault. Kühlhorn (1984) reports that 82 % of the offenders convicted of crimes of violence (wider definition than that used here) were intoxicated.

Also the victims of violence have to a high degree been found to be intoxicated (Pitman & Handy, 1964; Kühlhorn, 1984; Koch, Roes &

Nordström, no year given for the last two studies), although the proportion is lower than for the offenders.

The variations in the reported proportion of intoxicated offenders may be a consequence of the difficulties in finding this information from records of crime. As mentioned in the introduction (Chapter 1), this is a variable that requires careful examination of the police investigations.

In the Gävle Study it was found that 75 % of the offenders and 54 % of the victims were intoxicated. In 46 % both the offender and the victim were intoxicated, while in 37 % one of the parties was intoxicated and in 17 % both the victim and the offender were sober.

It should be mentioned that fairly strict demands were placed on the information before classifying an offender (victim) as intoxicated. For example, information that the offender had consumed a glass of wine or beer a couple of hours before the crime has not been coded as intoxication. If the offender (victim) was charged for drunkeness or other information in the investigations clearly showed that he was highly intoxicated, he was classified as seriously intoxicated.

The intoxication of the victim and the offender is given in Table 36. As evident from the table, alcohol has it greatest role in situational conflicts, in which both the victim and the offender were intoxicated in 74 % of the cases. Serious intoxication was coded for 37 % of the offenders and 25 % of the victims.

Other circumstances with a low proportion of cases between sober victims and offenders are molestation and intervention by officials or

Table 36. Alcoholic intoxication of victim-offender by preceding actions. The crime sample

	Intervention		Non–intervention– verbal arguments			Non–intervention no verbal argument	
	By offi– cials etc	By civi– lians	Soc. Rel.	Econ. Rel.	Situa– tional	Moles– tation	Sudden attack
Both victim and offender sober	8	22	29	32	8	7	31
Victim sober, offender intoxicated	41	23	42	4	13	41	27
Victim intoxicated, offender sober	42	4	3	6	5	7	0
Both victim and offender intoxi– cated	9	51	26	57	74	45	42
Total	100	100	100	99	100	100	100

person at work. The latter cases are somewhat special in that they have the highest proportion of cases with sober offenders and intoxicated victims, which is mainly "explained" by cases in which an official/person at work (who generally are sober) was the offender.

The highest proportions of cases in which both the victim and the offender are sober are among social relationship and economic conflicts and sudden attack[7]. The latter may be somewhat misleading since cases with sober parties are air-gun cases in which many offenders are very young, mostly below the age of 15.

4.4.2 Type of Violence/Weapons and Injuries to Victim

One way to get some indication of the seriousness of crimes of violence, instead of looking at the legal classifications, is to see what type of violence/weapons was used and what injuries the victim suffered.

Before presenting the results, it should be mentioned that especially the variable "injuries to victim" is somewhat difficult to code. In most cases there is a medical examination as the basis for classification. But in other cases the data are based, in the first instance, on the observations of the policeman making the report and, secondly, in cases reported some time after they occurred, the victim's statement.

Considering type of violence/weapons, this information is based on victims' and possibly offenders' and witnesses' statements. The principle of coding has been to refer a case to the class of most serious violence used, e.g. if a person is assaulted both with blows, kicks and cuts with a knife, the case is coded in the category pointed weapons, which is regarded as more serious than, e.g., kicks.

Weapons have been used in 14 % of the cases. Only in 3 cases do firearms appear. In more than half of the cases (55 %) the victim suffered bruises or less injury. Four victims were killed, 2 males and 2 females.

The distribution of type of violence/weapons and victims' injuries according to actions preceding the violence is shown in Table 37.

Considering the violence used, weapons (excluding air-guns) are less common in cases of molestation and sudden attack. The proportion of cases of minor injury (bruises) or no injury to the victim is higher in relationship conflicts and intervention by officials or person at work. It is of interest to note the comparatively smaller injuries in cases of

---

[7] It is worth noting in this connection that McClintock (1978:90) reports that neither the offender or the victim had been drinking prior to the crime in 82 % (!) of the studied cases of family violence. A rather surprising result.

Table 37. *Type of violence/weapons and injuries to victim by preceding actions. The crime sample*

	Intervention		Non—intervention—verbal arguments			Non—intervention—no verbal argument	
	By offi—cials etc	By civi—lians	Soc. Rel.	Econ. Rel.	Situa—tional	Moles—tation	Sudden attack
TYPE OF VIOL—ENCE/WEAPONS:							
Box on the ear or less serious	12	5	7	2	5	6	2
Blows	44	56	58	58	49	52	60
Kicks	17	2	8	2	6	5	2
Blows and kicks	15	21	17	21	27	32	9
Striking weapon	11	10	6	10	7	4	0
Pointed weapon	1	3	4	6	4	1	2
Fire arms	0	0	0	0	0	0	0
(Air—guns)	0	3	0	0	0	1	25
Total	100	100	100	99	99	100	100
VICTIM IN—JURIES:							
No injury	28	11	23	25	12	17	22
Bruises or less	45	44	49	38	37	35	31
Bleeding	5	19	10	4	24	19	16
Minor fracture	20	14	10	19	16	18	18
Broken limbs, unconsiousness	1	5	3	2	5	8	9
Wounds from cuts	0	6	4	8	4	2	2
Other severe injuries	1	0	0	4	0	2	0
Deaths	0	0	0	0	1	0	2
Total	100	99	99	100	99	101	100

social relationship conflicts, which conflicts somewhat with the results from some Swedish studies of convictions and victim surveys (see Section 2.1.2).

4.4.3 Place of Occurrence

Place of occurrence were classified in 44 categories. Of all cases 74 % had happened either in an apartment (24 %), in or around a place of public entertainment (29 %) or on streets and squares (21 %).

Of the cases occurring in apartments 38 % were in the home of both the victim and the offender, 36 % in the home of the victim, 13 % in the offender's home and the rest in the home of another person. Of cases in and around places of public entertainment 35 % occurred in restaurants and 39 % in entrances to restaurants.

The most common places of occurrence according to circumstances of the violent event are shown in Table 38.

Table 38. Place of occurrence by preceding actions. Only places where more than 5 % of the cases occurred are shown

INTERVENTIONS BY OFFICIALS/PERSON AT WORK

	%
Entrance to restaurant	36
Restaurant	21
Police station	17
Total	74

INTERVENTION BY CIVILIANS

Entrance to restaurant	17
Street, square	12
Restaurant	8
Other place of public entertainment	6
Hot dog stand	6
A wood	6
Offender's home	6
Other's home	6
Total	67

VERBAL ARGUMENTS, SOCIAL RELATIONSHIP

Home of victim and offender	38
Victim's home	19
Street, square	11
Offender's home	5
Other's home	5
Total	78

VERBAL ARGUMENTS, ECONOMIC RELATIONSHIP

Street, square	23
Park	10
Restaurant	10
Entrance to restaurant	8
Public transport	8
Proximity area, offender's home*	6
Total	65

VERBAL ARGUMENTS, SITUATIONAL CONFLICTS

Street, square	21
Entrance to restaurant	17
Restaurant	11
Victim's home	8
Total	57

MOLESTATION

Street, square	60
Restaurant	14
Entrance to restaurant	7
Total	81

SUDDEN ATTACK

Street, square	43
Victim's home	10
Total	53

*By proximity area is meant a cellar, staircase or garden.

Comparing the types of places of occurrence of the different circumstances it is social relationship conflicts that clearly differ from the rest in occurring predominatly in apartments. Very many of the other types of circumstances are likely to occur in relation to public entertainment.

4.4.4 Time of Occurrence

Different types of human activities have a different incidence on different days of the week and hours of the day. Crimes of violence are concentrated to weekends and nighttime, a consequence of their close association with homes and public entertainment, since home-life and public entertainment are leisure activities. Considering the crimes of violence that occur in the daytime, there is a predominance of cases related to alcoholic problems of the offenders (and in many cases the victims).

The proportion of cases occurring at weekends by circumstances (preceding actions) is shown in Table 39. As evident from the table, relationship conflicts tend to be less concentrated to weekends than other types of circumstances, which is likely to be explained by the concentration of public entertainment to weekends.

Table 39. Proportion of cases occurring at weekends (Friday 19.00–Sunday 04.00) by preceding actions

	Intervention		Non–intervention– verbal arguments			Non–intervention– no verbal argument	
	By offi– cials etc	By civi– lians	Soc. rel.	Econ. rel.	Situa– tional	Moles– tation	Sudden attack
% Cases occur– ring at week– ends	56	55	36	23	48	57	46

4.5 Discussion

As reported in many studies of crimes of violence a verbal conflict preceded the use of violence in the vast majority of cases (Wolfgang, 1958; McClintock, 1963; Pittman & Handy, 1964; Curits, 1974; Kühlhorn, 1984). An approach that considers the occurrence of conflict situations, and their relationship to violent outcomes, seems therefore to be of great theoretical interest. However, as mentioned in the introduction to Part 2, it is very difficult to sample situations, so that most studies are made on a sample of violent crimes. The risk then arises of misjudging the importance of different types of circumstances as antecedents to violent action. For example, although relationship conflicts are as common as situational conflicts in our data, it might well be that the proportion of relationship conflicts not resulting in violent action largely outnumbers the situational conflicts not resulting in violence.

Despite these problems some comments on the basis of the analysis of the circumstances of the violent event seem to be justified. First it is striking that, if **human activities** are divided into work and leisure, crimes of violence are greatly related to the latter. More specifically, it is in home-life and during participation in public entertainment that most violent actions occur. As regards those involved in violent crimes during work, it is mainly persons who have contact with leisure activities as part of their work e.g. employees of public establishments, those having as work to keep the peace (policemen, watchguards), those transporting people to and from public entertainment (bus and taxi drivers) and those taking care of injuries to people as a result of public entertainment (personnel at hospitals' casualty departments)[8] (see Section 5.7). It may be mentioned in this connection that the results of the Swedish victim surveys (Person, 1977; SCB, 1981), as well as other studies of recorded crimes (Knutsson, 1984), also support such a conclusion.

Work is not likely to be any particular conflict-free human activity, as probably most people will confirm. Yet there are very few of these conflicts that result in violent actions, a result that would hardly be changed if we had the opportunity to consider not only recorded but also hidden crimes.

This seems to be of great significance for the development of situational explanations of violent actions. One may speculate on the reasons for the low incidence of violent actions as a result of conflicts during work. One is maybe that the proportion of the population more prone to violent actions is outside the labour force. As shown in the preceding sections, there is hardly a representative sample of the population that gets involved in violence, rather they are recruited among those having greater individual social problems. Another, not necessarily conflicting, explanation is the clear regulation and hierarchies of authority that govern work and the importance of these for keeping work and good relationships with those one meets daily. Further, one is likely to have a good knowledge of one's work mates' normal behaviour and reactions.

Public entertainment, on the other hand, may be regarded as less organized. Strangers, with different behavioural customs – perhaps marked by clothing and other traits – , are met within small areas. One major activity, as it appears, of public entertainment is to get in contact with persons of the opposite sex, efforts which may be

---

[8]Some exceptions concern those, e.g. social welfare officers, who meet in their work people with social problems.

disappointing and frustrating. Alcohol is a major ingredient in public entertainment and may contribute to the development of conflicts into violent actions. Some research indicates that people who get aggressive after drinking alcohol are especially found among individuals with social problems, which is also often related to low self-esteem (e.g. Boyatzis, 1975:1205; Deardorff et al., 1975:1193–1194). In this connection it might be mentioned that a recent Swedish study of criminals in prisons showed that they (while free) were likely to be frequent participants at public entertainments (Åkerström, 1983). Another Swedish study, of the relationship between leisure time activities and criminality among youth in Stockholm, shows that the most criminal of the youths tends to engage more in commercial spare-time activities and spend more spare-time in inner city areas than other youths (Sarnecki, 1983).

All in all, then, there is much to indicate that the opportunities for confrontations between people are comparatively great in the course of public entertainment. It might be illustrative to describe briefly the milieu of the place in Gävle that had the highest incidence of outdoor crimes of violence in the city.

It was a small cross-street where the entrance to one restaurant, often frequented by pupils of upper secondary schools, and one high-class dance-restaurant, frequented by somewhat older people, was located on one side of the street, while a hot dog stand was located on the other side. The latter was a place in and around which many of the rockers of the city spent some of their time at night. So there was every opportunity for confrontation between different kinds of people.

Just as I think that the results presented in Chapter 4 indicate the advantage of an analysis of how human activities are related to the occurrence of conflict situations and the latters relation to violent outcomes, the data also point to the importance of life-styles, especially **life-styles of socially loaded persons** as an area worthy of exploration when violent actions are concerned.

Based on my experience from reading about 7,000 police investigations of violent crimes, a "normal" activity pattern for some of those living outside conventional society may be described as follows. A usual meeting place to start the day's activities is the city centre. Hanging around and meeting "friends", perhaps entering a department store, getting into conflict with the personnel or guards. Meeting in a park to drink alcohol, perhaps being approached by the police, occasional conflicts with them or other conventional citizens who comment upon some behaviour. Going with "friends" to someone's flat, generally in the outer-city areas, perhaps a confrontation with a taxi-driver over the payment. Heavy drinking parties in the apartment, perhaps confrontation with the others about alcohol, girl-friends, (illegal) affairs or whatsoever. An occasional confrontation with a complaining neighbour. Perhaps the police turn up and there is confrontation with them. In the evening, if not still in the apartment, going down town to a public entertainment. Getting into conflict with other people, perhaps commenting upon something or not approving of being passed in a queue. Occasional conflicts with personnel at restaurants.

Needless to say, a description like this is likely to be very superficial and, of course, all mentioned confrontations are not likely to occur during a single day, but I believe it grasps some essential aspect of a life-style highly related to violence.

Considering violence in the home, this is where most females get victimized, and also the place where most of the small proportion of female violent offenders commit their crimes. It is possible to distinguish between two main types of circumstances of violence in the home. Besides the "family violence cases" there are those that occur during heavy drinking parties, between males and often as a result of conflicts (e.g. concerning booze, brides, and physical strength) or intervention, the owner of the apartment trying to get rid of or refuse someone entrance into the apartment. The offenders in these cases are generally older than in others (with the notable exception of cases occurring during "youth parties"). The "heavy drinking party cases" are often attended by criminals and alcoholics as indicated above.

Many cases of family violence, notably wife assault, occur in families which may be described as social problem families, or at least the husband, or male, is to be regarded as socially problematic (alcoholic, criminal). This is also the result published in most other studies (e.g. McClintock, 1978). It has been argued in the general debate that wife assaults occur in all types of families (according to social background) and that is undoubtedly true. But there is a concentration to socially problematic families that would hardly vanish if all hidden violent crimes within the family were known.

5 Structural Aspects of the Violent Event

Chapter 5 focusses upon an exploration of the violent event in terms of victim-offender characteristics and relationships of those characteristics to selected crime characteristics. The analysis will take as point of departure empirically derived clusters of victim-offender characteristics that are not exclusive but rather describe dimensions on the basis of which to analyse the violent event.

5.1 Structural Aspects of Violent Events in Stockholm in 1982

In this section I shall analyse the violent event on the basis of data from the Big City Crime Study. Instead of taking a classification of preceding actions as point of departure as in Chapter 4, I shall start by attempting to empirically isolate dimensions of the violent events from variables measuring victim and offender characteristics. The steps of the analysis will be as follows:

1. First a factor analysis is carried out on offender and victim characteristics to isolate clusters of victim-offender characteristics. The use of factor analysis in this context may be disputed, since many of the variables used (see Appendix 3) are dichotomies or measured at the ordinal level. However, as a means to search for clusters of variables the use of ordinal and dichotomized variables in factor analysis may be justified[9].

2. After a first interpretation of Varimax rotated factors I shall proceed with an oblique rotation (Promax) to see if the assumption of orthogonality holds and eventually to see what inter-factor correlations there are. Gorsuch (1974:212), in a comparison of techniques of rotation, recommended the combined use of Varimax and Promax rotations. If there are

---

[9]For example, Kim & Mueller (1978) point out, in a discussion of the use of dichotomies, that if the underlying correlations among variables are moderate, then the structure of clustering will not be affected. They also state that *"... the correlation coefficients are fairly robust with respect to ordinal distortions in the measurement..."* (Kim & Mueller, 1978:75). See also Labovits (1972).

apparently significant inter-correlations between factors in the Promax solution, this solution will be the choice. Otherwise the Varimax solution is chosen. According to Gorsuch, the Varimax-Promax strategy should be used in cases with clear simple structure.

3. The next step will be to compute scores for the extracted factors. The factor scores will then be correlated with crime characteristic variables to have a primary indication of the relationship between victim-offender and crime characteristics.

4. In the fourth step of analysis, the defining variables of each factor will be used to create variables of different types of victim-offender characteristics. Then I shall compute how many of the cases fulfil the characteristics of each factor, also how many cases overlap between the factor-derived classes and how many do not belong to any of the factor-derived classes.

5. In the final step of analysis I shall further explore the circumstances of each factor-derived victim-offender type group and a group comprising cases that do not meet the criteria of any of the factor-derived classes.

5.1.1 Factor Analysis of Victim-Offender Characteristics

Table 40 shows the results of the Varimax rotated factors. The criterion for the numbers of factors to be extracted was the conventional one of including only those factors with an eigenvalue above 1. Inspection of a scree-plot indicated that a point of intersection after the sixth factor would not be inappropriate with regard to decay in eigenvalues. Together the six extracted factors explained 60 % of the variance.

The interpretation of the factors seemed fairly straightforward. The first factor was interpreted as **gang-fights**, the second as **fights between addicts/criminals**, the third was labelled **fights between older persons**, with high loadings on offenders' and victims' age but also on offenders' previous criminality and unemployment of offender. On the basis of what is known about older criminals one may speculate whether this not is a factor covering mainly cases with involvement of older alcoholics with a previous criminal record? Had we had any good indicators of alcoholic abuse, which we do not, a fairly good guess is that these indicators would have belonged to this factor[10]. The fourth factor is labelled **foreigners' fights**. It may be noted that this factor has a high negative loading on female offenders.

---

[10] Note the relationship between indicators of alcoholic abuse and offenders' age shown in Chapter 4.

98

The fifth and sixth factors deviate from the previous four in that they rather describe victim groups than violence among people with similar characteristics. The fifth factor is labelled **female victims**, and the sixth **victimization during work**. It is of interest to note that the sixth factor, besides high loading on the variable "victim at work", also has higher loadings on offender's unemployment and offender's intravenous drug use, which indicates that this factor covers a group of cases of confrontation between officials and socially loaded individuals.

Table 40. Factor loadings and communalities. Varimax rotated factors. Victim-offender relationships. Data from the Big City Crime Study

Variable	I	II	III	IV	V	VI	h²
Female offenders	−25	−23	−27	−51*	1	17	61
Female victims	−23	0	4	2	81*	−21	76
Offender's age	−23	−12	69*	− 4	10	−24	62
Victim's age	−16	− 5	72*	− 3	3	9	55
Foreign offenders	− 9	−18	−13	69*	− 1	2	55
Foreign victims	− 9	− 5	− 8	75*	− 1	17	61
Offender's previous criminality	13	44*	55*	− 4	7	12	54
Victim's previous criminality	1	58*	14	− 7	−40*	−23	59
Offender intravenous drug user	0	71*	4	− 5	12	35*	65
Victim intravenous drug user	−13	72*	−16	− 5	7	−19	62
Offender unemployed	− 4	11	40*	−33*	21	38*	48
Offender at work	−23	− 9	−18	11	−62*	−15	55
Victim at work	− 3	− 5	− 1	12	− 5	79*	64
Offender in youth gang	85*	− 2	−12	3	− 3	4	74
Victim in youth gang	83*	− 6	−14	−12	3	− 9	75
Contribution of factor, %	15	12	10	8	8	7	

Note: Coefficients have been multiplied by 100. No data of victim's employment status were gathered. Loadings 30 and higher marked with an asterisk.

The Promax rotation of these factors turned out to give the same factor structures although, of course, the factor loadings were not exactly the same. The interfactor correlations are shown in Table 41.

On the whole the interfactor correlations do not seem to be so strong as to justify the use of an oblique solution. The strongest correlation has a coefficient of 0.21 and is between fights between addicts/ criminals and between older persons.

Table 41. Interfactor correlations. Promax rotated factors

	Fights between addicts/ criminals	Fights between older persons	Foreigners' fights	Female victims	Victimization during work
Gang–fights (FI)	14	0	− 4	− 5	8
Fights between addicts/criminals (FII)		21	−11	2	3
Fights between older persons (FIII)			−13	16	7
Foreigners' fights (FIV)				−12	− 6
Female victims (FV)					14
Victimization during work (FVI)					100

Note: Coefficients have been multiplied by 100.

5.1.2 Relationship between Victim-Offender Characteristic Factors and Selected Crime Characteristics

The scores of the six extracted victim-offender characteristic factors were correlated with selected crime characteristics (Table 42).

Gang-fights show an association with occurrence on streets, at weekends and nighttime which seems to be reasonable. Fights between addicts/criminals show some association with occurrence in apartments and with the use of weapons. Fights between older persons are associated with occurrence in apartments, involvement of acquaintances, but not at nighttime and weekends. Foreigners' fights are related to occurrence at places of public entertainment.

The factor scores that show the highest correlations with crime characteristic variables are those for female victims. Strong correlations with occurrence in apartments and between acquaintances appear. These correlations are likely to indicate the presence of a large number of family-violence cases in the female victim factor. Finally, the factor describing victimization during work shows that these cases tend to occur at other places than those specified. Since offenders known for intravenous drug use and unemployment have a high loading on this factor, this correlation is likely to express those cases in the factor between officials and socially loaded persons occurring in offices, shops, police stations, and so forth.

The preliminary exploration of the relationship of victim-offender characteristic factors and crime characteristic variables seems to make a lot of sense. This will encourage us to further studies along this line.

Table 42. Zero-order correlations between factor scores of victim-offender relationship factors and crime characteristic variables. Data from the Big City Crime Study

Selected crime characteristics	Factors (see Table 40)					
	Gang fights	Fights between addicts/ criminals	Fights between older persons	Foreigners' fights	Female victims	Victimization during work
Apartments	−21*	17*	26*	− 6	40*	−17*
Street, square	25*	1	−10	− 8	− 7	− 2
Park	2	2	9	− 3	−11*	− 3
Public entertainment	8	−14*	−20*	21*	−32*	0
Public transport	5	− 4	− 6	− 9	−13*	7
Other place of occurrence	− 9	−10*	− 3	5	− 3	25*
Inner−city area	13*	−12*	−16*	− 4	−35*	5
Weekends	21*	− 5	−12*	− 3	− 5	− 7
Nights	22*	− 5	−22*	6	−16*	−13*
Weapons present	5	16*	2	− 3	−13*	3
Victims' injuries	13*	7	11*	− 6	−10*	6
Acquaintance	−23*	9	21*	1	46*	−25*

Note: Coefficients have been multiplied by 100. Correlations statistically significant at the 5 per cent level have been marked with an asterisk. Definitions of crime characteristics variables given in Appendix 3.

5.1.3   Creating Subgroups of Cases on the Basis of Extracted Factors

Having isolated six dimensions of the violent event in terms of victim-offender characteristics a natural next question is how many of the studied cases would fulfil the criteria of each of these dimensions.

To study this, new variables were created on the basis of the variables with high loading on each factor. One subgroup of cases was selected among those in which both the offender and the victim were members of a youth gang at the time of the crime (gang-fight). A second subgroup was created with the condition that the included cases should fulfil the criteria that the offender either was known for intravenous drug use or recorded for previous criminality or both, and that the victim also was known for intravenous drug use or recorded for previous criminality or both (fights between addicts/ criminals). The third subgroup was created so that the included cases had both an offender and a victim more than 40 years old (fights between older persons). The fourth subgroup was defined by the fact that both the offender and the victim were of foreign nationality (foreigners' fights). The fifth subgroup simply consisted of cases with female victims (female victims), while the sixth was made up of those cases in which the victim was victimized during work (victimization during work).

Of the 2,532 cases 1,460 (58 %) fell within any one the six defined subgroups. The remainder (42 %) were lumped together in a seventh group tentatively labelled other fights. There is no overlapping of cases between the latter subgroup and the six factor-derived subgroups. However, between the six factor-derived subgroups there are overlapping cases. In Table 43 it is shown how many cases overlap with another subgroup and with how many subgroups they overlap.

Table 43. Overlapping of cases in the six factor-derived subgroups by number of overlaps with other subgroup. Percentages in brackets

	No over-lapping	Overlapping with number of other subgroups	
		1	2
Cases	969 (66)	431 (29)	60 (4)

One third of the cases in the six factor-derived subgroups overlap with at least one other and at most two other subgroups. The two subgroups with the greatest number of overlapping cases are fights between older persons and foreigners' fights. In both instances the major overlap is with the subgroup female victims, accounting for 72 % of the overlaps in the subgroup foreigners' fights and 87 % in the subgroup fights between older persons.

Although the subgroups are not fully exclusive, this need not bother us much since the major obstacle in the coming analysis is to explore separately each of the factor-derived subgroups. The questions to be considered are, e.g., what characterize gang-fights, what characterize violent events with female victims, etc? In these explorations I shall also expand the scope of inquiry a bit in relation to the defined subgroup.

So what will come next is an exploration of the violent event, taking as point of departure extracted dimensions of victim-offender characteristics.

5.2 Gang Fights

Of all violent crimes only 2 % were gang-fights, signifying that both offender and victim were members of a youth gang at the time of the crime. However, considering also those cases in which youth gangs appeared as offenders against non-gang victims (6 %) or the more rare occasions when gang-members were victimized by a non-gang offender (1 %) brings up the total of the cases in which youth gangs were involved to 9 %. Here only gang-fights will be considered. Summary Table 1 shows various data about the gang-fights. No data of preceding actions were collected in the Big City Crime Study, but the experience from the Gävle Study makes it likely that the types of crime in which youth-gangs are predominantly involved are molestation and sudden attack, but also to some degree situational conflicts[11].

Nearly half of the victims and offenders have a previous criminal record. Notably, as many as 34 % of the offenders, in spite of their youth, have previously been recorded for crimes of violence[12]. Nearly one fifth of the victims are known for previous violent crimes. The rather strong association between the sex of the offender and the victim indicates that male gang members tend to fight other gangs' male members and that female gang members tend to fight other gangs' female members.

Gang-fights are extremely concentrated to nighttime at weekends. The victim and the offender are nearly always strangers and they fight predominantly outdoors (streets, in and around places of public entertainment and on public transport). The victims get fairly bad injuries in these cases, more than 20 % had bad injuries. This might be a consequence of an especially high dark figure in these cases, although that should not be taken for granted.

Yablonsky describes the types of gangs he refers to as "near-groups" (or violent gangs) as having a prime function "... of providing a channel for acting out hostility and aggression to satisfy continuing momentary emotional needs of its members. The gang is a convenient and malleable structure quickly adaptable to the needs of emotionally disturbed youths, who are unable to fulfil the responsibility and demands required for participation in constructive groups" (1968:232). The near-groups are characterisized by such factors as diffuse role definition, impermanence, shifting membership and unclear membership expectations (p. 226).

Although experience of the character of violent gangs from other countries may be of some general value in the understanding of violent gangs, our data do not permit us to draw any such conclusions. All we know is that the offender (or victim or both) was in a youth

---

[11] Data of the number of persons involved as victims or offenders in the Gävle Study (not shown in Chapter 4) showed that cases with more than one offender or victim were predominantly of the three mentioned categories.

[12] These figures are about the same when considering all cases in which the offender was member of a youth gang.

SUMMARY TABLE 1   Gang—fights   N = 57

CHARACTERISTICS	OFFENDER	VICTIM	CORRELATIONS VICTIM—OFFENDER CHARACTERISTICS		
Mean age	(22)	23	Age	(r.)	(.15)
% Females	10	26	Sex	(phi)	.57
% Foreigners	20	10	Nationality	(phi)	−.14
% Previously recorded for crime	(47)	(45)	Previous criminality	(r.)	(−.07)
Mean years	(2.0)	(1.0)			
% Previously recorded for violent crime	(34)	(19)	Previous crime of violence	(r.)	(−.30)
Mean violent crimes	(0.5)	(0.2)			
% Intravenous drug users	(0)	(0)	Intravenous drug use	(phi)	(.00)
% No regular work, excl. students	(9)	—			
% In youth gang	100	100	Youth gang	(phi)	.00
% At work	(0)	0	At work	(phi)	(.00)

VICTIM—OFFENDER RELATIONSHIP			VICTIMS' INJURIES		
	N	%		N	%
Family incl. relatives	0	0	No injury	3	5
Other close acquaintances	3	5	Bruises or less	15	26
Casual acquaintances	4	7	Minor fractures etc	27	47
Strangers	50	88	Severe injuries	11	19
Missing cases	0		Deaths	1	2
			Missing cases	0	

PLACE OF OCCURRENCE			TIME OF OCCURRENCE		
	N	%		N	%
Apartment	6	10	04.00—07.59	0	0
Street, square	26	46	08.00—11.59	0	0
Park	3	5	12.00—15.59	0	0
Publ.entertain.	10	17	16.00—19.59	4	8
Publ. transport	9	16	20.00—23.59	21	41
Shop, service institution	0	0	24.00—03.59	26	51
Other	3	5	Missing cases	6	
Missing cases	0				

WEEKENDS
% cases at weekends   87

Note: The numbers of missing cases may differ among variables.
Figures in brackets indicate that the percentage, mean or correlation
has been calculated on less than 50 cases. Some results are a direct
consequence of how gang—fights have been defined.

104

gang at the time of the crime, but not whether the gang shared any of the characteristics described by Yablonsky. Patrick (1973) has made a strong point, emphasizing the risk of "translating" results concerning gang characteristics from one country to another, and even from one city to another in a particular country. For example he finds no evidence that the "Glasgow gang" he describes in his study has counterparts in other British cities.

5.3   Fights between Criminals/Addicts

As already shown in Chapter 4, a large number of the offenders were recorded for criminality previous to the studied violent crime. Further, as stated on the basis of the readings of the police investigations, it appeared that a fairly large number of the crimes of violence studied were of the kind "internal fights" or fights related to what might be called a "the life-style of socially loaded persons".

It turned out, having access also to data of the victims' previous criminality, that as many as one in four (25 %) of the recorded crimes of violence in Stockholm (of cases where such data were available) ocurred between a victim and an offender both of whom were known for previous criminality and/or drug addiction. Being known for drug addiction generally meant also being known for criminality. In this section the focus will be on the cases occurring between previously recorded victims and offenders. But first some data will be given about the previous criminality and drug addiction for all cases.

Of all known offenders 58 % were recorded for previous criminality[13]. A point of reference here may be the figures given in Chapter 6, although not fully comparable, which show that, of a 1953 birth-cohort from the Greater Stockholm Area, 31 % of the males were recorded for criminality up to the age of 25/26 years. As is further evident (Table 44), most of the offenders recorded for previous criminality are multiple offenders, as many as 42 % of the offenders having a record in more than one year, and nearly one in twelve in 11 or more years previous to the studied violent crime. One third (33 %) of the offenders have a record of crime of violence, and 7 % are known for more than 5 crimes of violence.

Of the victims less are recorded for criminality, yet as many as 38 % appear in the police register previous to the studied violent crimes.

As stated above, being known for drug addiction (needle-marks) generally means also being known for criminality. Therefore the data about drug addicts cannot be added to those of recorded criminality,

---

[13]Note that data on previous criminality from the police register are used here (see Chapter 1).

Table 44. Previous recorded criminality and drug addiction. The Big City Crime Study

Number of years with a record in the police register	Offenders		Victims	
	N	%	N	%
No records	727	42	1 319	62
1	263	15	300	14
2— 4	305	18	294	14
5—10	270	16	147	7
11—	145	8	61	3
Total	1,710	99	2,121	100
Number of records for needle—mark	N	%	N	%
1979 — June 1982				
No records	1,546	90	2,030	96
1	61	4	26	1
2— 4	56	3	30	1
5—10	36	2	20	1
11—	11	1	15	1
Total	1,710	100	2,121	100
1981 — June 1982	N	%	N	%
No records	1 583	93	2 051	97
1	54	3	26	1
2— 4	58	3	22	1
5—10	12	1	16	1
11—	3	0	6	0
Total	1,710	100	2,121	100

Missing data, offenders: 822; victims: 411.

but rather show the group of recorded criminals as being known also for drug addiction. Since the indicator of drug addiction is recorded needle-marks, the data mainly refer to the group of more serious drug addicts, although it is likely that not all of them will be covered by the indicator needle-marks.

One in ten of the known offenders had a record of needle-marks some time during three to three and a half years before the studied violent crime. The corresponding figure for one to one and a half years before the violent crime was 7 %. Less victims are known as drug addicts (Table 40). It should be stressed that these figures do not tell anything about whether the offender/victim was under the influence of drugs when committing the violent crime.

Focusing on the fights between addicts/criminals (Summary Table 2) shows that a very large proportion of the offenders, but also of the victims, were known for previous crimes of violence; also that especially the offenders tend to have a long previous criminal record. Nearly one in six of the offenders were also known as serious drug addicts.

SUMMARY TABLE 2 Fights between addicts/criminals N = 347

CHARACTERISTICS	OFFENDER	VICTIM	CORRELATIONS VICTIM–OFFENDER CHARACTERISTICS		
Mean age	33	33	Age	(r.)	.27
% Females	4	31	Sex	(phi)	.05
% Foreigners	32	20	Nationality	(phi)	.53
% Previously recorded for crime	100	100	Previous criminality	(r.)	.25
Mean years	5.9	2.3			
% Previously recorded for violent crime	63	43	Previous crime of violence	(r.)	−.08
Mean violent crimes	2.2	1.1			
% Intravenous drug users	16	7	Intravenous drug use	(phi)	.41
% No regular work, excl. students	40	—			
% In youth gang	4	2	Youth gang	(phi)	.27
% At work	8	9	At work	(phi)	.01

VICTIM–OFFENDER RELATIONSHIP

	N	%
Family incl. relatives	74	22
Other close acquaintances	98	30
Casual acquaintances	19	6
Strangers	141	42
Missing cases	15	

VICTIMS' INJURIES

	N	%
No injury	11	3
Bruises or less	161	47
Minor fractures etc	144	42
Severe injuries	28	8
Deaths	0	0
Missing cases	3	

PLACE OF OCCURRENCE

	N	%
Apartment	156	46
Street, square	50	15
Park	4	2
Publ. entertain.	78	23
Publ. transport	42	12
Shop, service institution	0	0
Other	11	3
Missing cases	6	

TIME OF OCCURRENCE

	N	%
04.00—07.59	4	1
08.00—11.59	6	2
12.00—15.59	24	8
16.00—19.59	87	27
20.00—23.59	97	31
24.00—03.59	99	31
Missing cases	30	

WEEKENDS
Cases at weekends 48 %

Note: The numbers of missing cases may differ among variables. Some results are a direct consequence of how fights between addicts/criminals have been defined.

There is some association between the victim's and the offender's age and between their previous length of criminal involvement. There is a tendency that foreigners fight foreigners and that Swedes fight Swedes, that drug addicts fight drug addicts, and that cases involving youth gangs occur between two such gangs. This might be interpreted as a result of different interaction patterns among subgroups of those living outside conventional society. More experienced criminals, criminals of the same ethnicity, etc, tend to associate.

Nearly half of the crimes occurred in apartments, and places of public entertainment rank second. The cases occurred predominantly in evenings and nights, with some concentration to weekends. In the majority of cases the victim-offender had some sort of acquaintanceship.

5.4 Fights between Older Persons

As shown in Chapter 4, there is an association between the ages of the victim and the offender, especially in relationship conflicts. Further it was shown in Chapter 4 that the age of those involved in relationship conflicts was higher than in other types of circumstances preceding the violence. A greater proportion of the older offenders, and especially those with a criminal record, were known for alcoholic problems.

In this section data about the violent crimes in which both the victim and the offender were more than 40 years old will be presented (Summary Table 3). In these cases it is predominantly males assaulting females. There is a clear relationship between the offender's and the victim's age. More than half of the offenders have no regular work, and nearly half of them are known for previous criminality. Most cases occur between acquaintances and nearly half among those having a family or family-like relationship. These crimes occur mainly in apartments and are concentrated to evenings, but a comparatively large proportion occur during the daytime.

5.5 Foreigners' Fights

The foreign population in the municipality of Stockholm is 8 %. In the age-group 16–44 years foreign citizen are somewhat more numerous, 13 %. Of the recorded offenders in cases of crimes of violence 29 % are foreigners and among the victims 20 %. So clearly foreigners are overrepresented in crimes of violence, both as offenders and as victims. Such results are not confined to studies of recorded crimes of violence. The Swedish National Bureau of Statistics has reported victim-survey data from 1980/81 showing that foreign citizens are more victimized of violence than Swedish (SCB, Levnadsförhållanden, Rapport 38, 1984 p. 115).

SUMMARY TABLE 3   Fights between older persons   N = 208

CHARACTERISTICS	OFFENDER	VICTIM	CORRELATIONS VICTIM—OFFENDER CHARACTERISTICS		
Mean age	52	53	Age	(r.)	.40
% Females	4	68	Sex	(phi)	−.18
% Foreigners	9	10	Nationality	(phi)	.21
% Previously recorded for crime	45	18	Previous criminality	(r.)	.25
Mean years	3.9	1.2			
% Previously recorded for violent crime	35	9	Previous crime of violence (r.)		.03
Mean violent crimes	1.1	0.2			
% Intravenous drug users	1	1	Intravenous drug use	(phi)	−.01
% No regular work, excl. students	53	—			
% In youth gang	0	0	Youth gang	(phi)	.00
% At work	4	10	At work	(phi)	−.07

VICTIM—OFFENDER RELATIONSHIP

	N	%
Family incl. relatives	97	47
Other close acquaintances	43	21
Casual acquaintances	16	8
Strangers	49	24
Missing cases	3	

VICTIMS' INJURIES

	N	%
No injury	6	3
Bruises or less	118	57
Minor fractures etc	66	31
Severe injuries	13	6
Deaths	4	2
Missing cases	1	

PLACE OF OCCURRENCE

	N	%
Apartment	143	69
Street, square	6	3
Park	4	2
Publ.entertain.	21	10
Publ. transport	18	9
Shop, service institution	3	1
Other	12	6
Missing cases	1	

TIME OF OCCURRENCE

	N	%
04.00—07.59	7	4
08.00—11.59	19	12
12.00—15.59	19	12
16.00—19.59	73	45
20.00—23.59	37	23
24.00—03.59	7	4
Missing cases	46	

WEEKENDS
% Cases at weekends 42

Note: The numbers of missing cases may differ among variables. Some results are a direct consequence of how fights between older persons have been defined.

In 43 % of the recorded crimes of violence with a foreign offender, also the victim was a foreigner, and in 51 % of the cases with a foreign

109

victim, also the offender was a foreigner. In one of eight (13 %) of all recorded crimes of violence both the victim and the offender were foreigners. The characteristics of the victim and the offender and the crimes in these cases are shown in Summary Table 4.

SUMMARY TABLE 4 Foreigners' fights   N = 241

CHARACTERISTICS	OFFENDER	VICTIM	CORRELATIONS VICTIM—OFFENDER CHARACTERISTICS		
Mean age	33	32	Age	(r.)	.13
% Females	4	51	Sex	(phi)	.04
% Foreigners	100	100	Nationality	(phi)	.00
% Previously recorded for crime	62	46	Previous criminality	(r.)	.16
Mean years	2.2	0.9			
% Previously recorded for violent crime	30	17	Previous crime of violence	(r.)	−.11
Mean violent crimes	0.8	0.2			
% Intravenous drug users	0	1	Intravenous drug use	(phi)	.00
% No regular work, excl. students	28	—			
% In youth gang	3	0	Youth gang	(phi)	.00
% At work	9	12	At work	(phi)	.16

VICTIM—OFFENDER RELATIONSHIP	N	%	VICTIMS' INJURIES	N	%
Family incl. relatives	107	45	No injury	7	3
Other close acquaintances	43	18	Bruises or less Minor fractures etc	141	60
Casual acquaintances	30	13		69	29
Strangers	55	23	Severe injuries	14	6
Missing cases	6		Deaths	4	2
			Missing cases	6	

PLACE OF OCCURRENCE	N	%	TIME OF OCCURRENCE	N	%
Apartment	142	60	04.00—07.59	12	6
Street, square	9	4	08.00—11.59	14	7
Park	1	0	12.00—15.59	23	12
Publ. entertain.	44	19	16.00—19.59	47	24
Publ. transport	9	4	20.00—23.59	51	26
Shop, service institution	3	1	24.00—03.59	50	25
Other	27	11	Missing cases	44	
Missing cases	6				

WEEKENDS
% Cases at weekends   37

Note: The numbers of missing cases may differ among variables. Some results are a direct consequence of how foreigners' fights have been defined.

110

In half of the cases the victim was a female. It is more common that males assault females in foreigners' fights (49 %) than in other cases (33 %). A majority of the offenders and nearly half of the victims were recorded for previous criminality. Most cases occurred between acquaintances and in nearly half of the cases the relationship was family or family-like. Very few cases occurred in the streets. Most occurred in apartments, with places of public entertainment ranking second. Compared with the previously discussed types of fights these are more evenly spread over the hours of the day and there is less concentration to weekends.

5.6 Female Victimization

More males than females appear as victims of recorded crimes of violence. In 36 % of all cases the victim was a female, but this is likely to be an underestimate as discussed in Section 2.2.2.

Females tend to be assaulted by someone of their own age and nationality[14] (Summary Table 5). If the female is a drug addict there is some tendency that her assaulter also is a drug addict. And in the rare occasions when she is assaulted while member of a youth gang her assaulter is likely also to be in a youth gang (and to be a female as shown in Section 5.2).

Females mainly get assaulted by acquaintances and in nearly half of the cases by a family member or one with whom she has a family-like relationship. Apartments are the dominating scene of crime and evenings and early nights the most usual time when she is assaulted. There is, as in most cases, some concentration to weekends.

5.7 Victimization During Work

In one of eleven of the violent crimes the victim was victimized during work. As discussed in Section 4.5, the work of the victims in these cases is mainly of a kind that brings them into contact with public entertainment activities or the consequences thereof. The distribution of persons victimized during work according to their profession is shown in Table 45.

---

[14] According to subdivision into Swedes and foreigners.

CHARACTERISTICS	OFFENDER	VICTIM	CORRELATIONS VICTIM–OFFENDER CHARACTERISTICS		
Mean age	37	36	Age	(r.)	.42
% Females	9	100	Sex	(phi)	.00
% Foreigners	26	21	Nationality	(phi)	.52
% Previously recorded for crime	55	24	Previous criminality	(r.)	.12
Mean years	3.2	0.7			
% Previously reorded for violent crime	34	4	Previous crime of violence	(r.)	.12
Mean violent crimes	1.6	0.1			
% Intravenous drug users	6	3	Intravenous drug use	(phi)	.29
% No regular work, excl. students	40	—			
% In youth gang	2	2	Youth gang	(phi)	.77
% At work	4	7	At work	(phi)	.02

VICTIM–OFFENDER RELATIONSHIP

	N	%
Family incl. relatives	480	53
Other close acquaintances:	157	17
Casual acquaintances	34	4
Strangers	229	25
Missing cases	22	

VICTIMS' INJURIES

	N	%
No injury	29	3
Bruises or less	612	68
Minor fractures etc	226	25
Severe injuries	24	3
Deaths	4	0
Missing cases	27	

PLACE OF OCCURRENCE

	N	%
Apartment	610	67
Street, square	125	14
Park	6	1
Publ.entertain.	48	5
Publ. transport	57	6
Shop, service institution	24	3
Other	43	5
Missing cases	9	

TIME OF OCCURRENCE

	N	%
04.00—07.59	30	4
08.00—11.59	58	8
12.00—15.59	77	10
16.00—19.59	219	29
20.00—23.59	248	32
24.00—03.59	133	17
Missing cases	157	

WEEKENDS
% Cases at weekends   44

Note: The numbers of missing cases may differ among variables. Some results are a direct consequence of the definition of the category female victims.

SUMMARY TABLE 6   Victimized during work   N = 236

CHARACTERISTICS	OFFENDER	VICTIM
Mean age	31	36
% Females	9	28
% Foreigners	34	31
% Previously re-corded for crime	64	26
Mean years	2.6	0.5
% Previously recorded for violent crime	34	12
Mean violent crimes	0.7	0.1
% Intravenous drug users	9	0
% No regular work, excl. students	38	—
% In youth gang	7	0
% At work	7	100

CORRELATIONS VICTIM—OFFENDER CHARACTERISTICS

Age	(r.)	.30
Sex	(phi)	.13
Nationality	(phi)	.12
Previous criminality	(r.)	.10
Previous crime of violence	(r.)	−.16
Intravenous drug use	(phi)	.00
Youth gang	(phi)	.00
At work	(phi)	.00

VICTIM—OFFENDER RELATIONSHIP

	N	%
Family incl. relatives	6	3
Other close acquaintances	13	6
Casual acquaintances	13	6
Strangers	194	86
Missing cases	10	

VICTIMS' INJURIES

	N	%
No damage	21	9
Bruises or less	131	58
Minor fractures etc	66	29
Severe injuries	4	2
Deaths	2	1
Missing cases	12	

PLACE OF OCCURRENCE

	N	%
Apartment	19	8
Street, square	27	11
Park	0	0
Publ. entertain.	74	31
Publ. transport	36	15
Shop, service institution	33	14
Other	47	20
Missing cases	0	

TIME OF OCCURRENCE

	N	%
04.00—07.59	5	2
08.00—11.59	15	7
12.00—15.59	28	12
16.00—19.59	69	30
20.00—23.59	66	29
24.00—03.59	44	19
Missing cases	9	

WEEKENDS
% Cases at weekends   41

Note: The numbers of missing cases may differ among variables. Some results are a direct consequence of the definition of the category victimized during work.

Table 45. Persons victimized during work according to their profession. Per cent. Data from the Big City Crime Study

Profession	%
Watchguard	20
Policeman	3
Other official	6
Public transport	17
Restaurant employee	15
Medical personnel	9
Shop employee	15
Other work	14
Total	99

Note: Crimes against officials — if not aggravated — are not included in the study. Despite this, such victims appear in the study which is likely to mean that some legal misclassifications have been made in the police reports. N = 236.

Data about the crimes in which victims were victimized during work are given in Summary Table 6. There is a concentration of these crimes to evenings and early nighttime. Nearly one third occur at places of public entertainment, while public transport and shops/service institutions are other frequent scenes of crime. A fairly high proportion of offenders and especially victims are of foreign nationality, which may partly be explained by the comparatively large proportion of foreigners employed in the public entertainment sector as, for example, restaurant employees.

5.8 Other Fights

Finally we have those cases that did not belong to any of the factor-derived subgroups. These are cases with male victims, in which neither the offender nor the victim were of foreign nationality nor drug addicts/criminals or members of a youth gang at the time of the crime. Further, the victim was not victimized during work.

As evident from Summary Table 7, these are cases in which mostly the victim and the offender are strangers. They have mainly occurred outside apartments, in streets, at places of public entertainment and on public transport. It is also the type of violent crimes most strongly concentrated to nighttime. One might hypothesize that this is a group of crimes in which situational conflicts are common circumstances preceding the violence.

CHARACTERISTICS	OFFENDER	VICTIM	CORRELATIONS VICTIM—OFFENDER CHARACTERISTICS	
Mean age	29	32	Age	(r.)	.04
% Females	4	0	Sex	(phi)	.00
% Foreigners	25	11	Nationality (phi)	−.16
% Previously re-corded for crime	46	36	Previous criminality (r.)	−.20
Mean years	2.0	1.4		
% Previously recorded for violent crime	23	16	Previous crime of violence (r.)	.10
Mean violent crimes	0.8	0.5		
% Intravenous drug users	3	3	Intravenous drug use (phi)	.03
% No regular work, excl. students	21	—		
% In youth gang	13	1	Youth gang (phi)	.05
% At work	19	0	At work (phi)	.00

VICTIM—OFFENDER RELATIONSHIP

	N	%
Family incl. relatives	30	3
Other close acquaintances	106	11
Casual acquaintances	100	10
Strangers	756	76
Missing cases	80	

VICTIMS' INJURIES

	N	%
No injury	44	4
Bruises or less	494	49
Minor fractures etc	396	39
Severe injuries	77	8
Deaths	1	0
Missing cases	60	

PLACE OF OCCURRENCE

	N	%
Apartment	221	21
Street, square	286	28
Park	31	3
Publ.entertain.	225	21
Publ. transport	183	17
Shop, service, institution	12	1
Other	104	10
Missing cases	10	

TIME OF OCCURRENCE

	N	%
04.00—07.59	28	3
08.00—11.59	55	6
12.00—15.59	95	10
16.00—19.59	171	17
20.00—23.59	330	33
24.00—03.59	307	31
Missing cases	86	

WEEKENDS
% Cases at weekends   50

Note: The numbers of missing cases may differ among variables.

5.9 Discussion

Hindelang et al. (1978), in an attempt to formulate a theory of personal criminal victimization, stressed the importance of different lifestyles; "...different lifestyles imply different probabilities that individuals will be in particular places, at particular times under particular circumstances, interacting with particular kinds of persons..." (p. 251). In their eight propositions they state, among other things, that similar lifestyles are related to frequency of social contact and interaction, and that there is a relationship between offenders' and victims' demographic characteristics, meaning that people with demographic characteristics similar to those of the offenders are more likely than others to be victimized.

The results presented in Chapter 5 may to some extent be interpreted as supporting the thesis of a relationship between similiar lifestyles and victimization, i.e. gang-fights, foreigners' fight, fights between older persons and between criminals/addicts.

6 Violent Offenders in a 1953 Stockholm Birth Cohort

All data about the violent offenders presented so far have been taken from cross-sectional studies of sample of violent crimes. In this chapter longitudinal data of violent offenders in a birth cohort will be explored. The data cover the ages up to young adulthood (25/26 years). The definition of crimes of violence is wider here than in the two preceding chapters (see Section 1.1.4), but it is likely that most of them committed by the cohort members involve assault. Further, on the basis of the results in Chapter 4 and considering the ages studied, it is reasonable to assume that it is predominantly situational conflicts, molestation and sudden attack (in that order) that are the circumstances of the cohort members' violent crimes. This may be of some importance for the patterns shown, since relationship conflicts are mainly a type of circumstance in violent crimes in which people get involved at older ages than those studied.

The main subject of my research was the age at onset, distribution, persistence and specialization in crimes of violence. Before focusing on crimes of violence, some notes on the cohort members' criminality will be presented[15]. Of the 15,117 members of the Project Metropolitan birth cohort, 19 % (2,387) were recorded at least once by the police at the studied ages. Twelve per cent were multiple offenders. Restriction to males, 31 %, was recorded at least once and 20 % were multiple offenders. The most common type of crime committed by the cohort members was, as might be expected, theft, with traffic crimes rankning second.

6.1 Incidence and Distribution

Four per cent (591) of the cohort members were recorded for a violent crime. Most of them were one-time offenders (58 %). Of those known for criminality of any kind one fifth (21 %) were known for at least one violent crime. There are 7.5 times more males than females in the cohort known for crimes of violence.

---

[15] Those interested in a fuller treatment of the cohort members' criminality than given here are referred to Wikström (1985b).

In Figure 6 is shown the incidence of violent offenders (shaded area) and of crimes of violence at each of the studied ages (years). There is a low incidence before the age of 16, then there are 100 to 150 crimes per year at the ages of 16–19, and a generally lower level at ages 20–25, about 75–125 recorded crimes per year.

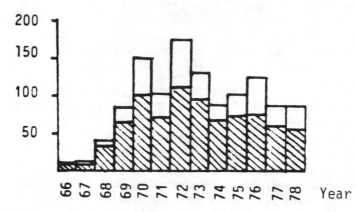

Figure 6. Age-specific incidence of crimes of violence and recorded offenders in cases of violent crime (shaded area).

6.1.1 Distribution of Recorded Crimes of Violence by the Cohort Members – the J-Shaped Curve

It has been argued, at least as far as certain "traditional" crimes are concerned, that there is good reason to believe that a minority of all offenders commit a large proportion of all offences (Carlsson, 1975).

In a study of break and enter offenders in Stockholm (Persson, 1976) the author shows that 10 % of the offenders during the studied period accounted for 50 % of the cleared-up break-and-enter cases.

Another Swedish example is a study of a representative sample of men in the General Criminal Register (Tham, 1978). It is shown (Table 7, p. 116) that 17 % of those convicted account for 45 % of the convictions.

Tham points out that those reconvicted several times are convicted of more offences than the others. With this in mind, and the fact that Tham works with data at the final stage of the selection process (i.e. from crime commission over detection, reporting, etc, to conviction), it is likely that there is some underestimation of the importance of a minor, highly active group, although it should be mentioned that Tham himself draws the conclusion that the hypothesis that few commit a major part of the crimes is probably not generally valid (ibid p. 117).

The observation that few commit a great number of the crimes is not limited to studies of recorded criminality; for example, Elmhorn's study of self-declared criminality among schoolchildren in Stockholm (Elmhorn, 1965:129).

In the present study it was possible to throw some light upon this topic. Most offenders in the cohort are known only for one or a few offences. As regards the significance of those few individuals committing a large number of crimes it may be mentioned that 6 % (161 individuals) of the 2,837 known offenders in the cohort were responsible for 50 % (11,937) of all offences (23,774) recorded for the cohort members.

Impressive as this figure is, it is however not without fault. It tends slightly to overemphasize the importance of the minor, highly active group, since the figure is calculated on the number of offences each offender is known for. Obviously, some of these offences might have involved several cohort members, so that some offences would be counted more than once. But it seems most unlikely that this would alter the conclusion that only a few offenders in the cohort are responsible for a great part of the cohort's criminality.

Focusing on violence (Figure 7), it is evident that there is also a highly skew distribution. The incidence of violent crimes varies between 1–16 and most offenders are only recorded for one violent crime. One

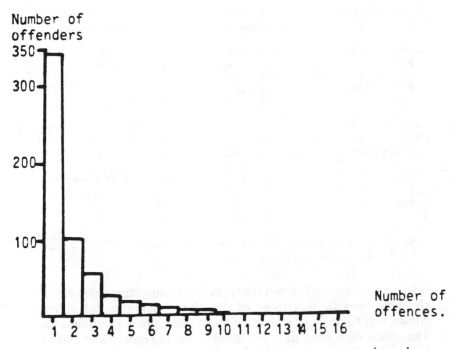

Figure 7. Incidence of recorded violent crimes among the cohort members up to the age of 25/26 (July 1979).

119

fifth (19 % or 122 offenders) are responsible for 50 % (645) of the 1,290 violent crimes recorded for the cohort members during the years studied.

This means that the significance of a small "highly" active group of offenders is less pronounced where violent crimes are concerned than with respect to crime in general.

6.2 Age at Onset

Of those cohort members whose first crime of any kind was committed up to and including the age of 25, 47 % had their debut before the age of 17, and nearly two thirds before the age of 20. In contrast, crimes of violence are likely to start at a higher age, only 19 % of them ocurring before the age of 17 and 58 % before the age of 20 (Table 46). A look at the percentage of reported crimes of all kinds each year by debutants shows this proportion to decrease with age. For crimes of violence a nearly perfect relationship (r. = –0,99) can be observed between age and percentage debutants. This is also well illustrated by figure 8.

Table 46. The recorded age-specific debuts in crimes of any kind and crimes of violence. Per cent in brackets. The Cohort Study

Year	Age	All crimes		Crimes of violence	
−1966	−13	454	(16)	8	(1)
1967	14	320	(11)	12	(2)
1968	15	266	(10)	34	(6)
1969	16	292	(10)	59	(10)
1970	17	279	(10)	85	(15)
1971	18	222	(8)	58	(10)
1972	19	221	(8)	81	(14)
1973	20	178	(6)	65	(11)
1974	21	186	(7)	39	(7)
1975	22	150	(5)	41	(7)
1976	23	90	(3)	39	(7)
1977	24	80	(3)	30	(5)
1978	25	64	(2)	18	(3)
Total		1,689	(99)	569	(99)

Note: Offenders with debut in the first half of 1979 excluded from the table.

A question of special interest relates to the results presented in earlier chapters, showing that many of the offenders known for violent crimes also have a fairly high record of other previous criminality. The cohort data allow us to see whether, for the multiple offenders, records of other criminality are likely to precede records of crimes of violence. This is also generally the case, which places greater

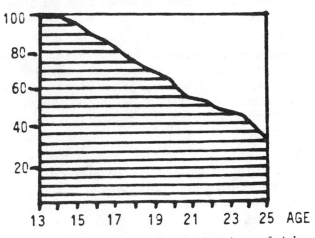

% DEBUTANTS

Figure 8. Age and per cent debutants in crimes of violence.

emphasis on the interpretation that many violent crimes may be related to a criminal or socially loaded person's life-style.

6.3 Persistence

Many researcher find it convenient, both empirically and theoretically, to divide criminals into subgroups according to their involvement in criminal activities. Differences in social background and seriousness of criminality are reported when temporary and persistent offenders are compared (e.g. Wolfgang et al., 1972:88; West & Farrington, 1977:36–37).

Also in discussions of crime prevention the distinction between temporary and persistent offenders has become important. The temporary offender is mostly viewed as an oppurtunistic offender and hence advocated crime prevention measures are aimed at reducing oppurtunities for crime (see, e.g., Clarke & Mayhew, 1980; Kühlhorn & Svensson, 1982).

Some researchers (e.g. Balvig, 1982) report that many of the persistent offenders' crimes are also opportunistic, but there seems to be a sceptical attitude among many researchers concerning the importance of opportunities (Persson, 1975:52–53) and opportunity-reducing measures in crime prevention (Clarke & Mayhew, 1980:11) for these offenders' criminality. This may be stated in somewhat simplified terms to the effect that temporary offenders run into opportunities, while persistent offenders seek out opportunities.

There is obviously a relationship between incidence of crime and persistence in criminality. Although these concepts in some cases have been used as equivalents, they differ in that persistence relates to duration in time; some highly frequent offenders may have their offences spread over a long period, while others may have them concentrated in time.

Persistence is measured as the number of years the cohort members are recorded for at least one of the crimes in question. Since all the individuals in the study are of the same age, there is no need to adjust for age, as would have been necessary in a study covering persons of different ages. The maximum possible duration of persistence is 14 years (1966–1979[16]).

As shown in table 47 55 % of offenders known for any crime and 72 % of those known for violent crimes are recorded only in one year. The mean duration of persistence in violent crimes is 1.5 years (the year of the first crime included[17]).

Table 47. Persistence (in years). All crimes and crimes of violence

Number of years	All crimes		Crimes of violence	
	N	%	N	%
1	1,551	54.7	424	71.7
2	515	18.1	94	15.9
3	273	9.1	38	6.4
4	142	5.0	14	2.4
5	101	3.6	11	1.9
6	67	2.4	4	0.7
7	54	1.9	4	0.7
8	49	1.7	2	0.3
9	28	1.0	—	—
10	17	0.6	—	—
11	22	0.8	—	—
12	10	0.3	—	—
13	6	0.2	—	—
14	2	0.1	—	—
Total	2,837	100.0	591	100.0

Taking as a criterion for separation of a persistent group of offenders from the rest that, in at least half of the studied years, they have minimally one recorded crime gives a group of persistent offenders in cases of violent crime of less than 1 %. The criterion may be regarded as very strict with regard to the offenders' hidden criminality and to the probability that some of the offenders have had times of incapacitation during the years studied (i.e. spent time in prison).

---

[16]Only the first half of 1979 is included in the study. In the calculations of years of persistence 1979 is treated as a full year.

[17]Exclusion of one-time offenders gives a mean persistence of 2.3 years in violent crimes.

One obvious problem in counting years of recorded criminality as measure of persistence is the differing age at onset among the offenders. Taking this into account and, counting how many offenders have at least one record in half of the years from the first to the final year (1979) gives a higher percentage of persistent offenders. With this criterion 6.2 % of the violent offenders are persistent.

However, the latter way of determining persistence is also problematic. The main problem of this criterion is that offenders with a late debut may constitute the bulk of the persistent group. Of the offenders who fulfil the criterion of persistence, most are late debutants – 51 % of the offenders in the persistent group had their debut after the age of 20.

A look at the relationship between persistence (in years) and incidence shows, as expected, that incidence of crime increases with persistence (Table 48).

Table 48. Frequency of crime by persistence

Persistence (in years)	Violent crimes	
	Mean incid. over the period	Mean incid. per year
1	1.3	1.3
2	3.0	1.5
3	4.3	1.4
4	6.8	1.7
5	7.8	1.6
6	11.5	1.9
7	13.0	1.9
8	13.5	1.7

The increase in mean incidence per year of persistence is at best slight; the most persistent violent offenders have about 0.5 more violent crimes per year of persistence than the least persistent.

6.4 Specialization

A widely discussed topic is whether criminality is a unidimensional phenomenon or not. The answer to this question depends, among other things, upon the definition of unidimensionality.

Hindelang et al. draw the conclusion from a review of self-declaration studies that *"These studies strongly suggest, then, that varieties of delinquency are not independent, but more or less consistent with each other. Thus, there is nearly universal support among the studies examined for the conclusion that at least one dimension, perhaps loosely configured, of delinquency exists"* (Hindelang et al. 1981:67–70). Authors of Swedish self-declaration studies disagree about the specificity of delinquent behaviour. Some interpret their results as showing unidimensionality (Elmhorn, 1969:93; Suikilla, 1983), others as showing multidimensionality (Olofsson, 1971:80; Dunér & Haglund, 1974:33). It should be remembered in this context that self-declaration studies mostly concern young people and to a great degree are confined to less serious offences (or delinquency).

Concerning recorded criminality Hindelang et al. write that *"...efforts to establish the dimensionality of official data, as we have seen, are extremely rare"* and they conclude that *"...official delinquent acts are only weakly correlated among themselves"* (Hindelang et al. 1981:71).

In a study (1964/1965) of 948 21-year old male recidivists in the Netherlands, Buikhuisen & Jongman report that *"Roughly speaking, recidivists relapse into the same kind of offence." "...it was found that more than 50 per cent of the recidivists could be classified if minimally 75 per cent of the offences on their record were of the same type"* (Buikhusen & Jongman, 1970:122). The four main offence categories used in the study were 1) economic offences, 2) aggressive offences, 3) sexual offences, and 4) traffic offences. Recidivists were defined as those offenders who had been convicted at least three times. A point to be made here is that it is probably of some importance for the results concerning specificity how broad are the offence categories that are used.

Walker et al. studied 4,301 Scottish males, who were convicted for the first time in 1947, during a period of eleven years in which their subsequent convictions were recorded. They also had access to a sample of 4,239 London males convicted in March or April 1957. In this case earlier convictions (this was not a first conviction sample) and subsequent convictions for a period of five years were studied. Focusing on violence, as they did, they drew the conclusion, among others, that 1) *"...with each successive conviction for violence the probability of a further such conviction increases sharply..."* (Walker et al. 1963:469), and 2) *"Loosely speaking, the table demonstrates an increasing tendency to 'specialise' in offences involving violence"* (ibid. p. 470). The increasing tendency to specialize refers to a relationship between number of convictions for violence and the percentage of subsequent convictions (within three years) that involve violence. The term "specialize" is perhaps not so appropriate here, since the criterion for specialization is that the conviction includes violence (perhaps among other types of crime).

In a study by Peterson et al., focusing on assaultive versus non-assaultive offenders, they present support for the hypothesis that *"...persons are arrested for assaultive crimes or non-assaultive crimes,*

124

but not both..." (Peterson et al. 1962:46). The study was conducted in St. Louis (USA) on a sample of 88 males aged 40 and above arrested for serious violent crimes (homicide, aggravated assault) or burglary or larceny. The high age of those in the sample, as well as the relatively small size of the sample, should be noted in comparisons with the other mentioned studies.

All these studies of recorded crimes indicate some "specialization". However, in a longitudinal study of recorded criminality among males in Philadelphia from their tenth to eighteenth birthday, Wolfgang et al. summarize their results concerning the repetitiveness according to type of offence among the cohort members in the following way;

> "*...the choice of the type of the next offense is only very slightly related to the type of prior offense or offenses. This finding leads us to the conclusion that the type of next offense – be it injury, theft, damage, combination, or nonindex – cannot well be predicted by examination of the prior offense history, at least when the history is represented by our typology.* **There is practically no evidence to support a hypothesis of the existence of offense specialization among juvenile delinquents.** *We are able to assert, however, that once an offense has been committed, the probability of a repeat of the same type of violation is somewhat greater than the likelihood of the initial offense. But as we earlier pointed out, these increased probabilities of repeats of the same type of offense can be explained, under the assumption of a stationary transition process, as the product of the accumulation of a large number of offenses rather than as the product of any special proclivity toward offense specialization*". (My emphasis, Wolfgang et al. 1972:254.)

Another U.S. study of 1,619 juvenile offenders in Pima County (Arizona) from the age of 8 to the age of 17, carried out by the same method as that of Wolfgang et al., reaches the same conclusion about specialization; "*...there was no evidence that male or female juveniles specialize in a particular type of offense as their official career develops, although the nature of their involvement differs*" (Rojek & Erickson, 1982:26).

Thus, to summarize the reports both of researchers occupied with recorded criminality as well as of those conducting self-declaration studies, there are differing opinions with regard to the specificity of criminal behaviour.

This issue appears to be complex and to depend on what meaning is given to specificity, and perhaps on what crime categories are used in the study and what ages the study covers.

It is certain that, if by specificity is meant the exclusive commission of one type of offence, then surely criminality is best regarded as a versatile phenomenon. On the other hand, if specificity is used as a concept describing tendencies to "prefer" certain types of offences to others, the answer is less obvious. In this case it is, of course, of utmost importance what strength of these "tendencies" is judged to be necessary before talking about specificity.

6.4.1 Zero-Order Correlations

In Table 49 and 50 the correlations between different types of crime are presented. In Table 49 the variables do not take into account the incidence of the crimes, i.e. the variables are coded according to whether the individual is known or not known for the type of crime in question, while in Table 50 the correlation is between the incidence of crime in the respective categories.

The results show that there are only weak positive correlations (or in some instances weak negative correlations) between the different crime categories when the concern is whether an individual who has committed one type of crime also has committed others (Table 49).

Table 49. Offence categories. Zero-order correlations. Dichotomies. Only cohort members recorded for criminality are included

	Violence	Damage	Fraud	Traffic	Narcotic	Other
Stealing	.06	.03	.10	−.12	.12	−.10
Violence		.22	.17	.07	.17	.22
Damage			.14	.04	.15	.10
Fraud				.02	.21	.09
Traffic					.06	.17
Narcotic						.25

Note: The variables are coded as 1 or 0 if the individual is or is not known for the offence. N = 2,837

Table 50. Offence categories. Zero-order correlations. Incidences. Only cohort members recorded for criminality are included

	Violence	Damage	Fraud	Traffic	Narcotic	Other
Stealing	.39	.44	.14	.40	.18	.18
Violence		.39	.13	.29	.16	.26
Damage			.08	.17	.13	.16
Fraud				.16	.09	.13
Traffic					.16	.53
Narcotic						.33

Note: The variables are coded as the incidence of offences in each offence category. N = 2,837

Another way of measuring the relationship between types of crime is to correlate the incidences of crime. Since we know that the distribution of crimes among offenders is highly skew, the highly frequent offenders (if versatile) are likely to play a great role in correlations between different crimes. The results (Table 50) show a rather strong interrelationship between the incidence of violent crimes, stealing and vandalism. Also traffic crimes appear to be a part of this interrelationship, although the correlation between traffic crimes and vandalism is comparatively low. On the other hand, fraud and narcotic crimes are neither strongly interrelated nor related to other crimes.

The result indicates that there exists a versatile pattern at least among more frequent offenders that might be labelled **conventional versatile criminality** (stealing, violent crimes, vandalism and traffic crimes).

6.4.2 The Specificity Ratio

Another way of studying specialization is what might be called the specificity ratio. This ratio attempts to answer the question how many of the criminals known for crimes of violence are to be regarded as specialized offenders.

The specificity ratio is calculated in the following way. First, all offenders with less than three crimes (all kinds) are excluded from the analysis. Second, of all remaining offenders known for a crime of violence a count is made of how many of their crimes are crimes of violence. Then what is shown (Table 51) is how much of the criminality of those recorded for violent crimes is violent crime.

Taking a specificity ratio above 75 % as a criterion of specialization, only 2 % of the violent offenders are specialized. Of all offenders in the cohort know for three or more crimes 27 % were specialized according to the criterion, mostly in crimes of theft.

Table 51. The specificity ratio. Offenders known for less than 3 crimes (all kinds) excluded

Per cent crimes of violence	Offenders known for crimes of violence	
	N	%
0— 25 %	330	73
26— 50 %	92	20
51— 75 %	23	5
76—100 %	10	2
Total	455	100

6.5 Some Further Explorations

As shown in the preceding section, there were rather strong correlations between the incidences of violent crimes and of stealing and damage. Further, few offenders known for violent crimes could be labelled as specialized according to the criterion used (2 %).

On this basis, it might be argued that there are really no "violent offenders" if by violent offender is meant a person who frequently and persistently commits crimes of violence and devotes most of his efforts to that type of crime.

In this section we shall go a bit deeper into the relationship between violent and other criminality and relate this to incidence, persistence and age at onset. Dividing the cohort members into those a) not known for criminality, b) those known for criminality but not for violent crimes, c) those known for both violent and other crimes, and d) those known solely for violent crimes gives the following table (Table 52).

Table 52. Cohort members in groups according to whether they are known for criminality or not and whether the criminality involves violent crimes

	N	%
No criminality	12,277	81.2
Criminality. No violent crimes	2,249	14.9
Criminality involving violent crimes	510	3.4
Only violent crimes	81	0.5
Total	15,117	100.0

Of those known for violent criminality 86 % are also known for other types of crime. Comparing violent offenders known with those not known for other criminality according to the incidence of violent crimes (Table 53 – top) shows that those known only for violent crimes are mainly one-time offenders (85 %) and that only 3 % of them are known for more than 2 violent crimes. Hence the more active violent offenders are to be found among those recorded both for violent and other types of crime. It is then hardly surprising that nearly all (97 %) of those known only for violent crimes have a persistence lasting only one year or less (Table 53- bottom).

A look at the relationship between total incidence of crimes (excluding violent crimes) by violent offenders also known for other crimes compared to offenders not known for violent crimes turns out

Table 53. Incidence of and persistence in violent crimes by groups of
violent offenders known and, respectively, not known for other types
of crime

Incidence of violent crimes	Both violent and other crimes		Only violent crimes			
	N	%	N	%		
1	276	54 (80)*)	69	85 (20)	345	(100)
2	93	18 (91)	9	11 (9)	102	(100)
3— 5	96	19 (98)	2	2 (2)	98	(100)
6— 8	29	6 (97)	1	1 (3)	30	(100)
9—16	16	3 (100)	0	0 (0)	16	(100)
Total	510	100	81	99	591	

Persistence (years) in violent crime	Both violent and other crimes		Only violent crimes			
	N	%	N	%		
1	345	68 (81)	79	97 (19)	424	(100)
2	92	18 (98)	2	2 (2)	94	(100)
3—5	63	12 (100)	0	0 (0)	63	(100)
6—8	10	2 (100)	0	0 (0)	10	(100)
Total	510	100	81	99	591	

*) = Row per cent.

to be rather interesting (Table 54). It is apparent that violent
offenders in general have a comparatively high incidence of other
crimes. Only 15 % are one-time offenders and as many as 27 % have
more than 25 other recorded crimes (24 % if the 81 offenders only
known for violent crimes are added).

Table 54. Incidence of criminality other than violent crimes among
offenders known for both violent and other crimes

Incidence of criminality (violent crimes excluded)	Offender known for both violent and other crimes		Offender not known for violent crimes	
	N	%	N	%
1	76	15	984	44
2— 5	137	27	833	37
6— 10	55	11	225	10
11— 25	102	20	147	6
26— 50	77	15	43	2
51—100	42	8	13	1
101—200	14	3	4	0
201—	7	1	0	0
Total	510	100	2,249	100

9

It is striking that a large proportion of the most frequent offenders are also known for violent crimes; of those recorded for more than 25 crimes (other than violent) as many as 70 % are known for at least one violent crime. All the seven offenders with more than 200 recorded crimes (other than violent) are known for at least one violent crime.

The conclusions seems to be straightforward;

• There are practically no pure violent offenders.

• Most offenders known for violent crimes have a rather high activity in other types of crime.

A look for any differences with regard to age at onset between the two groups of violent offenders (Table 55) shows a very slight tendency that the debut for violent offenders known only for crimes of violence is more spread over the ages. The differences are, however, small.

Table 55. Age at onset in cases of violent crime by groups of violent offenders known and, respectively, not known for other types of crime

Age at onset	Both violent and other crimes		Only violent crimes		Total	
	N	%	N	%	N	%
1966 (13)	4	50 (1)*	4	50 (5)*	8	100
1967 (14)	8	67 (2)	4	33 (5)	12	100
1968 (15)	29	85 (6)	5	15 (7)	34	100
1969 (16)	49	83 (10)	10	17 (14)	59	100
1970 (17)	79	93 (16)	6	7 (8)	85	100
1971 (18)	50	86 (10)	8	14 (11)	58	100
1972 (19)	72	89 (15)	9	11 (12)	81	100
1973 (20)	56	86 (11)	9	14 (12)	65	100
1974 (21)	36	92 (7)	3	8 (4)	39	100
1975 (22)	35	85 (7)	6	15 (8)	41	100
1976 (23)	36	92 (7)	3	8 (4)	39	100
1977 (24)	24	80 (5)	6	20 (8)	30	100
1978 (25)	17	94 (3)	1	6 (1)	18	100
	495	(100)	74	(99)		

* = Column per cent.

In this Chapter I have so far tried to describe the criminality of the cohort members, with special emphasis on their violent criminality and the relation of that to other types of criminality.

The results concerning the cohort members' violent criminality can be summarized in the following points:

- 4 % of the cohort members have been recorded by the police for at least one violent crime from the age of 13 to the age of 25/26 (July 1979).

- 21 % of those known for any criminality are recorded for at least one violent crime.

- 7.5 times more males than females are recorded for a violent crime.

- 58 % of the violent offenders are one-time offenders.

- 19 % of the violent offenders are responsible for 50 % of the violent crimes.

- The incidence of violent criminality over the studied ages is fairly stable after the take-off at age 16, although there are some peaks at the ages 17 and 19.

- Debuts in violent crime during the studied period are in many cases likely to come at a relatively high age; 56 % had their debut after the age of 18.

- The majority of those (multiple offenders) with a debut in violent crime have earlier been recorded for other types of crime.

- The highest incidences for the first commission of violent crime are between the ages 16 to 20.

- The proportion of recidivists increases linearly with the age of the cohort. At age 23 more than half of those recorded for a violent crime are recidivists in violent criminality.

- Few of the violent offenders can be regarded as persistent in violent criminality; 72 % are only known for violent criminality during a single year.

- There is no marked increase in incidence of violent crimes per year with increasing persistence in violent criminality.

- There are practically no specialized violent offenders.

The results presented so far in this chapter show that it seems fruitful to distinguish between two groups of violent offenders. First, we have those who only commit violent crimes. They are a minor part of all violent offenders (14 %), a group of **occasional violent offenders**. Most are one-time offenders (85 %) and their violent criminality is restricted to a single year (97 %).

Second, we have those offenders who have committed both violent and other types of crimes. Although nearly all violent offenders with a greater incidence of and persistence in violent criminality belong to this group; their distinguishing feature seems to be a great involvement in criminal behaviour of different kinds. A minority of these offenders are one-time offenders in crimes other than violence. This group may be labelled **criminal active violent offenders**.

It seems to be a plausible hypothesis that the violent crimes of the offenders belonging to this group in many instances may be offsprings – direct or indirect – of a "criminal life-style".

6.6 Some Notes on the Social Class Background of Violent Offenders

Chapter 6 will conclude with some notes on the social class background of the offenders.

The probably single most dominating explanatory variable in the history of criminology is that of the offender's social class background. However, its importance has from time to time been questioned (e.g. Hirschi, 1969:66) and recently there has been an intense debate on the issue, mainly in the American Sociological Review (e.g. Tittle et al., 1978; Hindelang et al., 1979; Braithwaite, 1979; Elliot & Ageton, 1980; Kleck, 1982; Thornberry & Farnworth, 1982). Two reviews of the literature (Tittle et al., 1978 and Braithewaithe, 1979), reaching different conclusions about social class-crime relationship, seem to have been the prime mover in that debate.

Restricting our attention to so-called "traditional crimes" (theft, vandalism, violence, etc) the state of knowledge may briefly be summarized as follows. There is a negative association between social class and traditional criminality (i.e. lower social classes commit more crimes), but it is comparatively weak. There is often a stronger association when the concern is adults than juveniles. A special problem in that context is, however, that the social class of the adult is likely to be affected by his (previous) criminality[18]. The results of the Swedish studies on the topic do not depart much from international experience (e.g. Jonsson, 1969:218–222; Olofsson, 1971:146–151; Werner, 1971; SOU 1976:72; Tham, 1979:130–136; Janson, 1982).

As shown in Chapter 4, many of the offenders in crimes of violence were recorded for different social problems, but no data were given about their social class. Most of the offenders in the Gävle Study were classified in the lowest social group of a division into three (86 %)[19]. It might be mentioned that the corresponding figure for the victims was 82 %. These figures refer only to those offenders (victims) who had regular work at the time of the crime (57 % of the offenders and 67 % of the victims, students not being counted as having regular "work").

---

[18] For more extensive discussion see Wikström (1983b).

[19] The classification is based on the professions and the ranking into social groups. It is an adjusted version of the social group classification formerly used in the official election statistics.

The problem of classifying violent offenders according to their present social class, partly for the reason that many are out of work and/or living an unconventional way of life, is well illustrated by the following quote from McClintock's London study:

> "...the majority of offenders were labourers, casual workers, street traders etc. /.../...most of the other offenders were semi-skilled factory workers or low grade clerical staff. These two groups accounted for more than 85 per cent of the offenders convicted of crimes of violence. The records show that a considerable proportion of these offenders frequently changed from one job to another .../.../ More than a third of the adult offenders who were classified under Group A were either described as unemployed at the time of their conviction for crimes of violence, or were describing themselves as 'labourer', 'street trader', or 'general dealer' as a facade for a living based on the proceeds of crime." (McClintock, 1963:132).

Thinking in casual terms, it is obviously difficult to use cross-sectional data of offenders' social class background to make any inferences about the importance of social class background for the propensity to commit crimes of violence. Longitudinal data, however, provide a better opportunity. In Table 56 is shown persistence in crimes of violence of the cohort members according to their parents' social class at their birth in four classes. The result shows that there is an association between persistence in crimes of violence and parents' social class, but at the same time the overwhelming majority of cohort members in any of the social classes are not known for crimes of violence, signifying that the explanatory power of parents' social class is slight.

Table 56. Social class of parents at cohort members birth and persistence in crimes of violence. Per cent in brackets

Persistence (in years)	Social class of parents			
	Lower working class	Working class	Middle class	Upper middle class
0	2,638 (94)	3,950 (96)	5,408 (97)	1,989 (99)
1	126 (4)	119 (3)	130 (2)	23 (1)
2—4	44 (2)	53 (1)	37 (1)	3 (0)
5—8	8 (0)	9 (0)	1 (0)	1 (0)
Total	2,816 (100)	4,131 (100)	5,576 (100)	2,016 (100)

Missing cases: 578; Gamma = -0.32; r. = -0.08; X^2 = 105.67; Significant at 1 % level

Regarding age at onset, the differences between the social classes were not significant at the 5 % level.

Part 3

Ecological Aspects

Temporal Variations

Regional Variations

Urban-Rural Differences

Intercity Variations

Intracity Variations

In Part 3 ecological aspects of crimes of violence will be the main concern. As a general background to the studies presented I shall, in the introduction to this part, a) give a brief overview of the ecological research tradition in the field of crime[1], b) focus in somewhat greater detail on research into the ecology of crimes of violence, and c) discuss some of the major methodological issues confronting ecological studies in relation to the present subject of research.

The Ecology of Crime

Roughly, the studies on the ecology of crime may be divided into an "old" and a "new" line of research. In both cases the inner differentiation of the city serves as a general frame of reference for the research (Table 57)[2].

Table 57. Main lines of study of the ecology of crime

General frame of reference	The inner differentiation of the city (population segregation and land use)	
	The "old" ecology of crime	The "new" ecology of crime
Main research interest	Neighbourhood effects on criminal motivation.	Local milieu (situational) effects on crime occurrence.
Main lines of explanation	Subcultures. Social disorganization — weak social control. (Relative deprivation)	Opportunity structures. Routine activity patterns.

The most vital result from the study of the "old" ecology of crime was the identification of high offender rate areas (Delinquency Areas). Besides a high juvenile delinquency rate, these areas were characterized by numerous other social problems, poor housing, low socio-economic status of inhabitants, declining population and often rapid changes in the composition of the population, often ethnical changes (see Shaw & McKay, 1969). Similar results have been reported in many other studies, although concentrations of juvenile delinquents as high as shown by Shaw & McKay are not always identified (e.g. Lander, 1954; Bagley, 1965; Bordua, 1958; Chilton, 1964; Wallis & Maliphant, 1967).

---

[1] More extensive reviews are given in Wikström (1982, 1983c, 1984).

[2] The discussion here is restricted to ecological studies of the city.

137

Shaw & McKay worked with two explanatory models. One was the transmission of criminality from young adults to juveniles (culture transmission or subcultures), the other emphasized social instability, resulting in weak social control in the area (Shaw & McKay, 1969:384–386). For example, it was assumed that it was difficult to create solidarity and consensus in areas with a mobile and ethnically heterogeneous population.

Shaw & McKay have been criticized for having contradictory explanatory models (e.g. Baldwin & Bottoms, 1976:16). Kornhauser (1978:69) strongly argued that subcultures are an unnecessary element in the theories of Shaw & McKay; subcultures arise only in socially instable areas where the social control is weak. Kornhauser (1978:70) further states that the data used by Shaw & McKay do not give convincing proof of any great importance of subcultures for the high rates of juvenile delinquency in the Delinquency Areas.

Relative deprivation (of the inhabitants of the Delinquency Areas) was not favoured as a major explanation of the high juvenile delinquency rate by Shaw & McKay (1969:186–187), although they claimed that it was "understandable" that inhabitants in these areas sometimes used unconventional measures (i.e. crime) to reach economic goals. Some of their arguments against relative deprivation as explanation was that even in the Slum Areas most youths became law-abiding citizen and that there were areas with poor conditions that did not have extremely high rates of juvenile delinquency. However, they did not regard weak economic and social conditions of the population as unimportant. For instance, weak social and economic resources contributed to the difficulties of the adults of Delinquency Areas to mobilize against a common problem: a high rate of juvenile delinquency.

The Delinquency Areas (Slum Areas) of Shaw & McKay were located near the city centre and that location was mainly related to ecological processes when the city centre expanded, which caused residential areas to decline when invaded by commercial establishments and light industry. Although valid for many big US cities, these patterns are not universal, as shown in various studies (e.g. Herbert, 1972:217; Harries, 1974:74–75).

In a discussion of British studies on the ecology of crime Baldwin (1975) notes that, with regard to slum clearance programmes, the interest over time has shifted from a study of Slum Areas to what Baldwin calls "difficult council housing estates", which in Sweden is nearest to what is often called Social Problem Areas. These areas are often a "result" of planning instead of a "result" of a housing market based on unrestricted free enterprise, and often located in the outer city areas.

The creation of Social Problem Areas has been discussed and studied in relation to a) differential rent levels, b) local housing authorities'

138

policies of distribution of apartments, c) self-selection of tenants, and d) the reputation of an area. For a discussion of this from British experience see Baldwin & Xanthos (1981:203–225). It is of interest to note that the "classical" causes subcultures and social instability appear as explanatory factors of high offender rates in the intense studies of four council estates made by Baldwin & Xanthos (p. 217 and 219)[3].

The "new" line of research into the ecology of crime, or environmental criminology as it has been called, is summarized in the following way by Brantingham & Brantingham: *"Environmental criminologists begin their study of crime by asking questions about where and when crimes occur. They ask about the physical and social characteristics of crime sites. They ask about the movements that bring the offender and the target together at the crime site. They ask about the perceptual processes that lead to the selection of crime sites and the social processes of ecological labelling. Environmental criminologists also ask about the spatial patterning in laws and the ways in which legal rules create crime sites. They ask about the spatial distribution of targets and offenders in urban, suburban and rural settings."* (Brantingham & Brantingham, 1981:8).

Since the "new" ecology of crime has been more interested in crime occurrence than criminal motivation – individual variations of the latter are often taken as one point of departure – the focus is rather on variations in land use than in segregation and composition of the population of areas. The built environment has been given a greater role than in the "old" ecology, where the social milieu was the main concern. The perhaps most well-known example of this is the theory of Defensible Space (Newman, 1972).

Just as it has been found that offenders show concentrations in some areas, also crime occurrences show such a concentration, notably to the Central Business District (e.g. Schmid, 1960). The overall explanation given for this is variations in opportunities for crime. Boggs (1965), for example, finds that the use of opportunity-based measures of crime occurrence drastically reduced the importance of the city centre as an area of crime. But there is no simple one-to-one relationship between opportunity and crime, especially if non-central city areas are considered, as shown by Baldwin & Bottoms (1976:61).

The concept of opportunity may either refer to a) the possibility to commit a crime – without cars no car theft – or b) good opportunities, e.g. unlocked cars. The latter may be divided into objectively good opportunity and perceived good opportunity. The latter is obviously

---

[3] Subculture is used for explaining differences in number of offenders between two council cottage-type housing estates, and "social instability" to account for differences in offender rates between two council high-rise deck-access developments.

the choice of the offenders – who are generally seen as acting rationally – and therefore psychospatial aspects (mental maps, offenders' search areas, etc) have occupied a major role in research (e.g. Carter & Hill, 1979; Rhodes & Conly, 1981; Brantingham & Brantingham, 1981).

While it is comparatively easy to apply the concept of opportunity to most property crimes, its use for crimes against persons often involves great difficulties. I shall return to this problem later on in the discussion of methodological issues.

The concept of criminals' mobility links together the offender and the crime distribution. A review of North American studies of the subject shows that criminals' mobility tends to be short (McIver, 1981). But this may vary between countries depending on the location of offender areas vis-a-vis crime areas (city centre).

Perhaps the most interesting line of theory and research in the "new" ecology of crime, considering crimes of violence, is that relating to the concept of routine activity patterns.

Cohen & Felson (1979) have outlined a routine activity approach for direct-contact crimes. They establish that such types of crimes are likely to occur when there is a motivated offender, a suitable target and an absence of capable guardians, i.e. people who can and are likely to intervene to prevent the commission of crime. The main point made by Cohen & Felson is that the organization of the (legal) routine activities (work, leisure etc) in a society affects criminal opportunity. Further, they emphasis the time aspect that is crucial in ecological studies of crimes of violence. In the light of what has already been discussed in Chapter 4 such an approach may be fruitful.

After the brief overview of some main lines of study of the ecology of crime, I shall now turn specifically to studies concerned with crimes of violence. It is no exaggeration to say that crimes of violence have not been the major area of interest in the ecology of crime. Most studies concerned with offender distribution have not distinguished between offenders committing different types of crime, hence the patterns shown are largely determined by property crime offenders and may mask interesting patterns of offenders known for crimes of violence. Studies concerned with the ecology of crime occurrence have focused upon various forms of property crimes (I count robberies in this group), although there is far from being a total lack of studies on the ecology of violent crimes.

The Ecology of Crimes of Violence

Below I shall review selected research concerned with the ecology of crimes of violence. In that review I shall include some results from the

Gävle Study and the Stockholm Violent Crime Study and finally sum up some of the main findings from the former of these two studies.

Crimes of violence are generally found to be **strongly concentrated** in the urban setting (Bullock, 1955:567; Bensing & Schroeder, 1960:105; Downes, 1966:145; McClintock, 1963:201–203). In the Gävle Study it was found that 23 % of the crimes were committed within an area of 25 blocks, and in the Stockholm Violent Crime Study that 25 % of the outdoor crimes were committed within an area of 100 blocks. Note that Stockholm is a far bigger city than Gävle. (Stockholm has about 650,000 and the city of Gävle about 60,000 inhabitants.) Further, there were marked concentrations to special places within these areas of 25 and 100 blocks.

Considering the distribution of **victims and offenders**, research shows that there is a **tendency that they live in the same areas as have high rates of crimes of violence** (McClintock, 1963:40; Bensing & Schroeder, 1960:106; Lundsgaarde, 1977:48-49; Porkny, 1965b: 492). However, in the Gävle Study the areal correlations were rather moderate (scene of the crime – offender's residence r.=0.34, scene of the crime – victim's residence r.=0.43).

Crimes of violence tend to be **highly localized**, i.e. short criminals' mobility. The distance from the offender's home address to the address of the scene of the crime is generally shorter for crimes of violence than for property crimes (Bullock, 1955:570; Curtis, 1974:147; Pyle, 1976:88; Baldwin & Bottoms, 1978:81). This short criminals' mobility is likely to be related to the fact that, especially in cases of homicide, many victims and offenders share the same address, i.e. family violence cases. But there are results that show that, even after the subtraction of family violence cases, the mobility is short (Porkny, 1965b).

Areas with a higher level of crimes of violence have often been found to be either **Social Problem Areas** (Slum Areas) or **areas where public entertainment activities are concentrated**. McClintock (1963:40) states that "Apart from the Piccadilly and Soho areas where a number of fights in clubs and streets occur – most of the crimes of violence take place in poor neighbourhoods among people living in overcrowded tenement houses or under slum conditions.".

In a study of the Stepney and Poplar wards in London, Downes describes the places to which crimes of violence are concentrated in the following way: "One massive cluster along the short, club-infested stretch of Cable Street between its junctions with Leman Street and Christian Street. Other – much smaller – clusters on Brick Line (Spatialfields) and the clubs and restaurant portions of West India Dock Road ..." (1966:145).

In Curtis' study of the ecology of crimes of violence in five US Big

Cities some interesting observations concerning the importance of Slum Areas and public entertainment localization for the incidence of crimes of violence is reported. Concerning San Fransisco, Curtis writes: "The heaviest concentration of all and the most localization was in the Fillmore Ghetto. Second in concentration and location was the upper Tenderloin where assaultive violence in 1967 may have reflected hustling and drug related activities" (1974:145), "The Tenderloin district/.../ is a major tourist attraction, heavy in topless joints, bars, restaurants, dope sellers, male and female prostitutes." (1974:143).

As shown in Table 58, Swedish studies report that at least every tenth crime of violence occurs in places of public entertainment. Similar figures, varying between 8 % up to 29 %, have been reported in international studies (Bullock, 1955; Wolfgang, 1958; Pittman & Handy, 1964; Porkny, 1965; Dunn, 1976; McClintock, 1963).

Table 58. Proportion of crimes of violence occurring in places of public entertainment according to different Swedish studies

Author	Area of research	Data	N	% in places of public entertain- ment
Koch (no year given)	Stockholm, 1966	Convicted for crimes of violence	302	12
Lenke (1974)	Stockholm, 1969	Police- reported crimes of violence	1203	11
Charpentier (no year given)	Uppsala, 1954 and 1963	Police- reported crimes of violence	206	15
Wikström (1980)	Gävle, 1968— 1970, 1973— 1975	Police- reported crimes of violence	989	29*
Persson (1977)	Sweden, 1974. Representative sample	Victim survey	1120 (78 subjected to threats or violence)	36**
Lenke (1978)	Sweden, 1975. Representative sample	Victim survey	1000 (88 subjected to threats or violence)	15

*Including entrances.
**Persson reports that 46 % of those subjected to threats of violence were employees at the place of public entertainment.

142

Observations of the relationship of public entertainment to crimes of violence can also be found in data from the 19th century (e.g. Aschaffenburg, 1911).

Public entertainment activities are likely to be of greater importance for the occurrence of crimes of violence than the figures in Table 58 indicate. Many of the crimes occurring in streets happen when people are on the way to or from places of public entertainment. Further we have, of course, a public entertainment life that is not connected with specific locals but occurs on the streets, e.g. rockers' gatherings. These are often located in areas with many places of public entertainment. The relationship between violence and public entertainment is illustrated by the high areal correlations found between number of restaurants in an area (indicator of public entertainment activities) and crimes of violence outside apartments in Gävle (r.=0.85) and the high correlation between crimes of violence and restaurants in the inner city areas of Stockholm 1979 (r.=0.71). Further, as shown in Map 2, where crimes of violence occurring between strangers in the central areas of Gävle and the locations of restaurants are plotted, it is obvious that these crimes cluster around the restaurants. Note that crimes occurring in restaurants and their entrances not are included in Map 2.

The results of the preliminary efforts to study the ecology of crimes of violence made in the Gävle Study will be summarized below[4].

The starting point for the description is a division of the wards of the city of Gävle into a) Central-city wards, b) Multi-storey block dominated areas, c) One-family houses dominated areas[5].

It was found that crimes of violence were highly concentrated to the **central city wards**; 58 % of the crimes occurred there. Within the central city wards as well strong concentrations appeared. More than half (52 %) of the crimes occurred in one of twelve areas into which these wards were divided. The reason for this strong concentration was obviously the concentration of public entertainment to parts of the central city (see above).

Most of the circumstances of the crimes classified as intervention (80 %), molestation (69 %) situational conflicts (61 %) and sudden attack (56 %) occurred in the central city. It was only relationship conflicts that deviate from this, only 37 % of these cases occurring in the central city areas. In this connection it may be mentioned that, of the relationship conflicts occurring in central city areas, a higher proportion than in other areas were conflicts over economic relationships (see also Chapter 4 above).

---

[4] More detailed information is given in Wikström (1980).

[5] By "dominating" is meant that more than 50 % of the dwellings are either one-family houses or multi-storey blocks.

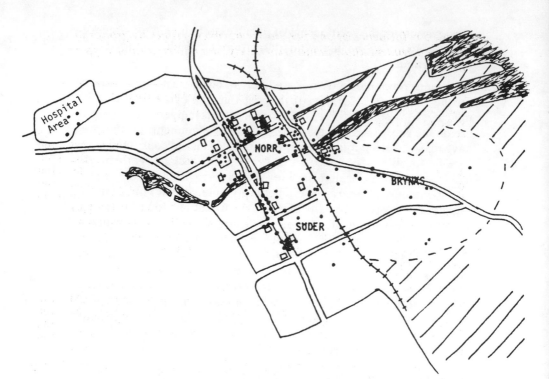

. = One case of assault outdoors between strangers.

□ = Block with one or more licensed establishment.

△ = The railway station.

/// = Industrial area.

Map 2. Key map of the central parts of Gävle showing the location of restaurants and scenes of crime in cases of violence occurring outdoors between strangers

Most of the offenders committing crimes of violence in the central city area had a home address outside the central city, and more than one third lived outside the city of Gävle. This is, of course, likely to be related to those visiting the central city area to participate in public entertainment. The offenders, and the victims, were generally younger in the central city than in other areas. About half of the offenders were previously recorded for social problems and/or criminality, which is not a higher figure than for all offenders committing crimes in the city of Gävle. Offenders living in the central city areas, and victims living in those areas, predominantly committed their crime, were victimized, in the central city areas. The proportion of the inhabitants known for crimes of violence in the central city areas was either the average for the whole of the city or below average. So the high incidence of crimes of violence in these areas cannot be explained by the presence among the inhabitants of a high proportion of violent offenders.

In the **multi-storey block dominated areas** 34 % of the crimes of violence occurred. The population of these areas is about one third more than in the central city areas and also one third more than in the one-family house dominated areas.

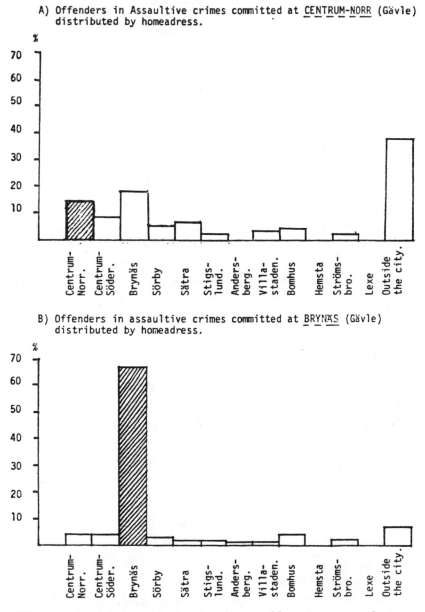

A) Offenders in Assaultive crimes committed at CENTRUM-NORR (Gävle) distributed by homeadress.

B) Offenders in assaultive crimes committed at BRYNÄS (Gävle) distributed by homeadress.

Figure 9. Distribution of offenders home address in two wards

10

While the scene of crime was mainly streets and places of public entertainment in the central city areas, there was a domination of crimes occurring in apartments/proximity areas in the multi-storey block dominated areas. Half (50 %) of the relationship conflicts occurred in these areas.

In contrast to the central-city wards, the offenders were mainly local. This is illustrated in Figure 9 where the distribution of the offenders home address in one central city ward and one multi-storey block ward is compared. The ages of the offenders and victims are higher than in the central city areas. The proportion of offenders recorded for previous social problems and/or criminality was higher than the average for the city.

In the **one-family house dominated areas** 8 % of the reported crimes of violence occurred. The structure of the crimes was largely the same as in the multi-storey block areas, with the notable exception that the proportion of offenders previously recorded for social problems and/or criminality was lower than in the latter areas. The main difference between the one-family house and multi-storey block dominated areas was a markedly lower level of crimes, offenders and victims in the former. This seems to be related to differences in social problems. The multiple R between indicators of social problems (social security, alcoholic problems, child welfare) and crimes of violence occurring in apartments was 0.82 in a division of the city into eleven areas, and 0.58 in a division of the city into 57 areas.

I shall conclude the introduction to this Part with a discussion of some of the several methodological issues that have to be considered when conducting research on the ecology of crimes of violence.

Methodological Issues

Spatially Differing Dark Figures and Clearance

The problem of spatially differential dark figures and clearance was discussed in Chapter 3 above. I shall not repeat that discussion here, but the analysis indicated that data of recorded crimes of violence give a fairly good picture of the areal distribution of the crimes, the victims and the offenders.

However, when comparing the crime structure between different areas – especially inner and outer city areas – more important differences between actual and recorded criminality were indicated, although not of the kind that the results would be seriously misleading.

Relative Incidences

There are several possible ways in which the areal variations of crimes of violence may be measured. However, there are no obvious best measures, as there are for example in cases of residential burglaries, i.e. the rate of residential burglaries/residents.

The reason for using relative incidences is often that one likes to account for differential opportunities to commit a crime in different areas. Strictly speaking, in case of crimes of violence there is an opportunity as soon as there is more than one person present. So the best measure of the relative incidence of crimes of violence would be the rate of crimes of violence/persons in the area.

However, this is for practical reasons a very difficult measure to obtain. First, it is hard to calculate how many people there are in an area, for example during a day. Second, there may be variations in the time people spend in the area, since people (in contrast to, e.g., residents) are mobile. Third, taking an average, if possible, of people in an area during a day is also problematic for other reasons, e.g. the incidence of crime may have its peak at one time of the day, while the number of persons in the area may have a peak at another time of the day. If, for example, one is interested in the risk of being a victim of violence when travelling on the underground, and using crimes of violence/travellers as a measure of the risk, this is likely to give misleading results since the peak of travel comes at other points of time than the peak of crimes of violence.

A common measure of relative incidences of crime (any kind) is in relation to the population of the area. This is clearly no good measure, as shown by Boggs (1965). In the case of crimes of violence it may lead to absurd consequences. For example, when I made such calculations in the Stockholm Violent Crime Study, it turned out that the most central area had an incidence of more than one crime of violence per person. This was a consequence of a high incidence of crimes of violence in that area but a low residential population. And the residents had very little to do with the crimes occurring there.

Some attempts to measure the relative incidence further illustrate the problem. Boggs (1965) used pairs of persons[6] (inhabitants) as denominator and found a very high correlation with the conventional measure with population as denominator.

Baldwin & Bottoms (1976:64) state that "The concept of 'opportunity' has perhaps limited direct applicability to crimes of violence.". In their efforts to account for varying opportunities they split up crimes of violence on the basis of McClintock's classification (1963) – see introduction to Part 2 above – into domestic disputes, attacks in public houses and other places of entertainment, and attacks in public throughfares.

Domestic disputes were studied in relation to rateable value of the house. No association was found. It might be remarked here that it is

---

[6]$N(N-1)/2$.

147

somewhat difficult to see the adequacy of "rateable value of house" as a measure of opportunity. More logical measures were used in the two other cases. Assaults in places of entertainment were found to be strongly positively correlated with an index of public houses and clubs, and assaults in public throughfares were closely associated with an index of Industrial and Commercial Premises.

Although Baldwin & Bottoms did not use opportunity measures as denominators in calculating relative incidences of crimes of violence, their approach indicates that it might be advantageous to make a division between types of crimes of violence when calculating the relative incidence. For example, with restriction to crimes of violence in apartments the populations of the areas may be a fairly good measure of varying opportunities. But, nevertheless, violence outside homes is clearly problematic. To be more specific, it is mainly outdoor crimes of violence in inner city areas that constitute the problem. In outer city areas also outdoor crimes of violence may be related without too much error to the number of inhabitants of the area on the assumption that these crimes are mainly local, in that both or either of the victim or the offender resides in the area.

All in all then, relating crimes occurring in apartments to the population of the area seems to be a fairly adequate measure, but there is no good solution when the concern is outdoor crimes of violence or when the incidences of all types of crimes of violence are measured.

When describing areal variations of violent offenders and victims, the use of the population of the area as denominator may be regarded as an adequate measure. However, one complication is the possibility of variations in the proportion of **multiple offenders** (victims) between areas. Had this been a study of, e.g., residential burglaries, this surely would have caused a problem (Wikström, 1985a). But in the case of crimes of violence, as shown in earlier chapters, most (recorded) offenders are one-time offenders. Further, most of the offenders known for a crime of violence will only be recorded once in a year. In the Stockholm Violent Crime Study a calculation was made separately for the years 1978 and 1979 how many of the known offenders appeared more than once during the year in records of crimes of violence in the municipality. In both of these years 82 % of the offenders were only recorded once, and 4–5 % had more than three records of crimes of violence (Table 59). When interpreting these data, it should be pointed out that as crimes of violence in the Stockholm Violent Crime Study were counted all from bag-snatching to murder and that most of the most frequent multiple offenders were in categories such as bag-snatching and robbery. Although multiple offence, and most likely also multiple victimization, in crimes of violence occurs during a single year in our research districts (cities), the problem cannot be regarded as a serious one for the population-based description of areal variations.

148

Table 59. Number of recorded crimes of violence* in the municipality of Stockholm. 1978 and 1979. Data from the Stockholm Violent Crime Study

Number of crimes of violence	1978 N	%	1979 N	%
1	2,000	81.8	1,936	82.2
2	317	13.0	330	14.0
3	81	3.3	56	2.4
4 or more	46	1.9	32	1.4
Total	2,444	100.0	2,354	100.0

*Wide definition of crimes of violence. All from bag–snatching to murder. Only crimes occurring in the municipality of Stockholm are included in the table.

Stability of Areal Distributions Over Time

A special problem when using data of areal distributions from a single year is the degree of stability that characterize them. If, for random or other reasons, there are marked variations from one year to another, the results may be dependent on the chosen year of research.

Table 60. Zero-order correlations of crime, offender and victim distribution in the wards of Gävle in the years 1968–1970 and 1973–1975. Data from the Gävle Study. N = 12

A/ Crime distribution

	1968	1969	1970	1973	1974
1969	94				
1970	76	87			
1973	90	97	93		
1974	92	97	87	96	
1975	89	96	87	97	94
Mean r. = 91					

B/ Victim distribution

	1968	1969	1970	1973	1974
1969	69				
1970	35	35			
1973	45	61	70		
1974	60	91	49	81	
1975	55	82	63	91	76
Mean r. = 64					

c/ Offender distribution

	1968	1969	1970	1973	1974
1969	74				
1970	48	42			
1973	42	52	14		
1974	45	22	52	59	
1975	58	68	49	81	65
Mean r. = 51					

Note: Coefficients multiplied by 100.

Since data in the Gävle Study were collected for six years, this gives an opportunity to study the areal stability of the distribution of crime, offenders and victims (Table 60). Taking the mean correlation as a stability coefficient shows that the crime distribution has a high degree of stability. In the case of the victim and the offender distributions the coefficients are markedly lower but clearly positive. It should be noted that the calculations are based on a very small number of data and that changes – especially for victim and offender distributions – may be expected over somewhat longer periods of time due to changes in age structure of wards, new-built areas, etc. The high stability of the crime distribution is likely to be due to the close relationship between public entertainment localization and outdoor violence. The former localization is very stable over time.

Areal Division

When using areas of cities as unit of research we have a variable in the division of the areas. Many different divisions are possible, and different divisions may yield different results.

Normally the option for practical-economical reasons is restricted to predefined areas if one wishes to study the relationship of criminality to population and other characteristics, although other techniques have been suggested and used, e.g. the isometric map (Mowrer, 1938; Hoiberg & Cloyd, 1971; Curtis, 1974).

When the scenes of crime, offenders' and victims' homes have been referred to areas, the areal division is that of areas for which population and other statistics are possible to obtain. However, there are several levels of divisions in such statistics, so a choice had to be made.

According to Baldwin & Bottoms "... the aim of urban analysis ought to be to provide categorizations of areas which are homogenous..." (1976:103). Areas may be homogenous in some respects and heterogenous in others, so there is no simple way to attain such a goal. Further, heterogeneity of an area may be an interesting feature of the milieu to relate to criminality.

I have striven to have wards as units in the intracity analysis. Wards of cities often have a history, and often certain types of housing (one-family, multi-storey blocks) dominate a ward and there are also often "natural" demarcations between wards such as major roads, rivers, parks. However, as a rule, inner city wards have no clear demarcations from other wards.

Wards were regarded as generally not too small units, so that the stability of, e.g., calculations of crime rates would be highly dependent on random variations. The ward unit was also regarded as not being so big as to have very heterogenous characteristics of, e.g., population and housing.

Although the ward level appeared to be the "best choice" in the respects discussed above, it is far from unproblematic. For instance, the plotting of the exact locations of the offenders' homes showed that in some wards these were highly concentrated to parts of the wards. One example was a ward consisting both of apartments that privately were rented by the tenants and apartments that were owned by a tenant-owners' association. In that particular area all recorded violent offenders were living in the parts with privately rented apartments and none in the other part of the ward.

When statistics from the municipal authorities were requested, it was stated that statistics were desired for the ward divisions of the city. When the statistics arrived from the various municipalities, it turned out that there were in some cases marked differences among the cities in the size of the areal units to which the statistics referred. So the areas of the cities in the 21 Police Districts Study differs in average size among the various cities (see Appendix 5).

The Ecological Fallacy

The probably most discussed problem in ecological research is that relating to the so-called ecological fallacy, i.e. errors arising when using aggregate correlations to make inferences about individual correlations.

The classic article on this problem is, of course, that by Robinson (1950) in which he showed that 1) correlations based on aggregated data generally are stronger than those calculated on the corresponding individual data, 2) that correlations based on aggregated data tend to increase in value with increasing size of aggregate, and 3) that the correlations based on aggregate data may even have a reverse direction to that of the corresponding individual correlation, e.g. a positive individual correlation might be changed to a negative correlation if the individual data are aggregated and the correlation is computed on the aggregate data.

The main source of the first two problems is that there will be less variations among observations when aggregated data (e.g. mean values) are used. Hammond proposed as a solution to this problem that the regression coefficients should be used instead of the correlation coefficients: "... *the regression coefficients define a straight line through a scatterplot. If points in the scatterplot are divided into subgroups, the means of those subgroups will be represented by points which cluster around the same straight line (leaving the regression coefficient unchanged), but the points will be less widely dispersed around the line (increasing the correlation coefficient)."* (Hammond, 1973:767).

151

However, this solution is applicable only when you know that there is no aggregation bias, which is indeed very difficult to know. Aggregation bias arises when individual data are not homogenously grouped on the aggregates (Hammond, 1973). This points to the importance of the areal division used, as discussed above. It is the "third variable", the grouping of individuals on areas, that comes into play and causes the aggregation bias.

Some authors have remarked that there is no technical solution to the problem of aggregation bias. Langbein & Lichtman state that aggregation bias is a result of inadequate theory or that an important variable has not been possible to measure. They advocate the formulation both of a model of the individual relationship one is interested in and a model of how the grouping of individuals on areas may affect this relationship (Langbein & Lichtman, 1978). The obvious problem here is to specify the correct model of the effects of the grouping.

The problem of the ecological fallacy falls into another light if the prime interest in the study is not to explore individual correlations through the use of aggregate data, but rather to explore milieu effects on behaviour. In the latter case differences in milieux may be regarded as represented by different areas and the main problem appears to be concerned with the creation of an adequate areal division.

In practice it seems that many researchers conducting ecological studies on crime are unclear whether they are concerned with exploring individual correlations using aggregate data as a (poorer) alternative to individual data or whether the prime interest is in milieu effects on criminal behaviour. In many cases it appears that such considerations arise when the results from the ecological studies are interpreted (for an example see Lander, 1954).

The problem is, however, not so simple as stated above, since areal variations of, e.g., crime may be caused both by variations among areas in individual characteristics connected with criminality and in milieu characteristics affecting criminality. Having access to the same data both for individuals and for aggregates gives the opportunity to try and separate these two effects. In the "normal" case of research, as in the present study, such an opportunity does not exist, but there are some studies of this type which indicate that both individual and milieu effects are of importance (e.g. Carlsson in SOU 1976:72, chapter 2).

Spatial Crime Spillover

Dorein has pointed to the possible problem of spatial autocorrelation when using "conventional linear models": "... *the methodological problems hinge upon the issue of whether or not observations for a variable at one point of geographical space are interdependent with other observations for that variable at other points in geographical space."* (1980:30). I shall not go into Dorein's discussion and offered solutions to the problem here, but rather take his mention of the possible problem of spatial autocorrelation as point of departure to discuss a problem of special relevance for studies of crime occurrence, namely, the possibility of a spatial crime spillover.

If, for example, as shown earlier, there is an areal association between measures of public entertainment and outdoor violence, such an association may be disturbed if there are spillovers of crimes of violence from areas with many public entertainment activities to adjacent areas with less or no public entertainment activities. The "cause" of many of the crimes of violence in these adjacent areas may then lie outside the area. When correlating measures of public entertainment activities and crimes of violence, the result then tends to underestimate the importance of public entertainment for areal variations of crimes of violence. The same type of problem may arise e.g. when correlating measures of social problems of areas to the incidence of crimes of violence, since the offenders living in social problem areas may commit some of their crimes in adjacent areas.

One way to grasp this problem is to study the patterning of residuals. If, for example, it turns out that positive residuals of the regression of a measure of public entertainment activities on the incidence of outdoor crimes of violence cluster around areas with many places of public entertainment, this might be taken as an indication of a crime spillover.

The ecology of crimes of violence in the city is a topic to be treated in Chapters 10 (together with intercity variations) and 11. But before that, temporal patterns (Chapter 7), regional variations (Chapter 8) and urban-rural differences (Chapter 9) will be considered.

7 Temporal Patterns

All behaviour occur in time and space. Identification of regularities in temporal and spatial variations of the incidence and type of crime may be both of theoretical and practical (preventive) interest. When considering the relationship between routine activities (see Section 4.5 and introduction to this Part) and crimes of violence, temporal patterns – especially weekday and hourly variations – are an important area to study. Furthermore, a knowledge of temporal variations of the incidence and structure of crimes of violence is of importance for the interpretation of spatial variations.

The study of temporal patterns of crime may be divided into four major areas; a) crime trends, b) seasonal variations, c) weekday variations, and d) hourly variations. In this Chapter I shall focus on weekday and hourly variations although some notes on crime trends and seasonal variations of crimes of violence will first be presented.

7.1 Crime Trends

Official statistics of crimes of violence reported to the police for the whole country are available from 1950 onwards[7]. The period covered in this section will be 1950–1983. The development of crimes of violence during this period may roughly be divided into four phases.

First, during the years 1950–1964 there was a stable level of crimes of violence, with a slight increase over the period. Second, in the second half of the 1960s there was a marked increase, which was followed by a period during the 1970s with a moderate average increase of a couple of per cent per year. Finally in the 1980s there has been a marked increase (see Figure 10).

The marked increase in the late 60s coincides with changes in the procedure for compiling the statistics, which has been judged to be at least partially responsible for that increase. The marked increase in 1982 is related to a change of the law concerning the possibility for people assaulted on private premises to withdraw their charge. This

---

[7] However, data of convictions are available for a long previous period.

154

INCIDENCE

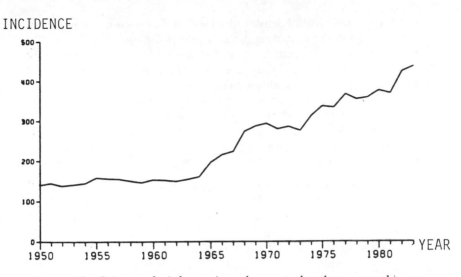

Figure 10. Crimes of violence (murder, manslaughter, assault) per 100,000 inhabitants reported to the police, 1950–1983.
Source: Brottsutvecklingen, Lägesrapport 1984, BRÅ Forskning 1984:5, p. 31.

right was abolished in 1982. Since all crimes reported to the police, regardless of whether the charges were withdrawn or not, were included in the statistics before 1982, this is not the reason for the increase. But there are many other circumstances connected with this change that are likely to have affected the dark figure of crimes of violence, i.e. more cases were reported. I have discussed this in Brottsutvecklingen, Lägesrapport 1983, pp. 17–22, and shall not go into details here, but merely conclude that in all likelihood the marked increase in reported crimes of violence in 1982 is at least partially explained by the mentioned change of law.

Apart from these two factors, both believed to have lowered the dark figure of crimes of violence, the crime trend has been discussed in relation to A) a general increase in the propensity to report crimes of violence among the population, B) the increase in alcohol consumption, and C) a growth of the part of the population involved more regularly in criminality and/or abuse of alcohol and drugs.

No special research has been made in Sweden on changes over time in the propensity to report crimes of violence. Instead, the hypothesis of a higher propensity to report crimes of violence seems to be an inference drawn from the intense public debate on several issues relating to violence over the past years, e.g. on the problem of family violence, child abuse, police violence, etc.

The central factor in the general debate on the increase of crimes of violence has been their relationship to the increase of alcohol consumption. It has even been argued in a research report that every

155

change in total alcohol consumption will be followed by a corresponding change in the rate of reported crimes of violence (Lenke, 1975).
However, the issue seems to be more complex than that. First, only a
very small proportion of the occasions when people consume alcohol
result in violent actions, although (as shown in Section 4.4.1 above) in
most cases of crimes of violence some or both participants are
intoxicated. Second, while the total alcohol consumption decreased
in the late 70s, the rate of crimes of violence continued to increase.
The relationship between total alcohol consumption and crimes of
violence is shown in Figure 11.

A third hypothesis concerning the reason for the rise of crimes of
violence is that it is related to an increase in the proportion of the
population engaged more actively in general crime and drug abuse
(Gustafsson & Kühlhorn, 1980). This hypothesis is especially
interesting in the light of the results that have been presented in
Chapters 4, 5 and 6 above. A fairly high proportion of the violent
offenders seem to be describable as socially loaded persons (criminals, addicts, alcoholics).

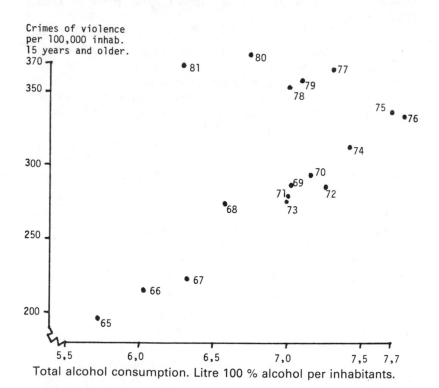

Figure 11. Total alcohol sales and police reported crimes of
violence.
Source: Brottsutvecklingen, Lägesrapport 1984, BRÅ Forskning
1984:5; Can rapport 83.

156

To these three hypotheses – which are not necessarily contradictory – one may add the possible importance of increasing public entertainment. From the previously presented results we know that a fairly high proportion of crimes of violence are connected with public entertainment activities. It seems clear that public entertainment has expanded over the past years. There has been an expansion in the number of restaurants, people have more spare time, etc. Studies have also shown that while 59 % of a representative sample of the Swedish population maintained they had been actively engaged in public entertainment in 1968, the corresponding figure was 67 % in 1974 and 71 % in 1981 (Tåhlin, 1984:326, Table 14:12). This is, of course, no proof that an increase in public entertainment is related to the increase in crimes of violence, but indicates that it might be an area worthy of special study.

7.2 Seasonal Variations

In a simplified way the seasonal variations of crimes of violence may be described as crimes having their minimum incidence at the beginning of the year, especially in February, increasing during the spring, and having a roughly speaking stable level over the rest of the year. Of some interest to note is the drop that occurs each year in July – the main holiday month in Sweden. This is illustrated by Figure 12, showing the incidence of simple assaults by month in the years 1977–1981.

Incidence.

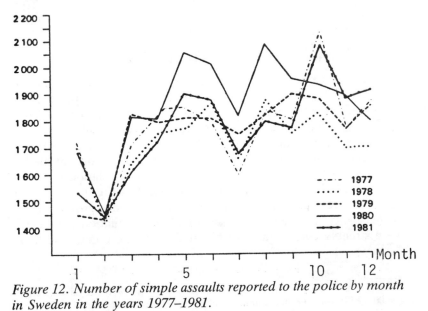

Figure 12. Number of simple assaults reported to the police by month in Sweden in the years 1977–1981.
Source: Socialdepartementet Ds S 1982:2, p. 110.

157

However, separating the assaults into those that occur outdoors and indoors show that the seasonal variations have a different patterning (Figure 13). While outdoor violence generally has its peak during the summer months, the opposite is true of indoor violence.

INCIDENCE

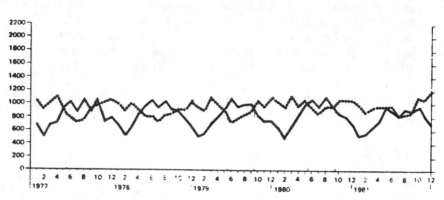

Figure 13. Number of simple assaults reported to the police by month in Sweden in the years 1977–1981. Dotted line = indoor assaults. Full line = outdoor assaults.
Source: Socialdepartementet Ds S 1982:2, p. 117.

It seems reasonable to attribute these patterns to the differing human activity patterns – outdoor as against indoor activities – over the year.

7.3   Weekday and Hourly Variations

Weekday and hourly variations in crimes of violence have already been touched upon in Chapters 4 and 5. It was clear that these crimes are concentrated to nighttime and weekends. It was further evident that not only the incidence but also the circumstances of the violence showed temporal variations. In Section 4.4.4 it was shown that intervention and molestation were the crimes most concentrated to weekends, while conflicts over social or economic relationships were less so[8]. In Chapter 5 it turned out that especially gang-fights, but also fights between addicts/criminals and the remainder group labelled "other fights" (presumably consisting of many situational conflicts), were strongly concentrated to nighttime. On the other hand fights

---

[8]In this connection it might be mentioned that, while 46 % of the daytime crimes (08.00–19.59) concerned relationship conflicts, the corresponding nighttime figure was 22 % (data from the Gävle Study).

158

between older persons were concentrated to daytime and evenings. In the latter cases there are reasons to believe that these cases involve a greater number of alcoholics. In this Section I shall make a more systematic analysis of weekday and hourly variations than has hitherto been done.

The lowest incidence of crimes of violence is in the early morning hours; the incidence may then be described as steadily increasing to the evening hours, when it takes a jump upwards and assumes a fairly stable level interrupted by peaks in the hours around midnight, finally decreasing and dropping significantly between 03.00 and 04.00 (Figure 14).

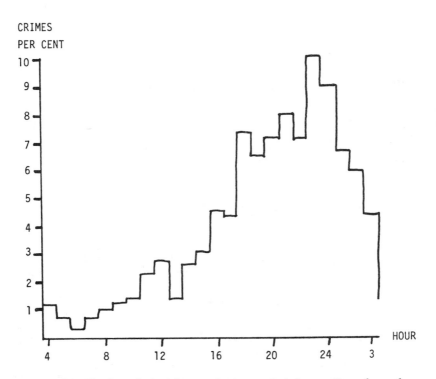

Figure 14. The hourly incidence of crimes of violence. Data from the Big City Crime Study. Per cent.

As regards weekday variations the clear concentration to Fridays and Saturdays is well illustrated by Figure 15.

It is important to note that the "natural" day has another rhythm than the official day. The highest incidence of crimes of violence is around the midnight hours of Friday and Saturday. The hours after midnight of the "natural" Saturday are referred to Sunday in Figure 15.

159

INCIDENCE

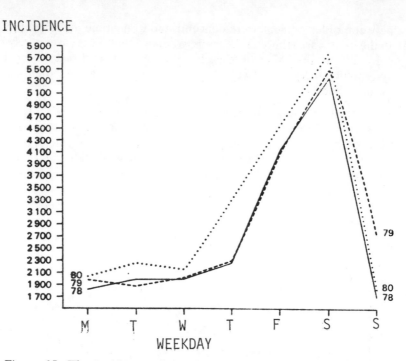

Figure 15. The incidence of simple assaults reported to the police by weekday in Sweden in the years 1978–1980.
Source: Socialdepartementet DS S 1982:2, p. 111.

Dividing the week into four periods (Table 61) illustrates the concentrations to weekend nighttimes.

Table 61. The distribution of aggravated and simple assault by weekday and time of occurrence. Per cent. Data from the Stockholm Violent Crime Study. 1978 and 1979

	Weekend – nighttime		Weekend – daytime		Weekday – nighttime		Weekday– daytime	
	1978	1979	1978	1979	1978	1979	1978	1979
Aggravated and simple assault, %	22	24	16	15	32	32	30	30
The periods' proportion of a total week, %	9		19		24		48	

N = 2,919 (1978); 2,871 (1979).
Definitions: Weekend–nighttime = Friday 20.00 to Saturday 03.59 and Saturday 20.00 to Sunday 03.59.
Weekend–daytime = Saturday 04.00–19.59 and Sunday 04.00—19.59.
Weekday–nighttime = Sunday 20.00—23.59, Monday—Thursday 20.00—23.59 and Monday—Friday 24.00—03.59.
Weekday–daytime = Monday—Friday 04.00—19.59.

Of special interest for the coming analysis of intracity variations (Chapters 10 and 11) is the relationship of spatial and temporal variations of crimes of violence in the city. There are good reasons to expect both temporal and spatial variations in the incidence as well as in the structure of the crimes.

I shall conclude this Section with an analysis of temporal variations in the structure of crimes of violence in Stockholm.

7.3.1 Temporal Variations in the Structure of Crimes of Violence

Different human activities in the city take place at different points of time and space. Both the incidence and the character of different activities show temporal and spatial variations. The temporal variations in main activities may be illustrated in a simplified way as in Figure 16 (see Walldén, 1975 for a detailed study of time use). As shown in Part 2, crimes of violence are events that mainly occur

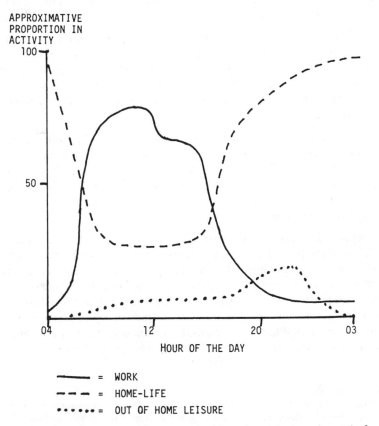

Figure 16. Schematic illustration of hourly variations in main human activities (weekdays).

during home-life and participation in public entertainment, but not in the course of work. Hence it is natural that the hourly distribution of the incidence of crimes of violence (Figure 14) has a shape similar to those of home and leisure activities.

People with different life-styles use their time and urban space differently. The proportion of people with certain characteristics present at given places is likely to vary through the week and the hours of the day. Of special interest when studying crimes of violence, in the light of the results presented in Part 2, is information on how socially loaded persons use their time and urban space. Not many Swedish studies have been made on this topic. Some relevant studies were mentioned in Section 4.5.

When analysing the temporal patterns of the structure of crimes of violence I shall use a broad division of the day into daytime and nighttime which is believed to embrace some essentials in the temporal variations of main activities.

Since weekends are so clearly different from weekdays as regards human activities, it was judged desirable to make a separation between weekends and weekdays.

Finally, in the analysis of data from Stockholm presented below, I have also made a spatial division of the city into inner- and outer-city areas. This was done in order to cover some of the essential spatial variations of human activities that occur. Further, as shown for instance in Section 3.1, the crime structure of inner- and outer-city areas differs markedly[9].

The temporal-spatial division used is shown in Table 62 together with the hourly incidence of violent crimes. The highest incidence is in inner-city areas at nighttime on Fridays-Sundays, followed by crimes in the inner-city areas occurring at nighttime on other weekdays. The lowest incidence is at daytime on Saturdays-Sundays followed by daytime on other days of the week.

As regards the **scene of the crime** there are clear temporal (and spatial) variations. Of the crimes in streets and in connection with public entertainment around half occur in the inner-city areas at nighttime on Fridays–Sundays. Also a greater part of the crimes on public transport (38 %) occur at nighttime on Fridays-Sundays in inner-city areas. On the other hand crimes in apartments occur predominantly in outer-city areas and are concentrated to nighttime, around half occurring in outer-city areas at nighttime[10].

---

[9] In Chapter 11 a more detailed analysis of the variations in crime structure among different types of areas in Stockholm will be made, including temporal variations.

[10] The population of the inner-city areas is about 200,000 and of the outer-city areas about 400,000.

162

Table 62. Number of crimes of violence by place (inner- or outer-city area) and time of occurrence. Data from the Big City Crime Study

	Incidence of crimes per hour
INNER–CITY	
Daytime:	
Monday—Friday	0.10
Saturday—Sunday	0.07
Nighttime:	
Monday—Thursday	0.29
Friday—Sunday	0.51
OUTER–CITY	
Daytime:	
Monday—Friday	0.09
Saturday—Sunday	0.08
Nighttime:	
Monday—Thursday	0.13
Friday—Sunday	0.27

Note: The incidence of crimes per hour calculated as the crimes divided by the total hours of the period and multiplied by the number of studied weeks.

Comparison of the distribution of crimes according to scene of the crime by time of occurrence for the whole city of Stockholm (Table 63) shows that the daytime crimes predominantly occur in apartments and streets. The difference between weekdays and weekends at daytime is that a higher proportion of the crimes in the former case occur in other places than apartments or streets. This may be regarded as a natural consequence of the fact that, e.g., many public institutions (part of the other category) are closed at weekends.

At nighttime there are more marked differences in the scenes of crime. A much higher proportion of the weekday cases occur in apartments. Comparison of the scene of the crime at day- and nighttime clearly shows the importance of public entertainment for nighttime crimes, and especially at weekends. Recall, as stated in the introduction to this Part, that a major proportion of the crimes in streets and on public transport at nighttime, especially at weekends, occur between people out to participate in public entertainment.

When Stockholm is divided into inner- and outer-city areas it is evident (Table 63) that the scenes of crimes differ markedly. At all times apartments are the dominating scene of crime in outer-city areas, while places outside the home are the dominating scene of crime in inner-city area. Note that the figure of the proportion of cases occurring in apartments in outer-city areas is most likely an underestimate (see Section 3.1).

163

Table 63. Scene of crime by time of occurrence. Total city, inner-city and outer-city areas separately. Data from the Big City Crime Study

	Street, park	Public entertainment	Public transport	Shop, service institution	Apartment	Other	Total	N
DAYTIME								
Monday—Friday								
Total city	25	8	8	5	40	14	100	298
Inner—city	32	10	10	8	28	12	100	153
Outer—city	17	6	6	2	53	15	99	145
Saturday—Sunday								
Total city	37	6	4	0	49	3	99	95
Inner—city	39	13	0	0	41	7	100	46
Outer—city	35	0	8	0	57	0	100	49
NIGHTTIME								
Monday—Thursday								
Total city	11	24	16	2	43	4	100	529
Inner—city	13	34	20	3	25	5	100	364
Outer—city	4	2	7	2	83	2	100	165
Friday—Sunday								
Total city	27	26	17	2	25	3	100	727
Inner—city	33	37	18	2	7	3	100	477
Outer—city	16	5	13	1	60	4	99	250

Note: Daytime = 08.00—19.59; Nighttime = 20.00—07.59; N = 1,649; Missing cases = 883. The definition of day- and nighttime is different here from that applied in Table 61.

Cases of crimes of violence in places of public entertainment are for natural reasons concentrated to the inner-city areas, since the vast majority of such places are located there. About one third of the crimes in inner-city areas at nighttime occur in places of public entertainment.

On the basis of the marked temporal-spatial differences in distribution of scenes of crimes one may expect, on grounds reported in Part 2, that these differences will be accompanied by differences in **victim-offender interpersonal relationship**. In the inner-city areas at all times, but especially at nighttime on Fridays-Sundays, there is a domination of crimes between strangers (Table 64). In fact as many as 42 % of all crimes of violence between strangers in Stockholm occur in inner-city areas at nighttime during weekends (Fridays-Sundays).

As is evident from Table 64, there is a smaller proportion of cases occurring outside apartments between strangers at daytime than at nighttime, and there is also a smaller proportion of cases outside apartments that involve strangers in outer-city compared to inner-city areas.

164

Table 64. Per cent **strangers** *in different categories of crimes according to time of occurrence, place of occurrence and scene of crime. Data from the Big City Crime Study*

	Apartments/ proximity area	Other place
DAYTIME		
Total city	**13** (155)	**79** (209)
Inner–city	20 (59)	86 (120)
Outer–city	8 (96)	71 (89)
NIGHTTIME		
Total city	**15** (393)	**88** (807)
Inner–city	15 (116)	89 (687)
Outer–city	15 (277)	79 (120)

Note: Number of cases in brackets. For definition of day– and nighttime see Table 63.

These patterns coincide with that of intermale fights (Table 65). There is a smaller proportion of intermale fights (or put otherwise, more fights involving females – generally as victims) in crimes occurring outside apartments in outer-city than in inner-city areas. As shown earlier (Section 4.2.1), females are mainly involved in relationship conflicts with acquaintances. However, in the crimes involving females daytime outside the home in outer-city areas two thirds occurred between strangers. Comparing weekends and week-days (not shown), there is a higher proportion of intermale fights at weekends.

Table 65. Per cent **intermale fights** *in different categories of crimes according to time of occurrence, place of occurrence and scene of crime. Data from the Big City Crime Study*

	Apartments/ proximity area	Other place
DAYTIME		
Total city	**38** (157)	**71** (215)
Inner–city	39 (59)	79 (126)
Outer–city	38 (98)	59 (89)
NIGHTTIME		
Total city	**39** (406)	**83** (794)
Inner–city	40 (122)	84 (678)
Outer–city	39 (284)	78 (116)

Note: Number of cases in brackets. For definition of day– and nighttime see Table 63.

165

From the analysis in Part 2 we know that the **age** of those involved in crimes of violence is likely to be related to the circumstances of the crime (Section 4.2). For instance, older offenders are predominantly involved in relationship conflicts while the youngest offenders are mainly involved in situational conflicts, molestation and sudden attack. In Section 5.4 it was shown that, of those crimes in which both the victim and the offender were 40 years and above, it was predominantly males assaulting females, further that a comparatively high proportion of these cases occurred in the daytime, 69 % occurring between 08.00–19.59. Finally, among the offenders 40 years and above a significant proportion were known as alcoholics, and to a much higher degree than the younger offenders (Section 4.3.2.2). The proportion of offenders 40 years and above by time and place of occurrence and scene of crimes is shown in Table 66.

Table 66. Per cent **offenders aged 40 or above** *in different categories of crimes according to time of occurrence, place of occurrence and scene of crime. Data from the Big City Crime Study*

	Apartments/ proximity area		Other place	
DAYTIME				
Total city	**37**	(144)	**29**	(154)
Inner–city	34	(50)	27	(94)
Outer–city	39	(94)	33	(60)
NIGHTTIME				
Total city	**22**	(328)	**13**	(535)
Inner–city	11	(107)	11	(460)
Outer–city	27	(221)	24	(75)

Note: Number of cases in brackets. For definition of day– and nighttime see Table 63.

There is a clearly higher proportion of older offenders in daytime than in nighttime crimes. There is a higher proportion of older offenders in crimes taking place in outer-city than in inner-city areas. This difference is much greater at nighttime than at daytime.

That there are marked temporal-spatial variations in the crimes of different age-groups may further be illustrated by the fact that, while 46 % of the crimes committed by offenders aged 0–19 years occurred in the nighttime at weekends (Friday–Sunday) in the inner-city area, the corresponding figure for offenders aged 20–29 was 35 %, for offenders aged 30–39 years 16 % and for offenders aged 40 years or above only 6 %.

The differences at daytime in mean age of offenders between weekdays and weekends are marginal. However, at nighttime there is

166

a marked difference between cases on weekdays and at weekends. The offenders are much younger in the latter case. This difference is greater for inner- than for outer-city areas. For example, while the mean age of offenders in crimes outside apartments in inner-city areas at weekends is 25 the corresponding figure for crimes in outer-city areas in apartments on weekends is 40.

Offenders' age may be regarded as an indirect but crude measure on crime circumstances. Hence, the results point at substantial temporal variations of crime circumstances which is in line with the results presented in Section 4.4.4 and in Chapter 5.

Consideration of the **employment status** of the offenders, according to a dichotomy employed/student or other, (Table 67) shows that the proportion of those out of work who are not students is markedly higher at daytime than nighttime, and higher in cases occurring in apartments than elsewhere. In cases occurring outside apartments at nighttime these offenders are a very low proportion. The proportion of cases of offenders out of work is clearly higher on weekdays than at weekends.

Table 67. Per cent **offenders not employed/students** *in different categories of crimes according to time of occurrence, place of occurrence and scene of crime. Data from the Big City Crime Study*

	Apartments/ proximity area	Other place
DAYTIME		
Total city	49 (99)	46 (130)
Inner—city	46 (35)	40 (73)
Outer—city	50 (64)	51 (57)
NIGHTTIME		
Total city	39 (231)	14 (432)
Inner—city	42 (76)	15 (379)
Outer—city	38 (155)	13 (53)

Note: Number of cases in brackets. For definition of day— and nighttime see Table 63. The vast majority of those not employed/students are unemployed, early retirements, and casual workers.

Finally, consideration of the **previous criminal record** of those involved in crimes of violence (Table 68) shows that the proportion of cases in which at least one of the parties had a previous criminal record is higher at nighttime than at daytime and in outer-city areas than in inner-city areas.

Table 68. Per cent **cases in which at least one of the parties had a previous criminal record** *in different categories of crime according to time of occurrence, place of occurrence and scene of crime. Data from the Big City Crime Study*

	Apartments/ proximity area		Other place	
DAYTIME				
Total city	**60**	(110)	**59**	(109)
Inner—city	55	(44)	57	(60)
Outer—city	63	(66)	61	(49)
NIGHTTIME				
Total city	**72**	(261)	**76**	(412)
Inner—city	67	(76)	75	(366)
Outer—city	75	(185)	80	(46)

Note: Number of cases in brackets. For definition of day— and nighttime see Table 63.

7.3.1.1 Broad Temporal Variations of Crimes of Violence in the City – a Summary and Discussion

The overall conclusion from the exploration of broad temporal variations of crimes of violence in Stockholm is, as expected, that

- not only the incidence but also the circumstances and characteristics of persons involved in the violence show temporal variations – totally and in various parts of the city.

Considering first the incidence of crimes of violence, temporal variations in **the incidence of contacts[11] between people** may be one explanation to the temporal variation in the incidence of the crimes. A first glance at the data (Table 62) indicates however, that this is no good overall explanation. The incidence of contacts between people is likely to be highest at daytime weekdays in the course of work and movements in urban space related to work.

Separating crimes between strangers and crimes between intimates the latter seems to be possible to relate to the incidence of contacts between intimates. Both the crime and the contact incidence is likely to be highest at nighttimes (including evenings). In this connection it is important to remind of the fact that it is hardly a representative sample of the population that is involved in these crimes. But it seems likely that temporal variations in the incidence of interaction with intimates for socially loaded persons in large is similar to that of "conventional" people.

---

[11]The concept of contacts seem more adequate than the concept of opportunity discussing crimes of violence. I use the concept of contact here somewhat losely as to mean possibilities to interact on a face to face basis.

168

The high incidence of crimes of violence between strangers at nighttimes seems not to be easily explained by a especially high incidence of contacts between strangers at this point of the day. Contacts between strangers are likely to be much more frequent at daytime.

The latter draws the attention to the importance of the **incidence of different types of contacts**. There is much that indicate that it is mainly the incidence of contacts involving socially loaded persons and contacts during the course of public entertainment that are critical regarding the likelihood that the contact would result in an interaction that in turn would develop into conflicts and violence (see discussion in Section 4.5).

In Table 69 I have tried to summarize some of the broad variations in crime circumstances and persons involved by scene of crime and time of occurrence. I have not only used the results presented in this Section but also the results presented in Part 2 as basis for the description. I like to stress that the description given is an interpretation and a simplification, but I believe that it embraces some of the essentials of the variations concerned.

Table 69. Some main characteristics of crimes of violence by scene of crime and time of crime occurrence. A simplified description

Time of occurrence	Scene of crime Apartment/ proximity area	Other place
DAYTIME	Low incidence of crimes. Especially morning hours.	Low incidence of crimes. Especially morning hours.
	A significant proportion of the cases are inter-male fights between socially loaded persons (alcoholics). Situational conflicts, interventions.	A significant proportion of the crimes are male-male fights involving socially loaded persons (alcoholics). Strangers. Situational conflicts, intervention
	The next frequent group of crimes are family-violence cases. Female victims. Relationship conflicts.	In contrast to inner-city areas a marked proportion of the victims in outer-city areas are females assaulted by strangers.
	The proportion family violence cases is markedly lower in inner- compared to outer-city areas.	
NIGHTTIME	Medium incidence of crimes.	Medium incidence weekdays and high incidence of crimes in weekends. Especially around midnight.
	Domination of family-violence cases and alike. Mostly female victims. Relationship conflicts.	Most cases occur in the course of public entertainment. Situational conflicts, molestation, sudden attack. Overwhelming male to male fights. Strangers.
	The next frequent group is intermale fights between or involving socially loaded persons. Situational conflicts, intervention.	Markedly younger offenders (especially on weekends).

170

8 Regional Variations in Crimes of Violence in 1978 in Relation to General Social Problems, Labour Market Problems, Alcohol Consumption and Alcohol Abuse

A classical field of research in the study of criminality is the exploration of regional variations in crime. The ecological research tradition from the early 20th century was preceeded by the so-called Cartographic School in the 19th century. Although most studies in the 19th century were preoccupied with regional variations, for example de Guerry in France (see Elmer, 1933), some efforts were also made to study intracity variations, e.g. Mayhew's studies in London (see Levin & Lindesmith, 1937).

Today the most well-known studies of regional variations in violent crimes are probably those that resulted in the formulation of the thesis of a regional subculture of violence in the southern USA or, as it has been called, the Gastil-Hackney hypothesis (Gastil, 1971; Hackney, 1979). The research and the debate that followed the presentation of the Gastil-Hackney hypothesis illustrate the great methodological and theoretical problems arising in studies of large aggregates[12] when, as in this case, conclusions are drawn about cultural influences (southernness) on behaviour (violent crimes, especially deadly violence). To mention just one example, critics have pointed out that region and culture are equated and that no independent measure of culture is used (Loftin & Hill, 1974). An overview of this research and debate is given in Wikström (1982:3–9).

The background for the present analysis of regional variations is the results presented in Part 2 showing that a large percentage of the offenders, but also of the victims, were known for one and often several social problems, e.g. unemployment, previous criminal record, alcohol abuse, etc.

The research question asked is simply whether regional variations in such types of social problems as characterize many offenders and victims in cases of violent crime will be related to the violent crime rate of the region.

---

[12] Some of these problems were touched upon in the introduction to Part 3 and will not be repeated here.

The strategy of analysis is as follows. First, several indicators of each variable are chosen. The reason for choosing several indicators was that in some instances, e.g. labour market problems, it was believed that several indicators together would give a better estimate than any single indicator. Second, a factor analysis was made in which it was hypothesized that indicators of a variable would have a high loading on a single factor. Third, the factor scores of extracted factors were correlated with the violent crime rate. Fourth, regression analysis and inspection of residuals were carried out.

8.1 Variables, Indicators and Possible Bias of Indicators

Before proceeding to the analysis I shall discuss the indicators chosen in some detail.

8.1.1 General Social Problems

Three indicators of General Social Problems were chosen: a) general crime, b) LOB detention cases (drunkenness), and c) persons receiving social security.

First one may object that the indicator **general crime** has deficiencies since violent crimes are part of the indicator. But this is judged to be no great problem, since only a minor part of all crimes are violent crimes and variations between regions in general crime are largely determined by variations in crimes against property. In this connection it should also be mentioned that some of the reported crimes are missing in the regional official statistics, notably among traffic crimes and fraud[13].

LOB detention cases may be dependent upon regional variations in the intervention practice of the police. For example, it is possible that the practice is generally milder in larger than in smaller urban areas. No systematic knowledge is available concerning this, but conversations with some individuals in the police force support the existence of such variations. Of special interest is the studied years' closeness to the year 1977 when drunkenness was decriminalized. Some confusion as to how to apply the new law (Lagen om omhändertagande av berusade personer, LOB) that replaced the old one seems to have existed in the police force in 1977. There was a marked drop in interventions due to drunkenness in that year (see Ds S 1982:2, p. 75). It is possible, although not explored here, that there might have been regional variations in the interpretation of the new law concerning drunkenness, especially in the initial phase. If so, it might also have affected the figures for 1978.

---

[13] See SMR 1980:5, pp. 14–15.

172

Also in the case of **persons receiving social security** there might exist regional variations in practice. No efforts have been made to explore this possibility.

All in all, then, we have three indicators believed to measure different aspects of General Social Problems in regions. It is hypothesized that there will be a strong covariation among these indicators at the regional level.

8.1.2 Labour Market Problems

Three indicators were chosen to measure labour market problems in the regions: a) unemployment rate, b) relief work, and c) early retirement.

It was judged that it might be problematical to use only the unemployment rate as measure of labour market problems since there might be regional differences in the handling of unemployed persons, e.g. through relief work or giving persons early retirement pensions for reasons of unemployment. Studies have shown that great regional variations exist in the use of early retirement pensions (SOU 1977:88 p. 59–65). A relationship between high unemployment and the incidence of early retirement is also shown in that study. The author interprets the result to the effect that this is partly a consequence of the fact that in regions with high unemployment the less competitive on the labour market are eliminated from it (p. 80).

8.1.3 Alcohol Consumption

The data about alcohol consumption are based on delivery figures, which is not wholly satisfactory. But in general there is a close correspondence between deliveries to and sales from liquor stores (see Ds S 1982:2 p. 57). Further there may be a discrepancy between sales and consumption of alcohol. But since the data are for a full year, this is judged to be of no great significance.

More problematical may be that some customers may buy the alcohol in one region but consume it in another. Because the regional division used (A-regions) is created to cover functional areas of major urban areas, it seems likely that the major part of the consumption will be within the region. However, one may object that regions having many tourists as temporary population during, in most cases, the summer may have an inflow of alcohol consumed in the region but bought in another region. But it seems likely that tourists buy most of their alcohol in the region they are visiting.

A possible problem may be variations in illegal distilling of alcohol. No efforts have been made to explore this, which of course is a very difficult task.

8.1.4 Alcohol Abuse

The variable, among all those included, that presents the greatest problems with regard to the validity of indicators is that of measuring regional variations in alcohol abuse. Three indicators were used: a) male deaths in liver cirrhosis, b) admittances to temperance care, and c) psychiatric hospital care with the diagnosis of alcoholism or alcohol psychosis.

The indicator male liver cirrhosis has such small incidences in the regions that I considered dropping it from the analysis, but did not do so. Perhaps an unwise decision. The two other indicators of alcohol abuse are also clearly problematical since their incidence may be related to varying treatment resources among regions. Further, the indicator of treatment in psychiatric hospitals for alcoholism and alcohol psychosis may be affected by regional variations in diagnosis, just as may figures of liver cirrhosis.

8.1.5 Regional Characteristics

Almost no other data about population and other characteristics of regions than those concerning diverse social problems have been used. The reason for this is the aim of the inquiry as stated at the beginning of the chapter, but it seemed anyway necessary to keep the main influence of urbanization on crimes of violence under some control. Therefore three indicators thought to be of relevance for the urban dimension were used: a) total population, b) population in urban areas (localities), and c) population aged 20–44 years.

8.2 Factor Analysis

The result of the factor analysis (Varimax rotated factors) is shown in Table 70. Four factors with an eigenvalue above one were extracted. Together they explained 72 % of the variance. Three of the four factors were interpreted while the fourth did not make much sense.

The first factor was labelled **General Social Problems** (urbanization) with high loadings on the indicators of general social problems: social security (82), drunkenness (78) and general crime (77). Also with a high loading on these factors was the indicators measuring urbanization, showing the association between general social problems and urbanization. Further, indicators of wine and strong beer consumption had moderate loadings on this factor, which is probably a result of drinking habits characteristic of large urban areas. Also two of the indicators of alcohol abuse had some loadings on this factor.

The second factor is clearly a **Labour Market Problems** factor, with high loadings on all three of its indicators. Somewhat confusing is that

174

Table 70. Factor loadings and communalities. Varimax rotated factors. Regional variations. 1978 (N=70)

	I	II	III	IV	h^2
URBANIZATION					
Total population	60*	−23	34*	−27	60
Population in urban areas	74*	−18	−07	24	65
% 20—44 years	−84*	12	06	−09	73
GENERAL CRIME					
Crime per inhabitant	77*	−16	28	11	70
SOCIAL SECURITY					
Social security per inhabitant	82*	22	06	11	73
LABOUR MARKET PROBLEMS					
Unemployment in per cent of labour force	02	82*	−22	21	77
Relief work per inhabitant	−01	90*	−02	06	82
Early retirement per inhabitant	−10	83*	16	−17	75
ALCOHOL CONSUMPTION (Sales figures)					
Spirits. Litres per inhabitant	−17	11	91*	10	87
Wine. Litres per inhabitant	62*	−28	63*	−19	91
Strong beer. Litres per inhabitant	66*	23	47*	02	71
Pure alcohol. Litres per inhabitant	27	−03	95*	−02	97
DRUNKENNESS					
LOB detention cases per inhabitant 15— years	78*	17	05	−09	65
ALCOHOL ABUSE					
Male deaths in liver cirrhosis. Observed/expected incidence	13	47*	18	−53*	56
Admittances to temperance care per inhabitant 20— years	30*	15	14	76*	70
Psychiatric hospital care, diagnosis of alcoholism or alcohol psychosis	41*	−35*	23	12	37
Contribution of factor %	33	18	14	7	

Note: Coefficients have been multiplied by 100.
Loadings 30 and higher marked with an asterisk.

one indicator of alcohol abuse has a positive loading and one a negative on this factor. But the reader is reminded of the great problem of reliability there may be for these indicators.

The third factor is labelled **Alcohol Consumption** with high loadings on all four alcohol consumption indicators, but especially on total

175

alcohol consumption (litres pure alcohol) and consumption of spirits. It should be noted that this factor also has some loading on total population.

The fourth factor was, as stated above, not given any interpretation. The two variables with high loading on this factor were both thought to measure alcohol abuse, but one of them had a positive loading while the other had a negative, which is just as confusing a result as was the case for the alcohol abuse indicators in factor two.

An oblique rotation (Promax) of the factors resulted in the same factor structures. The inter-factor correlations are shown in Table 71. There is a negative correlation between the General Social Problems factor and the Alcohol Consumption factor (–30) and a positive correlation between the Alcohol Consumption factor and the non-interpreted factor four (31). Note that liver cirrhosis has a positive loading on the Alcohol Consumption factor but a negative on factor four.

Table 71. Inter-factor correlations. Promax rotated factors. Regional variations 1978

	Labour market problems (F II)	Alcohol consump– tion (F III)	Factor IV (F IV)
General social problems (F I)	10	–30	–09
Labour market problems (F II)		–07	–09
Alcohol consump– tion (F III)			31
Factor IV (F IV)			100

8.3 Relationship of Factors and Violent Crime Rate

After completing the factor analysis, factor scores were computed from the Varimax rotated factors and correlated with the violent crime rate of the regions. The result is shown in Table 72.

176

Table 72. Zero-order correlation of factor scores and violent crime rate. Regional variations in 1978. N=70

	Violent crime rate
General social problems (F I)	75*
Labour market problems (F II)	10
Alcohol con— sumption (F III)	19
Factor IV (F IV)	18

Note: Coefficients have been multiplied by 100. Correlations statistically significant at the 5 per cent level marked with an asterisk.

Crimes of violence in the regions show a strong relationship with general social problems, but not with any of the other factors. Comparison of the map of the regional variations of violent crimes in five classes (Map 3) with the map where the scores for the General Social Problems factor have been given in five classes (Map 4) well illustrates the close association of General Social Problems and Crimes of Violence.

12

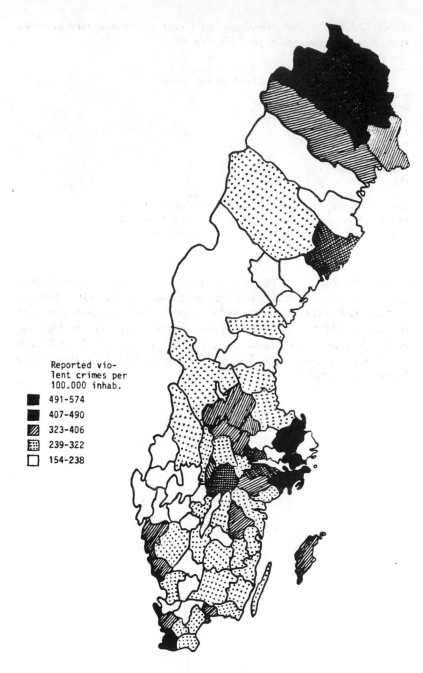

Map 3. Regional variations in violent crimes.

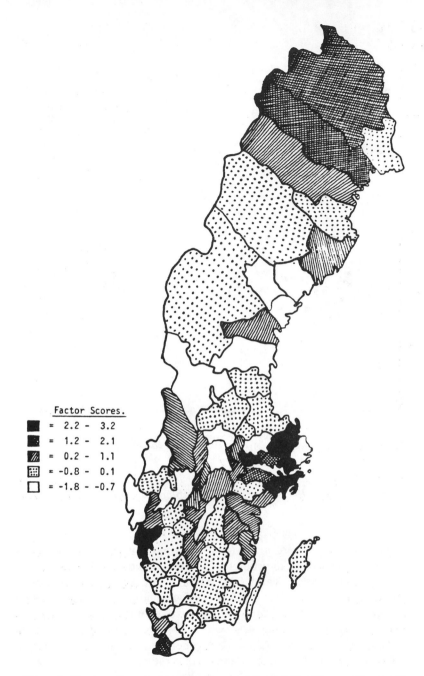

Map 4. Regional variations in General Social Problems (Factor I).

Some further explorations were made, confined to the relationship between violent crimes and general social problems. In Figure 17 is shown a plot of these two variables.

179

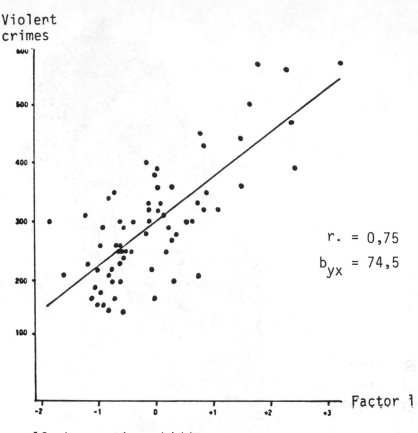

Figure 17. Plot of crimes of violence per 100,000 inhabitants and factor scores for Factor I, General Social Problems. Regional variations in 1978. N=70.

Plots of residuals were made (Map 5), predicting the violent crime rate from general social problems. Comparison of the distribution of violent crimes (Map 3) and the distribution of the residuals (Map 5) shows there is a tendency that negative residuals, i.e. less violent crimes than predicted from general social problems, occur in areas with low violent crime rates, while positive residuals, i.e. more violent crimes than predicted from general social problems, tend to occur in regions with high violent crime rates.

All in all, regions with a high level of crimes of violence are almost exclusively those with greater or big cities. The exception is the mining district in the north of Sweden (Kiruna/Gällivare). But there are regions with greater or big cities, notably Gothenburg, that do not belong to those with the highest violent crime rate. Of the 15 A-regions with a higher violent crime rate (>+50) than predicted

180

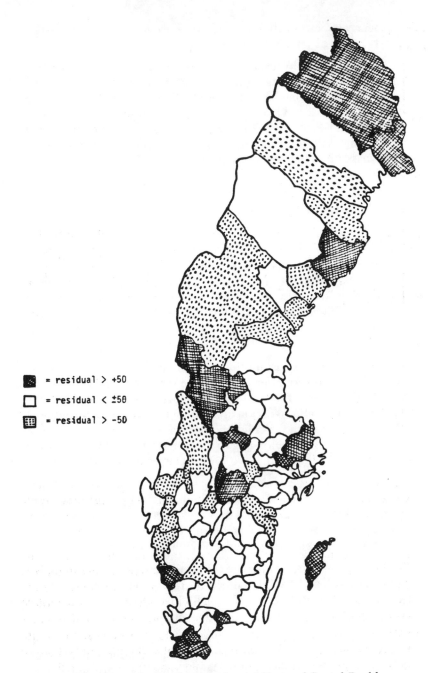

Map 5. Plot of residuals of regression of General Social Problems on violent crime rate.

from General Social Problems, 5 belonged to the 8 regions in the two highest classes of crimes of violence.

The 21 regions in the lowest class of violent crimes are characterisized by a lack of large localities. Few had a locality with more than 20,000 inhabitants, while none had a locality with more than 50,000. Of the 14 regions with less violent crimes (>–50) than predicted from General Social Problems, 9 belonged to the class with the lowest violent crime rate and 4 to the next lowest class. One was in the middle class of violent crime rates.

8.4   Discussion

The results from the Regional Study show that there is no association between regional variations in alcohol consumption and in labour market problems and crimes of violence. A look at the map of factor scores of labour market problems (not shown here) shows that with few exceptions the farther north in Sweden you get, the more labour market problems there are. Labour market problems are generally less in A-regions with big cities, which, as noted above, are those likely to have the highest violent crime rate.

Concerning alcohol consumption a map (not shown here) of the factor scores for Factor III shows that the regional variations are less marked for this than for the other two factors discussed. Only the Stockholm/Södertälje A-region falls within the class (of five) with the highest scores for the alcohol consumption factor. With a few exceptions the regions belonging to those in the two highest classes of violent crimes belong to the two lowest classes of alcohol consumption.

The indicators of alcohol abuse turned out to give no consistent pattern. One reason may be that they are as poor indicators of alcohol abuse as was suspected. No conclusions about regional associations between alcohol abuse and crimes of violence will be drawn.

The close association between the General Social Problems factor (as measured here) and the violent crime rates is interesting since it indicates that the proportion of socially loaded persons in a region will affect the region's violent crime level.

Considering the patterning of residuals, there are some explanations for this that might be hypothesized: a) the relationship between General Social Problems and Violent Crime Rate are not linear, although it is difficult to find any obvious non-linear function from inspection of the scatter diagram, b) a third variable intervenes, e.g. concentration effects, so that General Social Problems are not so important for the violent crime rate in small places as in large urban areas. It should be stressed that none of these possibilities has been explored here.

9   Some Notes on Urban-Rural Differences

Studies of criminality generally show that crime rates are higher in urban than in rural areas (e.g. Christie et al., 1965; Gibbs, 1979:2). Baldwin & Bottoms point out that although urban-rural crime differences are an important epidemiological variable "...criminology had made little progress in adequate explanation ..." (1976:14). Further they identify rural criminality as a much neglected subject of research.

In this Chapter some explorations will be made of urban-rural differences in rate and structure of crimes of violence. The data used are from the 21 Police Districts Study. Of the 56 municipalities in the study those with 25,000 inhabitants or less (generally less than 15,000, see Table 2) were referred to as rural. In addition, the parts of the other municipalities not within the area defined as city (see Section 1.1.2) were also referred to as rural. To be specific; as rural areas were counted small places and the countryside, while the cities were counted as urban. Hence the measure of urban-rural is somewhat crude.

With this division 56 % of the population of the studied police districts lived in urban areas and 44 % in rural areas. As expected, there was a much higher rate of crimes of violence in urban than in rural areas (Table 73).

Table 73. Rate of crimes of violence per 1,000 inhabitants in urban and rural areas. Data from 21 Police Districts Study

	Crimes of violence per 1,000 inhabitants
Urban areas	3.8
Rural areas	1.0
All areas	2.6

No data about population or other characteristics of the rural areas have been collected at this stage of research. The reader is therefore reminded that part of the differences between urban and rural areas may be "explained" by differential compositions of population.

9.1 Sex, Age and Nationality

Somewhat surprisingly to the author, it turned out that the urban and rural distributions of the sex of victims/offenders were nearly identical (Table 74). On the hypothesis that street violence would be less frequent in rural areas I had expected there would be a higher proportion of violent crimes between males in urban than in rural areas.

Table 74. Sex of victim and offender in urban compared with rural areas. The 21 Police Districts Study. Per cent

Sex*	Urban	Rural
Male, male	68	67
Male, female	27	28
Female, male	2	2
Female, female	3	3
Total	100	100
N	4,658	992

*Offenders' sex given first.

As regards the age distribution of the victims and offenders (Table 75) it was found that there was a higher proportion both of offenders and victims in the youngest and in the oldest age categories. This may be related to the fact that individuals in the most economically active ages have moved from rural areas to a greater extent than the rest of the population.

Table 75. Age of offender and victim in urban compared with rural areas. The 21 Police Districts Study. Per cent

Age of offender	Urban	Rural	Age of victim	Urban	Rural
0—19	15	17	0—19	17	22
20—29	40	34	20—29	36	27
30—39	28	23	30—39	23	20
40—	18	26	40—	24	30
Total	101	100	Total	100	99
N	3,759	875	N	4,735	1,014
Significant at 1 % level (X^2)			Significant at 1 % level (X^2)		

Finally, the proportion of offenders and victims of foreign citizenship was higher in urban than in rural areas; 24 % of the offenders in urban areas as compared with 16 % in rural areas were foreigners, while

16 % of the victims in urban areas compared with 12 % in rural areas
were foreigners. Again these differences may be related to differences in composition of population.

9.2 Interpersonal Relationship

One of the major contrasts between urban and rural areas is the
difference in interaction between strangers that can be expected to
occur in these two types of areas. In fact, a main feature of the city has
been described as being "A World of Strangers" (Lofland, 1973).

Comparing the urban-rural distribution of victim-offender interpersonal relationships (Table 76) shows also that a markedly higher
proportion of the cases in urban areas involved strangers. Of some
interest is that there was no real difference in the proportion of crimes
occurring within the family or between people with family-like
relationship. Instead, it was those crimes with less acquaintanceship
between victim and offender that were more numerous in rural
areas.

*Table 76. Victim-offender interpersonal relationship in urban compa-
red with rural areas. The 21 Police District Study. Per cent*

Interpersonal relationship	Urban	Rural
Married/cohabiting	9	10
Formerly married/cohabiting	5	5
Fiancés	3	2
Parent–child	1	1
Other relatives	2	3
Other close acquaintances	20	24
Casual acquaintances	3	2
Acquainted by recognition	12	17
Strangers	45	34
Total	101	99
N	4,655	990

Significant at 1 % level (X^2).

9.3 Scene of the Crime

Since crimes between strangers predominantly occur outside apartments and, as shown above, crimes between strangers are more
frequent in urban areas, it is to be expected that a higher proportion
of the crimes in urban areas would have occurred outside apartments.

185

This is undoubtedly true regarding street crimes (Table 77) but not with regard to crimes in places of public entertainment or on public transport. While urban areas have a higher proportion of the crimes occurring in streets, rural areas have a higher proportion occurring in the unspecified category "other places". It is worth noting in this connection that many of the crimes in rural areas occurring at "other places" are committed in weekend cottages, camping sites and similar places, where probably many urban dwellers are involved in the crimes. On the other hand it is also likely that, among cases occurring in the central parts of urban areas, a number of visiting rural dwellers are involved.

Table 77. Scene of the crime in urban compared with rural areas. The 21 Police Districts Study

Scene of crime	Percentage		Per 1,000 inhabitants	
	Urban	Rural	Urban	Rural
Street, square	27	17	1.0	0.2
Place of public entertainment	21	20	0.8	0.2
Public transport	3	3	0.1	0.0
Shop, service institution	4	2	0.1	0.0
Apartment, proximity area	38	43	1.5	0.4
Other place	6	16	0.2	0.2
Total	99	101		
N	4,748	1,012		

Significant at 1 % level (X^2).
Note: Crimes occurring in entrances to restaurants included in the category place of public entertainment. By proximity area is meant staircase, cellar or garden.

Looking at differences in scenes of crimes in relation to population (Table 77), the greatest difference is found to be in cases of street crime (5 times more in urban areas), followed by cases occurring in places of public entertainment (4 times more) and in apartments (nearly 4 times more).

9.4 Some Further Remarks on Other Urban-Rural Differences

A higher proportion of urban than of rural cases occurred at nighttime and at weekends. A higher proportion of the victims were victimized during work in the urban areas. Although the presence of weapons was about the same in urban and rural areas, there was a difference between the preference for striking or pointed weapons. Pointed weapons were somewhat more common in urban areas, striking weapons somewhat more common in rural areas.

9.5 Discussion

Since no other data referring to the urban-rural division than crime data and size of population have been collected at this stage of research, there was no possibility to explore the correlates of the variations in incidence and structure of crimes of violence. The results in Chapter 9 show, as expected, that

- there were marked differences in both the incidence and the structure of crimes of violence between urban and rural areas.

As mentioned several times previously, one reason for this difference may be the **difference in composition of population** that exists between urban and rural areas.

However, it seems to be a plausible hypothesis that the most important explanation of the urban-rural difference in crimes of violence lies in

- differences in the frequency and character of contacts between people, especially between strangers,
- differences in the amount and character of social problems.

Concerning the latter, it may be mentioned that a much higher proportion of the offenders in the urban areas (33 %) than in the rural areas (23 %) were unemployed or on relief work at the time of the crime. This might be taken as an indication that the proportion of socially loaded offenders is higher in urban areas. Further, as shown in Chapter 8, there is a close association between measures of urbanization and of general social problems at the regional level. It is reasonable to assume that this relationship would also hold in a comparison between urban and rural areas.

It is possible that some of the urban-rural differences in incidence of crimes of violence may be related to **differing dark-figures**, although the existence of such differences would hardly have any dramatic impact on the results. It might be argued, for instance, that as there are more crimes between acquaintances in rural areas (according to reported crimes), it is likely on the basis of what has been reported in Part 1 that the dark-figure would be somewhat higher in rural areas. On the other hand, it might also be argued that the tolerance of the urban dweller concerning street violence may be higher than that of the rural dweller. None of these speculations, or other possible sources of differential dark-figures between urban and rural areas, have been explored here. In this context it might be mentioned that Baldwin & Bottoms (1976), discussing crime and urbanism, note that

US victim surveys show larger urban-rural differences for crimes of violence than for property crimes, and that the reverse applies in US studies of reported crimes. Baldwin & Bottoms find this to be "... *a matter of considerable interest and worthy of more research effort."* (p. 7). This might indicate that data of reported crimes of violence underestimate the urban-rural difference in crimes of violence. However, when comparing data from victim surveys with data of reported crimes, such a result is to be expected. As discussed in Section 2.1.2, victim surveys are likely to miss most of the violence between intimates, and since (according to reported crimes) a larger proportion of crimes of violence in rural areas occur between acquaintances than in urban areas, the result will most likely be that victim surveys show greater variation between urban and rural areas. At least it seems reasonable to assume that this is an important "explanation" of the difference in results between victim surveys and studies based on reported crimes.

10 Inter- and Intracity Variations in Crimes of Violence in 21 Medium-Sized and Smaller Swedish Cities in 1978

In this Chapter an analysis of the general patterns of inter- and intracity variations in crimes of violence and their correlates in the 21 cities studied in the 21 Police Districts Study (see Section 1.1.2) will be presented. In Chapter 11 a more detailed analysis of intracity variations in Stockholm will follow.

In Section 10.1 intercity variations will be explored and discussed. In Section 10.2 intracity variations for the same cities will be the theme.

10.1 Intercity Variations

The principles of the demarcations of the 21 studied cities have been stated in Section 1.1.2 above. The population of the studied cities varied between 20,000 up to 100,000. Five of the cities had a population below 40,000 and four above 80,000.

The crime data, with the exception of Södertälje, have been taken from the year 1978. In the case of Södertälje the data are from 1979. The population data and other characteristics of the cities were taken from a special run made by the Swedish National Bureau of Statistics. These data are from the year 1980, mainly from the census carried out in that year. There is no one-to-one correspondence between the area for which crime data of the cities are shown and the area for which the population data and other characteristics are given. This was not possible to obtain for practical-economical reasons. However, the differences in boundaries are small. It is mainly some smaller areas on the outskirts of the cities that are either included or excluded. It is assumed that this fact will not significantly affect the analysis[14].

The population and other characteristic variables chosen are the same as for the analysis of intracity variations (see Appendix 2). However, it was not possible to obtain all the requested variables from the Swedish National Bureau of Statistics. Unfortunately most of the variables not available concerned socio-economic characteris-

---

[14] Generally the difference in population between areas for which crime data and areas for which population and other data are given is less than 2,000.

tics of the cities: mean and median income, females gainfully employed, and social security. Only the variable "workers", i.e. employees in manufacture, was then left in the group of variables thought to measure aspects related to socio-economic characteristics.

It is worth noting that the variable under the heading socio-economic variables that is the prime measure of social problems (social security) is not included in the analysis. This may be troublesome, since it is likely to be of significance for intercity variations according to the results previously presented in Part 2 and this Part[15].

10.1.1   Variations in Rates of Crimes of Violence

Table 78 shows the incidence of crimes of violence in the cities per 10,000 inhabitants. There are marked differences in the rates, from the highest of 53 to the lowest of 18 per 10,000 inhabitants. Hence there seem to be good reasons to expend effort on further exploration.

Table 78. Crimes of violence per 10,000 inhabitants in 21 medium-sized and smaller cities in 1978. Data from the 21 Police Districts Study

City	Crime of violence per 10,000 inhabitants
Uppsala	53
Umeå	53
Södertälje	52
Borås	48
Västerås	44
Eskilstuna	44
Kalmar	44
Örebro	40
Boden	40
Helsingborg	39
Linköping	36
Norrköping	35
Halmstad	33
Luleå	32
Falun	32
Jönköping	31
Karlstad	27
Gävle	25
Sundsvall	23
Sandviken	23
Östersund	18

[15] However, data of social security at the municipal level will be considered in Section 10.1.5.

10.1.2 Violent Crime Rate and City Characteristics

The zero-order correlations of the rate of crimes of violence and selected city characteristics are shown in Table 79. Only two variables show any statistically significant (5 % level) association with the level of crimes of violence: the proportion of foreigners that is positively related, and the proportion of one- and two-family houses that is negatively related, to crimes of violence.

Inspection of plots showed that there was one extreme observation (Södertälje) in the association between the proportion of foreigners and the violent crime rate. When this observation was omitted, the magnitude of the correlation coefficient decreased ($r = 0.50$) but was still significant at the 5 % level. A distinction between foreigners from Scandinavian countries (including Finland) and those from countries outside Scandinavia showed the correlation to be somewhat lower in the first case (0.45 as against 0.57), but significant in both instances.

Table 79. Zero-order correlations of population and other characteristics of cities with rate of crimes of violence. N = 21

Population and other characteristics	Crimes of violence per 1,000 inhabitants
Young persons, %	— 4
Old persons, %	— 8
Males, %	— 10
Foreigners, %	57*
Overcrowded households, %	25
Households with children, %	9
Single working parents with children, %	13
One- and two-family houses, %	— 43*
Dwellings in municipal housing, %	— 2
Large dwellings, %	— 18
Small dwellings, %	27
Old dwellings, %	3
Workers, manufacturing, %	— 13
Population size	33
Population size, log	28
Employees in shops, %	18
Employees in restaurants and hotels etc, %	— 27

Note: Correlations significant at the 5 % level marked with an asterisk. Coefficients multiplied by 100. See Appendix 2 for definitions.

However, the positive correlation between the proportion of foreigners and the rate of crimes of violence in the studied cities may merely be a reflection of the fact that foreigners tend to live in cities

191

with high rates of crimes of violence (for whatever reason) and not that they are more active in crimes of violence than those of Swedish nationality. But as shown in Section 5.5 above, with data from Stockholm, foreigners are overrepresented both among offenders and victims. A result well in line with other Swedish research (e.g. Sveri, 1980; Leiniö, 1983). Furthermore, of interest to note in the sequel is that many of the crimes of violence involving foreigners occurred between two persons of foreign nationality who were acquainted (see Summary Table 3, Chapter 5).

Since we have data about the offenders' and the victims' nationality for the 21 studied cities, this enables us to study the relationship between the proportion of foreigners in a city and their proportion among offenders and victims. As shown in Table 80, there are high and significant (1 % level) correlations. Plots of the associations are shown in Figure 18. The lines in the figures are not the regression line but the line showing the expected regression if the proportions of offenders/victims were equivalent to their proportions of the population. As is evident from the figure, the proportion of foreign offenders (victims) in the cities is clearly higher than is to be expected from their proportion of the population of the cities.

Table 80. Zero-order correlations for 21 studied cities of the proportion of inhabitants of foreign nationality, and of foreigners among victims and offenders in crimes of violence. Figures within brackets are those excluding Södertälje

	% foreign victims	% foreign offenders
% foreigners of all inhabitants	75 (69)	77 (71)
% foreign victims		96 (94)

Note: Coefficients multiplied by 100.

As mentioned above, most of the internal fights among foreigners in Stockholm occurred between acquaintances and in apartments. This results is replicated for the 21 studied medium-sized and smaller cities. A comparison of scenes of crimes by victim-offender nationality shows that crimes between foreigners to a markedly higher degree than in other cases occur in apartments (Table 81)[16].

---

[16] In this connection it may also be reported that while only 16 % of the crimes where both victim and offender were foreigners occurred between strangers, the corresponding figures in cases between Swedes were 40 % and in cases between Swedes and foreigners 54 %.

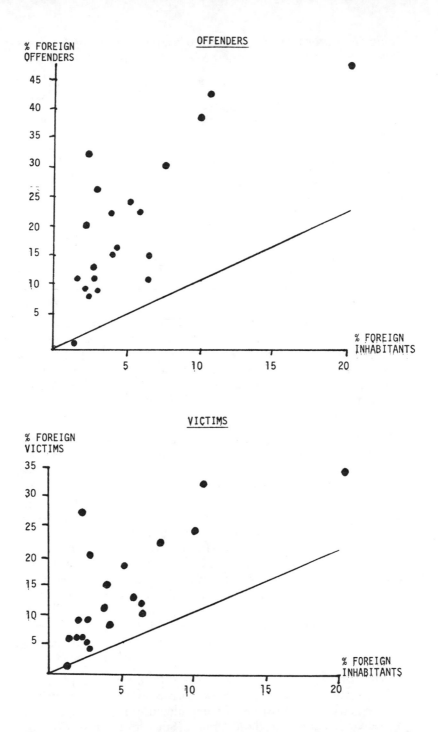

Figure 18. Plots of association between the proportion of foreigners in the population and of foreign offenders and victims. Note that the lines in the figures are not the regression line. N = 21.

193

Table 81. Nationality of victim and offender by scene of the crime. Data from the 21 Police Districts Study. Per cent

Scene of crime	Victims' and offenders' nationality		
	Both Swedes	Both foreigners	Mixed
Apartment/proximity	41	58	33
Street, square, park	26	18	25
Public transport	3	1	2
Place of public entertainment	19	16	27
Shops, service institutions	4	1	5
Other places	7	5	8
Total	100	99	100
N	2,889	453	771
Missing cases: 657			

The city with both the highest proportion of foreign inhabitants (20 %) and foreign offenders (47 %) had also the highest proportion of cases occurring in apartments/proximity area (47 %) of all cities studied. This was also the city with the highest rate the studied year (1978) of cases in which the police were called to apartments because of quarrels (data from a special run made by the Data Unit of the National Police Board).

Of special interest to report in this connection is that in cities with a higher proportion foreigners a larger proportion of the crimes involving foreigners are internal fights, than in cities with a lower foreign population. The average proportion in the studied cities of crimes involving foreigners that occur between two foreigners is 28 %. However, looking at those four cities with the highest proportion foreign inhabitants (between 8 and 20 %) show the proportion of the crimes involving foreigners that occurs between two foreigners to be much higher – between 39 and 53 %, where the rank order of that figures is the same as for their rank according to foreign population. To some degree such a result may be expected – due to that the increase in "pair of foreigners" will be greater than "the number of foreigners" with increasing foreign population – but the differences are much greater than to expect. This issue will be more directly dealt with in the section about intracity variations.

Calculation of a partial correlation between the proportion of foreigners and the rate of crimes of violence in the cities, controlling for the percentage of workers (in manufacture) resulted in a slightly higher correlation than the original[17]. So, with the restriction that

---

[17]The same results were obtained when controlling for all other predictors included.

194

there might be better socio-economic measures, there was no support for the hypothesis that the association between proportion of foreigners and the rate of crimes of violence could be "explained" by variations in socio-economic characteristics of the population between the cities studied[18].

Considering all predictors, and finding the smallest set of predictors producing the highest R^2 through the technique of Step-wise regression, results in a five predictor set when using 0.15 as significance level for entering the model, with an R^2 of 0.79 (Table 82).

Table 82. Step-wise regression analysis of population and other characteristics of the studied cities on the rate of crimes of violence

New regressor introduced	R^2 for all the regressors included so far	Increase in R^2 due to the new regressor
Foreigners (+)	32	32
Workers (—)	48	16
Restaurant, hotel etc employees (—)	65	17
One-family houses (—)	71	6
Overcrowded (+)	79	8

Note: Coefficients multiplied by 100. Sign within brackets indicate zero—order correlation direction of relationship with violent crime rate.

The predictive power of city characteristics increases considerably when adding three more variables to the proportion of foreigners and of one- and two-family houses. The squared mutiple correlation (R^2) of proportion foreigners and one- and two-family houses with rate of crimes of violence is 0.36.

10.1.3 Violence in Apartments and Violence between Strangers in Relation to City Characteristics

The rates of crimes of violence were also calculated separately for cases in apartments and for cases between strangers, since the circumstances of the crimes in these two types of cases are likely to differ markedly (see Part 2). On the basis of the results presented so far, there are reasons to believe that crimes involving foreigners will

---

[18]This should not be confused with the fact that persons of foreign origin are likely to live under poorer social and material conditions than persons of Swedish nationality, as shown, e.g., in the Swedish National Bureau of Statistics' recent report on immigrants (SCB, 1984).

show a stronger relationship to the level of crimes in apartments than to crimes between strangers. This was also the case.

The results (Table 83) show that the proportion foreigners and of overcrowded households have a significant association with crimes in apartments, while no city characteristic variable shows significant associations with crimes between strangers.

Table 83. Zero-order correlations of population and other characteristics of cities with crimes in apartments/proximity area and crimes between strangers. N = 21

Population and other characteristics	Crimes in apart- ments per 1,000 inhabitants	Crimes between strangers per 1,000 inhabitants
Young persons, %	9	— 17
Old persons, %	— 3	3
Males, %	9	— 23
Foreigners, %	77*	38
Overcrowded households, %	47*	16
Households with children, %	— 4	— 18
Single working parents with children, %	16	10
One- and two-family houses, %	— 40	— 41
Dwellings in municipal housing, %	27	— 16
Large dwellings, %	— 34	— 21
Small dwellings, %	36	27
Old dwellings, %	3	13
Workers, manufacturing, %	17	— 23
Population size	39	32
Employees in shops, %	— 6	26
Employees in restaurants, hotels etc., %	— 36	— 21

Note: Correlations have been multiplied by 100. Correlations significant at the 5 % level marked with an asterisk.

Step-wise Regression Analysis showed that only the variable "per cent foreigners" was significant enough (with 0.15 as significance level) to be included in the model when considering violence in apartments and "the proportion of one- and two family houses" (negative) when crimes between strangers were the dependent variable.

10.1.4 Some Further Explorations

As mentioned above, no data of social problems (social security) were available for the cities. However, since social problems in previous explorations in Part 2 and this Part have turned out to be an important variable, I decided to use data of social security for the municipalities as an estimate of variations in social problems among the cities.

196

Public entertainment has proved to be related to crimes of violence (Part 2, introduction to this Part), but the measure included in the analysis above of variations in public entertainment activities – proportion of employees in restaurants, hotels etc. – showed negative association with the rates of total crimes of violence and of crimes of violence between strangers. The measure is crude, so I decided to try a measure believed to be somewhat better; number of restaurants with alcohol sales per 1,000 inhabitants. Clubs and similar establishments not open to the public were excluded. These data were calculated on the basis of a list of these restaurants obtained from the National Social Health and Welfare Board. However, it should be stressed that this is also a somewhat crude measure since no regard is paid to the size and character of the establishments.

The results of these additional computations are shown in Table 84. The proportion of inhabitants receiving social security is positively related to the measures of crimes of violence, but it is only in cases of violence in apartments that the association is as strong as to reach statistical significance.

Table 84. Zero-order correlations of some additional population and other characteristic variables with total crimes of violence, violence in apartments and violence between strangers. N = 21

Population and other characteristics	Total crimes of violence per 1,000 inh.	Violence in apartments per 1,000 inh.	Violence between strangers per 1,000 inh.
Social security, %	37	59*	22
Restaurants with alcohol sales per 1,000 inhabitants	—5	—15	—1

Note: Coefficients multiplied by 100. Social security data refer to the municipality and not to the city. Correlations significant at the 5 per cent level marked with an asterisk.

As regards public entertainment the new indicator, just like the old one, shows negative associations with the measures of crimes of violence. So there is no support for the hypothesis that intercity variations in crimes of violence, totally and between strangers, are related to variations in public entertainment activities.

Since the proportion of inhabitants receiving social security – just as the proportion of foreigners – turned out to be rather strongly related to city variations in violence in apartments, I decided to test the hypothesis that the association between the proportion of foreigners and violence in apartments would be spurious. The partial correlations, controlling for social security, are shown in Table 85. The correlations decrease but are still quite high, signifying that the intercity association between the proportion of foreigners and crimes

197

of violence (totally and in apartments) cannot be fully "explained" by the variation in social problems (social security).

Table 85. Partial correlations, controlling for social security, between percentage foreigners with total crimes of violence and crimes of violence in apartments per 1,000 inhabitants. Zero-order correlation within brackets

	Foreigners, %
Total crimes of violence per 1,000 inhabitants	46 (57)
Violence in apartments per 1,000 inhabitants	63 (77)

Note: Coefficients multiplied by 100. Social security data refer to municipality and not to city.

10.1.5 Intercity Variations - a Summary and Discussion

In this Section some of the problems of studying intercity variations with special reference to the present study will be commented upon and the interpretation of the findings will be discussed. But first the main results may be summarized in the following points:

- Substantial variations in the rate of crimes of violence exist between the studied cities.

- The main correlates of the total rate of crimes of violence in the cities are the proportion of foreign population and the proportion of one- and two-family houses (negative). It is also worth noting in the light of the previously presented results that the proportion of population receiving social security shows some (although non-significant) association with the total rate of crimes of violence.

- Closer examination of the data indicates that it is mainly crimes of violence in apartments (among acquaintances) that are related to foreign population and social problems (social security). The analysis further indicates that the relative size of the foreign population has an association with the rate of crimes of violence (both totally and for cases occurring in apartments) that cannot be fully "explained" by variations in social problems.

- The proportion of crimes involving foreigners that were internal (i.e. both offender and victim were foreigners) was markedly higher in the cities with the highest proportions of foreign population compared to the average for the studied cities.

198

- The intercity variations in the rate of crimes of violence between strangers show no strong association to any of the variables included in the study. Consideration of variables measuring other aspects of city characteristics than those used may give better results on this point.

- No evidence was found to support the hypothesis that inter-city variations in rates of crimes of violence totally, or between strangers, were related to variations in the magnitude of public entertainment activities. However, the measures used are to be regarded as crude.

There are several problems in the study of the intercity variations that I would like to discuss before proceeding to a discussion of the findings.

First it is obvious that the results are dependent on the variables included in the study. The **set of variables used** was on the whole the same as for the study of intracity variations. One reason for that was to make possible comparisons between intercity and intracity correlates with the crime variables. However, it may well be that these variables are not the most adequate for exploring inter-city variations, although they may be fairly good for studying intracity variations.

The variables included describe main population and housing characteristics, while few concern **special characteristics of the city**. Especially when we are studying a limited number of cities, their special characteristics that might be thought to be related to life in the city may be of special relevance. For instance, some of the cities (Uppsala, Umeå) have major universities, which may affect the character of public entertainment. To give just one example, in Uppsala many places of public entertainment have restrictions regarding visits from non-students, which may be one source of conflict. Other cities (e.g. Boden) may be described as "military cities", since several large regiments are located there. Hence young males doing their military service will be a significant proportion of the young males of the city. Some cities (e.g. Örebro) have several prisons and similar institutions located nearby. A final example is those cities which are major travel terminals. In, e.g., Helsingborg the number of travellers passing through each year, going by ferry to Denmark, is many times the population of the city.

The last example draws attention to the possible importance of differences between cities in the size of **non-residential population** present in the city. It seems reasonable to assume that there are considerable variations between the studied cities in this respect. The proportion of offenders and victims from outside the city differs significantly. For instance, the proportion of offenders from outside the city varies from 7 up to 33 %. This may be a source of error when

199

exploring the relationship between population characteristics and the incidence of crimes for the cities[19].

Since the study of intercity variations concerns a single year and the number of studied cities is comparatively small (N = 21), **special events** occurring in a city in the studied year and related to crimes of violence may "disturb" the analysis. Let me give an example to illustrate this point. In the Gävle Study, which was a six year study, there was a marked peak of crimes of violence in one of the years. There were indications that this peak was related to an intense media debate on the issue of a high incidence of crimes of violence in a particular street in the city, which might have affected both the propensity to report outdoor crimes of violence and caused many curious and perhaps violence-prone people to go to that particular street at nighttime and get involved in violence (see Wikström, 1980). During my visits to the 21 studied cities I tried as far as possible to discover whether such events had occurred during the studied year. The result was negative, but of course I may not have been completely successful in tracing all such possible events. "Special events" are just one source of the year-to-year "random" variations in the incidence of crimes of violence that are likely to occur.

Despite these problems I think it is valid, on the basis of the results presented, to draw the conclusion that variations between cities in number of **individuals with social problems** and the existence of large **minorities** are factors worthy of consideration when explanations of intercity variations of crimes of violence, and in particular variations in crimes of violence within the family and among acquaintances, are discussed.

The result that the size of certain minority populations in cities is related to the rate of crimes of violence accords with findings from US research. Several authors (e.g. Schuessler, 1962; Harries, 1974) have found that the proportion of black population is the best predictor of intercity variations of crimes of violence.

However, a US study of intercity variations, using both data of recorded crimes and victim-survey data, reports that the result is the reverse when using victim-survey data compared to the use of data of recorded crimes (Decker et al., 1982). Correlation of victim-survey data of crimes of violence with the proportion of white population showed a positive association, while the same calculation using data of recorded crimes showed a negative association (p. 31)[20]. Consistently with this result Nelson (1980:84) reports that, while for most

---

[19]This possible source of error was taken into consideration by recalculation of some of the analyses, excluding crimes committed by offenders from outside the city. The result was only marginally affected. The zero-order correlation between the cities' violent crime rates excluding and including crimes by offenders from outside the city was (r.) 0.98. The step wise regression analysis picked out the same variables in both cases.

200

crimes there was a positive association between victim-survey data and police reported crime (at the intercity level), this was not so for aggravated and simple assault, for which no or negative association resulted. These results are, of course, confusing and may raise questions of validity, although it is not clear whether it is data of police-reported crimes or victim surveys that are invalid in this respect. As reported in Section 2.1.2, victim surveys are likely to miss cases of violence among intimates to a higher proportion than police records. Nelson (1980:81) reports a methodological study comparing victim-survey data with police-reported crimes, which shows that more than half of the police-reported crimes of assault did not appear in the victim survey, i.e. were not mentioned to the interviewer. I shall assume that data of police reported crimes of violence are more adequate than the corresponding victim-survey data, although such a conclusion must be tentative.

10.2   Intracity Variations

In this Section, when considering intracity variations of crimes of violence, I shall treat all the 21 studied cities as one city for the purpose of finding out general as opposed to city-specific patterns.

The units of analysis in this Section are the wards of the cities. I have discussed the choice of that level of analysis in the introduction to Part 3 and shall not repeat myself here. Not all of the wards of the studied cities were included. First I decided to exclude all wards with less than 500 inhabitants so that the measures of offender and victim rates would not be too much affected by random variations. However, I changed this decision and excluded all wards with less than 481 inhabitants. This odd figure was chosen because exclusion of all wards with less than 500 inhabitants would have meant the exclusion of one of the city centre wards, which of course would have been problematic since a large proportion of crimes occur in inner-city areas (see below). As things turned out, the now excluded wards are mainly industrial areas in which generally no or only a few crimes of violence occur. I judged this to be no great problem for the analysis.

The total number of included wards was 399. While data of the crimes, offenders and victims, and the population, were available for all these wards, this was not so for the other variables (see Appendix 2). There were, in particular, four variables for which it was difficult

---

[20] It is of interest to note in this connection that Decker et al. (1982) also report that the same discrepancy occurs for the variable "persons receiving public assistance". A positive relationship with crimes of violence occurs when data of recorded crimes, but a negative when victim survey data, are used.

to get ward-level data; social security (N = 45), income heterogeneity (N = 137), females gainfully employed (N = 179) and mean income (N = 265). For the rest of the variables information was available for between 324 and 373 wards (see Appendix 5). I wish to stress that for some of the variables information is lacking for whole cities, notably in the case of the four variables mentioned above. This is, of course, far from satisfactory. The large number of missing cases for some variables also restricted the "possibility" to use multivariate regression techniques.

10.2.1   The Crime, Victim and Offender Distributions

The problem of measuring the relative distributions of crime, offenders and victims in the wards was and victims was discussed in the introduction to Part 3. This discussion will not be repeated here. It was concluded that the residential population was a fairly adequate denominator when the concern was the offender and the victim distribution, but not so in the case of the crime distribution. However, if inner-city areas are excluded from the analysis, the residential population may serve as a fairly adequate denominator in calculating the relative incidence of the crimes. I have used "per 1,000 inhabitants" instead of, e.g., "per 1,000 inhabitants 15 years and older" as denominator. This choice may be disputed, However, some comparison of the use of these two measures showed no other than marginal differences in the results.

As might be expected, the distributions of crimes, offenders and victims among wards in the city are highly skew. This is especially so for the crime distribution. A large proportion are concentrated to the inner-city area[21]. Of all crimes of violence in the studied cities as many as 34 % occurred in the inner city (23 of 399 wards). As already shown with regard to Stockholm (see e.g. Table 19 in Section 3.1), the structure of criminality in outer- and inner-city areas shows marked differences. That is also the case for the medium-sized and smaller cities, as illustrated in Table 86 concerning the scene of crime by place of occurrence (inner- and outer-city areas). Note that the actual differences are likely to be greater than those shown according to the analysis in Section 3.1.

---

[21] For the sake of clarity it should be pointed out that the concept of inner-city area used here refers to the ward, in some cities the two wards, containing the city centre (CBD), usually a square surrounded by big department stores. When referring to the inner-city area of Stockholm, the area covered is much larger (see Chapter 11).

Table 86. Scene of crime by place of occurrence (inner- or outer-city area). Data from the 21 Police Districts Study. Per cent

Scene of crime	Inner–city	Outer–city
Apartment/proximity area	6	55
Street, square, park	41	19
Public entertainment	36	14
Public transport	5	2
Shop, service institutions	7	3
Other	6	7
Total	101	100
N	1,630	3,183

Comparing the crime, offender and victim distributions (Table 87) there is a close association between offender and victim distributions. Wards with higher offender and victim rates are generally located in the outer parts of cities. Excluding the inner-city areas, also the crime distribution shows a close association with the offender and victim distributions.

Table 87. Zero-order correlations of crime, offender and victim distributions per 1,000 inhabitants. Correlations excluding inner-city areas within brackets. N = 399 (N = 376). Data from the 21 Police Districts Study

	Offenders per 1,000 inhabitants	Victims per 1,000 inhabitants
Crimes per 1,000 inhabitants	19* (83*)	27* (88*)
Offenders per 1,000 inhabitants		86* (82*)

Note: Coefficients multiplied by 100. Correlations significant at the 5 % level marked with an asterisk. Wards with less than 481 inhabitants excluded. N = 399.

10.2.2 Basic Correlates of Crime, Victim and Offender Distributions

The variables chosen for the analysis of the intracity variations of crimes of violence, offenders and victims are presented in Appendix 2. The zero-order correlations are presented in Table 88.

Table 88. Zero-order correlations of ward characteristics with crimes, offenders and victims per 1,000 inhabitants. Total cities and with inner-city areas excluded. Data from the 21 Police Districts Study

Ward characteristics	Crimes Total	Excluding inner-city	Offenders Total	Excluding inner-city	Victims Total	Excluding inner-city
Mean income	− 7	−19*	−15*	−15*	−15*	−15*
Income heterogeneity	− 5	− 9	−13	−12	−18	−18
% aged 0—14 years	−22*	− 9	0	0	0	0
% aged 60— years	10	4	− 8	−10*	− 8	− 9
% females aged 15— years	−11*	− 2	− 4	− 6	− 6	− 6
% foreign nationality	5	32*	35*	35*	38*	39*
Household size, mean	−22*	−21*	−12*	−12*	−14*	−13*
% dwellings in one- and two family houses	−20*	−29*	−27*	−27*	−29*	−29*
% dwellings in municipal housing	− 2	25*	30*	31*	32*	33*
% small dwellings	16*	25*	19*	19*	21*	20*
% large dwellings	−10*	−24*	−23*	−23*	−24*	−25*
% old dwellings	16	4	− 5	− 6	− 3	− 6
% households with children/youth	−21*	−13*	− 3	− 3	− 5	− 3
% children with single working parents	29*	42*	33*	40*	43*	43*
% vacant dwellings	9	21*	23*	23*	23*	23*
% work places	44*	18*	4	2	5	0
Industrial work, number of employees	29*	3	3	2	5	2
Commercial centre	55*	23*	5	11*	9	10*
Distance from city centre	−26*	−17*	− 8	− 8	−12*	−11*
% overcrowded	8	23*	26*	26*	26*	26*
% blue—collar workers	− 3	3	5	6	2	3
% social security	25	40*	47*	45*	40*	38*
% females, gainfully employed	− 6	− 9	− 4	− 5	− 2	− 2

Note: Differing N due to lack of data for some of the studied cities, see Appendix 4. Few observations for the variable "social security". Coefficients have been multiplied by 100. Coefficients significant at the 5 % level marked with an asterisk. Wards with less than 481 inhabitants excluded. For definitions of ward characteristic variables see Appendix 2.

Inspection of the correlations shows that the correlates of the offender and victim distributions are nearly identical, which is to be expected since these distributions showed such a close association. Considering all studied wards, the crime distribution shows a differing pattern of correlates, but with inner-city areas excluded has almost the same correlations with the variables as have the offender and victim distributions.

The strongest association between ward characteristics and the total crime distribution is, between the variables "commercial centre" and "work places", which of course is a result of the mentioned concentration of crimes to inner-city areas. This concentration is likely to be explained by the localization of public entertainment to these wards, as discussed in the introduction to Part 3, which is also well illustrated by Table 86 above.

Considering the interrelationship between variables positively and negatively related to offender and victim distributions (and crime distribution excluding inner-city areas), there is a tendency that these variables are positively intercorrelated, especially those negatively related to the crime variables (Table 89).

Table 89. Intercorrelations of variables that are (significantly) positively (top table) or negatively (bottom table) related to the offender and victim distributions. Data from the 21 Police Districts Study

Intercorrelation variables positively related to offender and victim distributions					
	Foreigners	Municipal housing	Over-crowded	Single working parents	Vacant dwellings	Small dwellings
Social security 67*	45*	57*	59*	48*	13*
Foreigners	35*	42*	15*	26*	8
Municipal housing		33*	36*	20*	23*
Overcrowded			40*	25*	55*
Single working parents				10*	53*
Vacant dwellings					16*

Intercorrelation variables negatively related to offender and victim distributions		
	Large dwellings	Household size	Mean income
One- and two family houses	85*	80*	56*
Large dwellings		74*	56*
Household size			56*

Note: Coefficients (r.) have been multiplied by 100. Correlations significant at 5 % level marked with an asterisk. Differing numbers of observations (see Appendix 4). Few observations for the variable "social security". Wards with less than 481 inhabitants excluded.

Higher rates of offenders, victims and (excluding inner-city areas) crimes tend to occur in wards which, on the basis of the result obtained, may be described as "social problem areas". This finding accords with results from previous research and the preliminary findings from the Gävle Study reported in the introduction to Part 3. Wards with lower rates of offenders, victims and (excluding inner-city areas) crimes tend to be high social ranking areas dominated by single family houses (see also Appendix 6).

205

10.2.3   Some Further Explorations of the Offender Distribution

In this Section I shall make some further explorations of the offender distribution, concentrating on differences in wards according to their offender rate with regard to a) ward characteristics, b) offender characteristics, and c) characteristics of the crimes committed by them.

As already mentioned, the distributions among wards of offenders, victims and crimes are highly skew. One way to get some information about the concentration of offenders is to calculate a **segregation index** (see e.g. Andersson-Brolin, 1984:77–78) of the offender distribution. This index shows the proportion of offenders who have to move to another ward for the offender distribution to be the same as for the whole population. The segregation index for the offender distribution is 32 %.

Figure 19 shows the distribution of offenders among wards classified in three groups according to offender rate. All classifications may be disputed since different cutting points between classes may yield different results. To explore that source of error I tried out some other cutting points than those finally used. The result showed that the data presented are not highly sensitive to variations in cutting points, although radical changes would of course have some impact on the results.

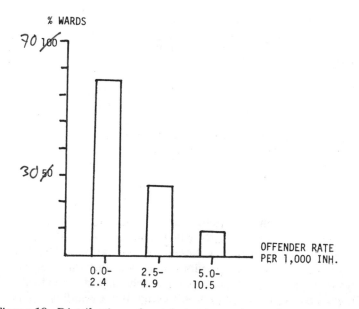

Figure 19. Distribution of wards in classes by offender rate per 1,000 inhabitants.

Mean characteristics of the wards in the different classes according to offender rate are shown in Table 90. The result is in close accordance with the findings of the correlational analysis. At the bottom of the table is shown the victimization rate. Wards with high offender rates have also high victimization rates, and vice versa, which is to be expected since, as shown above, the offender and victimization rates in the wards are closely correlated.

Table 90. Selected mean characteristics of wards grouped by offender rate. Data from the 21 Police Districts Study

Ward characteristics	Offender rate per 1,000 inhabitants		
	0—2.4	2.5—4.9	5.0—10.5
Mean income (Sw. Cr.)	49,375	44,140	41,255
% aged 0—14 years	18.0	16.6	18.9
% aged 60— years	20.9	20.2	15.8
% females aged 15— years	49.7	49.5	47.6
% foreign nationality	2.8	6.3	12.2
Household size, mean	2.3	2.1	2.2
% dwellings in one— and two family houses	41.5	18.6	1.6
% dwellings in municipal housing	14.0	31.2	42.9
% small dwellings	35.7	47.3	44.8
% large dwellings	20.8	10.1	10.5
% old dwellings	34.6	30.1	31.4
% households with children/youth	33.5	29.1	34.0
% children with single working parents	13.5	18.2	20.7
% vacant dwellings	0.1	0.2	0.8
Distance from city centre in kilometres	2.6	2.1	2.3
% overcrowded	3.7	5.1	6.4
% blue—collar workers	26.4	27.3	29.3
% social security	2.9	5.6	11.0
% females, gainfully employed	66.6	64.9	62.5
Victims of violence per 1,000 inhabitants	1.7	3.8	6.4

Note: Differing numbers of observations due to missing values. Few observations for the variable "social security". See Appendix 2 for definitions of variables.

Comparison of **offender characteristics** of the ward classes according to offender rate (Table 91) shows no difference with regard to the offenders' sex and no marked difference with regard to their age, although there is some tendency to older age in the low offender rate wards[22]. As regards offender nationality there are great differences between the classes of wards; while 15 % of the offenders in the low offender rate wards are foreigners, the corresponding figure in the high offender rate wards is 35 %. This is to be related to the fact that the latter have a higher proportion of foreign inhabitants (see Table 90). Considering the offenders' employment status, there is a clearly higher proportion of offenders who are unemployed or on relief work in the high than in the low offender rate wards. This might be taken as an indication of a higher proportion of socially loaded offenders in the high offender rate wards.

Table 91. Selected offender characteristics by offenders' home address grouped according to offender rate of ward. Data from the 21 Police Districts Study. Per cent. Number of cases within brackets

Offender characteristics %	Ward offender rate per 1,000 inhabitants		
	0—2.4	2.5—4.9	5.0—10.5
OFFENDER'S SEX			
Male	93	94	93
Female	7	6	7
	(1,033)	(1,402)	(903)
OFFENDER'S AGE			
0—19	15	15	16
20—29	36	38	41
30—39	26	28	27
40—	23	19	16
	(1,012)	(1,371)	(886)
OFFENDER'S NATIONALITY			
Swedish	85	76	65
Other Scandinavian*	8	13	18
Outside Scandinavia	7	11	17
	(1,024)	(1,393)	(895)
OFFENDER'S EMPLOYMENT STATUS			
Employed/Student	58	54	51
Unemployed/relief work	29	35	39
Pensioner**	8	7	7
Other	5	4	3
	(840)	(1,139)	(728)

*Including Finland
**Mostly early retirement

Turning to a comparison of the **characteristics of the crimes** committed by offenders from different wards according to offender

---

[22] The offenders' mean age in the low rate wards is 31 as compared to 29 in the high rate wards.

rate[23] (Table 92) there are no marked differences with regard to victim-offender interpersonal relationship or sex relationship of victim-offender. With regard to scene of crime a somewhat smaller proportion of the cases committed by offenders from low offender rate wards occurred in apartments. The most marked differences concerned the victim-offender nationality.

Table 92. Selected crime characteristics by offenders' home address grouped according to offender rate of ward. Data from the 21 Police Districts Study. Per cent. Number of cases within brackets.

Crime characteristics	Offender rate per 1,000 inhabitant		
	0—2.4	2.5—4.9	5.0—10.5
SEX RELATIONSHIP			
Intermale	62	62	61
Male offender, female victim	31	32	33
Other	7	6	6
	(1,033)	(1,402)	(903)
VICTIM—OFFENDER NATIONALITY			
Both Swedes	81	69	58
Both foreigners	5	12	18
Mixed	14	19	24
	(1,024)	(1,393)	(895)
VICTIM—OFFENDER INTERPERSONAL RELATIONSHIP			
Family or the like	23	24	23
Acquaintances	42	43	42
Strangers	35	33	35
	(1,031)	(1,390)	(900)
SCENE OF CRIME			
Apartment	42	47	48
Street, square, park	21	23	23
Public entertainment	20	18	17
Public transport	4	2	3
Shop, service institution	3	3	5
Other	9	6	5
	(1,029)	(1,402)	(903)

10.2.3.1 Some Additional Explorations with Regard to Ethnicity of Victims-Offenders

As already noted on several occasions, foreigners are overrepresented in crimes of violence in relation to their proportion of the population. As shown in Table 91, this is also the case in all three

---

[23] Which is not to be confused with the characteristics of crimes occurring in the different wards, since the offenders need not have committed their crimes in their home ward.

209

groups of wards according to the offender rate of the ward. Focusing on the victim-offender relationship in terms of nationality in the simple division into Swedes and foreigners shows that the proportion of crimes committed by offenders from the high offender rate wards that were internal fights between foreigners is nearly four times as high as in the low offender rate wards, while the proportion of fights between Swedes and foreigners is nearly twice as high in high as in low offender rate wards. This might also be illustrated from a somewhat different angle, as in Figure 20, where, of crimes involving at least one foreigner either as victim or offender, the proportion between two foreigners is shown for the different groups of wards.

Since the proportion of foreigners varies between the groups of wards considered, the likelihood that a crime of violence would occur between a given combination according to victim-offender nationality would be expected to vary under the (unrealistic) assumption that the crimes were to occur at random.

Taking this into consideration, the expected distribution of crimes for combinations of victim-offender nationality was calculated for the

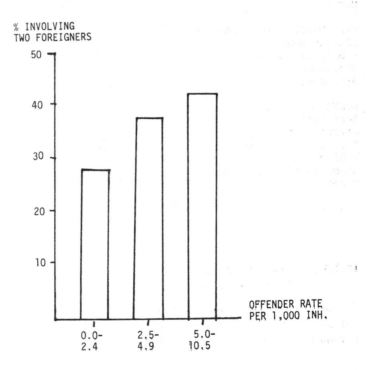

Figure 20. *Proportion of crimes involving at least one foreigner that occurred between two foreigners by offender rate of ward. Data from the 21 Police Districts Study.*

210

different groups of wards[24] and compared with the actual distributions according to victim-offender nationality of A) all crimes
committed by the offenders and B) with restriction to those
committed in the offenders' home ward. The result of these
computations is shown in Table 93.

*Table 93. The expected and the observed distribution of crimes of
violence by victim-offender nationality in different groups of wards
according to offender rate. Per cent*

EXPECTED DISTRIBUTION

Offender rate per 1,000 inhabitants	Victim–offender nationality			
	Swede–Swede	Swede–foreigner*	Foreigner–foreigner	Total
0 — 2.4	94	6	0	100
2,5— 4.9	87	13	0	100
5,0—10.5	76	22	2	100

OBSERVED DISTRIBUTION

Offender rate per 1,000 inhabitants	Victim–offender nationality			
	Swede–Swede	Swede–foreigner*	Foreigner–foreigner	Total
0 — 2.4	81 (82)	5 (6)	14 (12)	100 (100)
2,5— 4.9	69 (70)	12 (13)	19 (17)	100 (100)
5,0—10.5	58 (56)	18 (22)	24 (22)	100 (100)

Note: Figures within brackets in bottom table are those when only crimes
committed in the home ward of the offender are included.
* = or vice versa.

The result shows

• that, while fights involving both Swedes and foreigners are about
as might be expected from their proportions of the population, the
fights that occur between two foreigners are much higher than
expected. This is so in all the three groups of wards according to
offender rate.

This result is interesting since it indicates that it is rather internal
problems in the "foreign community" than frictions between
minority and majority populations that are related to the overrepre-

---

[24]The expected distribution of crimes was calculated on the basis of the relative
frequency of Swedish and foreign inhabitants in the different groups of wards. The
expected proportion of crimes between Swedes was calculated as the relative
frequency of Swedes multiplied by itself. The same type of calculation was made to get
the expected proportion of crimes between foreigners. The expected proportion of
crimes between Swedes and foreigners was calculated as the relative frequency of
Swedes multiplied by the relative frequency of foreigners. Since the probability that a
fight would occur between a Swede and a foreigner is the same as that of a fight
between a foreigner and Swede, these probabilities were added.

sentation of foreigners in crimes of violence. A more detailed analysis taking into consideration variations between different groups of foreigners according to ethnical background seems to be warranted, since differences may be hypothesized to exist. This issue was, however, beyond the scope of the present study.

Of further interest to note from Table 93 is that the proportion of fights between two foreigners is not only markedly higher than expected in all groups of wards considered, but also that there appears to be

● an increasing proportion of internal fights among foreigners with increasing offender rate of ward that cannot be fully explained by an increasing foreign population.

Taking into consideration the difference between the expected and observed proportions of internal fights among foreigners shows that it increases with offender rate of ward.

10.2.4   Crime and Distance in the City

The results presented so far have, among other things, shown that crimes have a different distribution in the urban area than that of the offenders and victims. However, when the inner-city areas were excluded, the crimes as well showed a distribution similar to that of the offenders and victims. The latter indicates that outer-city area crimes are mainly of a local nature (i.e. offenders from the neighbourhood). In this Section I shall consider more specifically the question of crime and distance in the city.

The topics to be dealt with are summarized in the following paragraphs:

A. The distribution of crimes according to distance "travelled" by offender and victim respectively.

B. The distribution of crimes according to distance between the residences of the victim and the offender.

C. Differences in distance "travelled" between crimes occurring in inner- and outer-city areas, and between offenders from different groups of wards according to offender rate of ward.

D. Differences in distance "travelled" according to demographic characteristics of victim and offender.

E. The creation of a Distance Typology.

F. Exploration of crime and victim-offender characteristics by classes of Distance Typology.

G. Relating the Distance Typology to the offender rate of the ward.

Before presenting the results, several limitations and problems when studying crime and distance should be discussed. First, the study of crimes and distance is limited to those offenders (victims) living in the studied cities who have committed their crimes (been victimized) in the city. Hence offenders and victims from outside the cities committing their crimes (being victimized) in the city are not included. Nor are those offenders (victims) living in the city included who have committed crimes of violence (been victims of violence) outside the cities. In the latter case we have no information about the offenders and victims[25]. However, for the offenders (victims) from outside the city involved in crimes of violence in the city there are data. In Table 94 crimes involving offenders from outside the city are compared with those involving offenders from within the city.

Table 94. A comparison of offender, victim and crime characteristics between offenders from outside and from within the cities. Data from the 21 Police Districts Study

Offender, victim and crime characteristics %	Crimes by offenders from within the city	Crimes by offenders from out- side the city
Female offenders	6	4
Female victims	36	31
OFFENDER'S AGE		
0—19	15	16
20—29	38	39
30—39	27	25
40—	19	20
VICTIM'S AGE		
0—19	16	19
20—29	34	32
30—39	24	21
40—	25	27
Foreign offenders	24	6
Foreign victims	17	12
Offenders unemployed or on relief work	34	22
Crimes between strangers	34	37
Crimes in apartments	46	39

Note: Differing number of observations for variables, around 3,000 for crimes by offenders from within cities and around 1,000 for crimes by offenders from outside cities.

---

[25] These crimes, and hence their offenders and victims, are not included in the study.

213

The results of the comparison show that there are no great differences in the sex and age of the offenders or of their victims, although there is a somewhat greater involvement of females and slightly older victims in the crimes committed by offenders from within the city. The much higher proportion of foreign offenders among those from within the city may partly be related to the fact that foreigners tend to be involved more than Swedes in crimes between acquaintances, and these crimes are more local than others.

Offenders from outside the city tend more often to be involved in crimes between strangers and less so in crimes occurring in apartments. This may be related to the fact that a greater proportion of the "visiting" offenders get involved in crimes of violence during visits to the city to participate in public entertainment. Finally, the markedly higher proportion of offenders from within the city who are unemployed or on relief work may be interpreted to the effect that a higher proportion of these offenders are socially loaded persons. Overall,

- Offenders living in the city seem to a higher degree to be socially loaded persons and more often involved in crimes in apartments between acquaintances than those coming from outside of the city.

The **distance** from, e.g., the offender's home to the scene of the crime may be measured in several different ways. The two most common measures are a) the shortest way between the two points (*line distance*) or b) the shortest way by road (*wheel distance*).

Arguments may be raised against the use of both these measures. I have used *line distance*. Wheel distance is a much more time-consuming measure to obtain and, as Phillips states, "*... there is no reason to assume that the shortest street distance measured from a map has any relation to actual travel routes, ...*" (1980:173). He states further that both these methods yield very similar results, although that opinion is not agreed with by all researchers. Rhodes & Conly (1981:178) point to such factors as natural barriers (e.g. rivers) that make wheel distance a more appropriate measure.

In measuring the distance on the maps of the various cities the goal has been to have errors of the various measured points not above 100 metres. Although larger errors are likely to occur in some instances, there is no reason to believe that these would in any way be systematic (i.e. correlated with other studied variables) but rather to be random. Crimes occurring just outside the apartment of the offender or victim have been referred to zero distance since, as noted, it was not judged possible to have a precision finer than "hundreds of metres".

214

10.2.4.1 Distribution of Distances from Offenders' and Victims' Home and to the Scene of the Crime

Phillips notes that not much research has been done on the topic of crime and distance, but states that "*All researchers have reported finding a* **distance-decay** *relationship ...*" (my emphasis, 1980:168). He includes crimes of violence in that statement, although he recognizes that there are differences in average distance travelled between different types of crimes as stated above in the introduction to Part 3. The reported relationship refers to criminals' mobility. I know of no study (of crimes against persons) that has in detail considered distance and victimization.

Phillips' generalization is well supported by the data from the 21 studied cities (Figure 21).

- Both the incidence of crimes committed and of victimization show a decrease (of J-shaped form) with increasing distance from the offenders' (victims') home.

As is evident from the figures, offenders commit their crimes and victimizations occur to a great proportion in and around the home. More so in the latter case. But also a fairly high proportion of the crimes are committed, and persons are victimized, in the neighbourhood if by that is understood crimes occurring within 500 metres of the offenders' (victims') home.

Few of the offenders commit their crimes, and few persons are victimized, further than 4 kilometres from the home. The "possible" distances that may occur must, of course, be seen in relation to the size of the studied cities, and the reader is further reminded of the other limitations mentioned in Section 10.2.4 above.

In the text below I shall refer to distance between offenders' home and scene of crime as **criminals' mobility** and distance between victims' home and scene of crime as **victimization distance**.

10.2.4.2 Distance between Victims' and Offenders' Homes

As shown in the previous Section, the shapes of the distributions of criminals' mobility and victimization distance were very similar. The question to be raised here is what association there is between the location of the offender's residence and that of the victim. This was possible to study since not only the criminals' mobility and victimization distance were measured, but also the distance between victims' and offenders' homes.

In about one fourth of the crimes (24 %) the distance was zero, meaning generally that the victim and the offender shared the same apartment or in a minor number of cases were close neighbours. In a further 18 % of the crimes the victim and offender lived nearby each

215

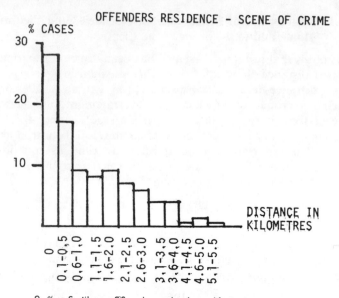

OFFENDERS RESIDENCE - SCENE OF CRIME

2 % of the offenders had a distance
travelled longer than 5.5 kilometres.

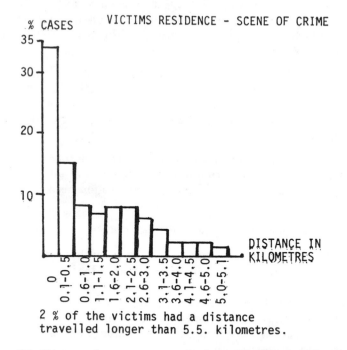

VICTIMS RESIDENCE - SCENE OF CRIME

2 % of the victims had a distance
travelled longer than 5.5. kilometres.

Figure 21. Distance between scene of crime and offenders' home (top figure) and victims' home (bottom figure). Data from the 21 Police Districts Study.
Note: The zero distance refers to no distance or a distance less than 100 metres.

other, defined here as that the residents were located within 500 metres from each other.

- In 4 out of 10 cases (42 %) the victim and offender were living at the same address or within 500 metres of each other.

Exclusion of those cases with zero distance between victims' and offenders' homes, shows that, also with this restriction, a significant proportion of the cases (24 %) occur between a victim and an offender living nearby each other (within 500 metres).

10.2.4.3 A Comparison between Crimes Occurring in Inner- and in Outer-City Areas according to Distance to Offenders' and Victims' Homes

It is reasonable to assume that crimes involving offenders and victims in cases occurring in inner-city areas would be less local. This is in fact the case, as shown in Table 95. Note that offenders from outside the city are not included and that a high proportion of the offenders (victims) in crimes occurring in inner-city areas are likely to come from outside of the city, as previously shown by data from the Gävle Study (see Figure 9 in introduction to Part 3). The result accords closely with general findings from research into criminals' mobility (e.g. Baldwin & Bottoms, 1976).

Table 95. Mean distance in kilometres "travelled" by offender and victim according to whether the crime occurred in an inner-city or an outer-city area. Data from the 21 Police Districts Study

| | Scene of crime occurrence | |
	Inner–city area	Outer–city area
Mean distance "travelled" by offender	2.1 (1.4) N = 879	1.1 (1.5) N = 2,225
Mean distance "travelled" by victim	2.0 (1.4) N = 1,217	0.9 (1.5) N = 2,670

Note: Standard deviation given within brackets. Offenders (victims) living outside the city not included.

10.2.4.4 A Comparison of Distance "Travelled" by Offenders according to Offender Rate of Offenders' Home Ward

Baldwin & Bottoms (1976:88) report the general finding on crime and distance that "... *the higher the rate of delinquent residence in any ward, the shorter distance do offenders who live in that ward tend to travel when committing their offences.*" This general pattern is also replicated for the 21 studied cities, as shown in Table 96 where the

217

distances travelled by offenders have been grouped in three classes[26]. Of special interest to note is that the difference in proportion of cases occurring in the offender's neighbourhood is larger than that of cases in and around the home.

Table 96. Distance from offenders' home to scene of crime in three classes by offender rate of the offender's home ward. Data from the 21 Police Districts Study. Per cent

Distance	Offender rate per 1,000 inhabitants		
	0—2.4	2.5—4.9	5.0—10.5
In and around the home of the offender	26	28	31
In the offender's neighbourhood	13	18	23
At other place in the city	61	54	46
Total	100	100	100
N	892	1,329	874

It may further be of interest to show (Table 97) that a smaller proportion of cases of offenders from high offender rate wards occur in inner-city areas than in low offender rate wards. This may be partly interpreted to the effect that crimes by offenders from low offender rate wards to a higher degree than from high offender rate wards are related to participation in public entertainment.

Table 97. Per cent crimes committed in the inner-city areas by offender rate of offenders' home ward. Data from the 21 Police Districts Study. Per cent

	Offender rate per 1,000 inhabitants		
	0—2.4	2.5—4.9	5.0—10.5
Per cent crimes committed in inner—city areas	30	27	22

10.2.4.5 Distance to Scene of Crime by Offenders' and Victims' Demographic Characteristics

In studying various correlates of distance travelled by offenders (e.g. type of offence, sex of offender, age of offender, recidivism of

---

[26]This grouping of the crimes according to distance will be discussed in Section 10.2.4.6. By neighbourhood is understood within 500 metres from offender's home excluding cases in and around the home.

offender, social class of offender) Baldwin & Bottoms reach the conclusion that "... *age and type of offence are the two most important variables influencing the distance travelled by offenders ...*" (1976:91). Young criminals tended to have a shorter mobility, a finding that has also been reported in other studies of criminals' mobility (e.g. Rhodes & Conly, 1981).

Focusing on crimes of violence, as in this study, the data from the 21 studied cities show that no great difference in distance travelled by *offenders* appears as regards their sex and nationality. As regards age the result is the reverse of the general finding concerning criminals' mobility and age presented above. Older offenders tend to commit their crimes of violence at a shorter distance from home than do younger offenders (Table 98). However, this is likely to be related to

Table 98. Mean distance in kilometres between scene of crime and homes of offenders and victims by sex, age and nationality of offender (victim). Figures within brackets excluding zero distance. Data from the 21 Police Districts Study

	Mean distance in kilometres	Standard deviation	N
OFFENDERS' SEX			
Male	1.3 (1.9)	1.6 (1.6)	2,894 (2,088)
Female	1.2 (1.8)	1.5 (1.6)	200 (134)
VICTIMS' SEX			
Male	1.5 (1.9)	1.6 (1.5)	2.585 (2,030)
Female	0.7 (1.9)	1.4 (1.7)	1.301 (521)
OFFENDERS' AGE			
0—19	1.6 (1.8)	1.5 (1.5)	461 (418)
20—29	1.5 (1.9)	1.5 (1.5)	1,171 (929)
30—39	1.3 (2.0)	1.7 (1.7)	842 (553)
40—	0.8 (1.6)	1.4 (1.6)	580 (305)
VICTIMS' AGE			
0—19	1.4 (1.7)	1.5 (1.6)	641 (503)
20—29	1.4 (2.0)	1.6 (1.5)	1,352 (989)
30—39	1.2 (2.0)	1.6 (1.7)	889 (537)
40—	0.9 (1.7)	1.4 (1.5)	989 (516)
OFFENDERS' NATIONALITY			
Swedish	1.3 (1.9)	1.6 (1.6)	2,309 (1,659)
Other Scandinavian	1.2 (1.7)	1.5 (1.5)	410 (287)
Outside Scandinavia	1.3 (1.8)	1.5 (1.5)	364 (269)
VICTIMS' NATIONALITY			
Swedish	1.3 (1.9)	1.6 (1.6)	3,204 (2,148)
Other Scandinavian	0.9 (1.8)	1.4 (1.5)	353 (178)
Outside Scandinavia	1.1 (1.7)	1.4 (1.5)	312 (215)

Note: The distance referred to is between offenders' home and scene of crime in cases when offenders' demographic characteristics are concerned and between victims' home and scene of crime in cases when victims' demographic characteristics are concerned. Offenders (victims) living outside the city not included.

the fact that a higher proportion of the older offenders' crimes occur in and around the home. Consequently, when excluding cases occurring at zero distance (figures within brackets in Table 98), the distance travelled by offenders increases with age of the offender with the exception of offenders in the oldest age category, whose crimes are even more local than those of youngest offenders.

Comparing the results for *victims* and offenders there are some notable differences. Female victims tend to be assaulted at a much shorter distance from home than male, which is "explained" by the fact that a vast proportion of female victims are assaulted in the home. Excluding cases occurring at zero distance from victims' homes (figures within brackets) the male-female difference disappears. There is also a tendency that persons of foreign nationality tend to be victimized closer to home than Swedes. Exclusion of the zero distance cases does not result in full disappearance of that difference. Instead, there is a decrease in victimization distance from Swedes, over other Scandinavians to those from outside Scandinavia.

10.2.4.6 Distance Typology of Crimes of Violence

After presentation in the previous Sections of some basic facts about crimes of violence and distance, I shall now turn to the topic of developing a Distance Typology of crimes of violence. In that effort I shall take into consideration simultaneously, instead of separately as has been done so far, the distances from scene of crime to the homes of the victim and the offender. For instance, discussing localness of crimes, a truly "local crime" may be regarded as one where both the victim and the offender live near the scene of the crime, while a truly "non-local crime" may be regarded as a crime occurring at a longer distance from both the home of the victim and of the offender and where these two are not resident nearby each other.

The first step in the development of the typology was to make a classification of the distances. I judged that it was mainly three "distances" from the home of the victim and the offender to the scene of the crime that were of interest from an ecological point of view, namely

1. Crimes in and around the home, zero distance

2. Crimes in the neighbourhood, defined as within 500 metres from the home, excluding crimes in and around the home

3. Crimes at other places in the city.

The distance division is illustrated in Figure 22. Note that the circles are in no way proportional to the area which they cover.

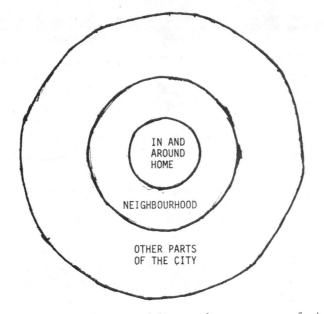

Figure 22. The classification of distance between scene of crime and offender's (victim's) home illustrated.

In the second step the distance travelled by the victim was related to that travelled by the offender according to the classification given above. Taking this into consideration there were nine possible combinations of distance travelled by victim and offender, as illustrated in Figure 23.

Reading Figure 23 from the left to right beginning from the top, the first four circles may be regarded as various types of **local crimes**[27]. The next two circles represent cases which occurred in one of the parties' homes but where the other party was from outside the neighbourhood. Together with the crimes illustrated by the next two circles – crimes in neighbourhood of one of the parties when the other was from outside the neighbourhood – these crimes may be labelled **semilocal**. Finally, represented by the last circle, we have those crimes where both the victim and the offender were outside their neighbourhoods when the crime occurred. These crimes may be called **non-local** crimes. Hence, we have three main types and nine subtypes in the distance typology of crimes of violence.

So far we have not considered the **distance between the residences of the victim and the offender**. Calculation of the proportion of cases in which the victim and offender lived within 500 metres of each other for the various distance types produced a very satisfactory result (Figure 23, percentage given at the upper right of the circles).

---

[27]Note that the circles in Figure 23 are those defined in Figure 22.

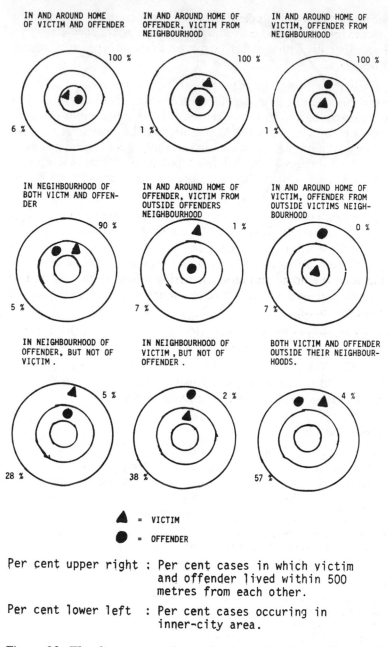

IN AND AROUND HOME OF VICTIM AND OFFENDER — 100 % — 6 %

IN AND AROUND HOME OF OFFENDER, VICTIM FROM NEIGHBOURHOOD — 100 % — 1 %

IN AND AROUND HOME OF VICTIM, OFFENDER FROM NEIGHBOURHOOD — 100 % — 1 %

IN NEGIHBOURHOOD OF BOTH VICTM AND OFFENDER — 90 % — 5 %

IN AND AROUND HOME OF OFFENDER, VICTIM FROM OUTSIDE OFFENDERS NEIGHBOURHOOD — 1 % — 7 %

IN AND AROUND HOME OF VICTIM, OFFENDER FROM OUTSIDE VICTIMS NEIGHBOURHOOD — 0 % — 7 %

IN NEIGHBOURHOOD OF OFFENDER, BUT NOT OF VICTIM. — 5 % — 28 %

IN NEIGHBOURHOOD OF VICTIM, BUT NOT OF OFFENDER. — 2 % — 38 %

BOTH VICTIM AND OFFENDER OUTSIDE THEIR NEIGHBOURHOODS. — 4 % — 57 %

▲ = VICTIM

● = OFFENDER

Per cent upper right : Per cent cases in which victim and offender lived within 500 metres from each other.

Per cent lower left : Per cent cases occuring in inner-city area.

Figure 23. The distance typology of crimes of violence illustrated.

In three out of four of the subtypes of local crimes the proportion of cases of victim and offender living within 500 metres of each other was 100 % and in the fourth 90 %. So these crimes are definitely to be regarded as local.

222

In the rest of the five subtypes the highest proportion of cases in which the victim and the offender lived within 500 metres of each other was 5 %, consistently with the classification of these subtypes as semilocal and non-local.

As stated at the beginning of Section 10.2.4, on the basis of the close correspondence of crime, victim and offender distributions (excluding inner-city) areas there was reason to believe that outer-city area crimes are to a large degree local and that the reverse is true for inner-city area crimes. A calculation of the proportion of crimes in the various subtypes of the distance typology occurring in inner-city areas supports that hypothesis (Figure 23, percentage given at the lower left of the circles).

Of different types of local crimes the highest proportion of cases occurring in inner-city areas was 6 %, while of the non-local crimes as many as 57 % occurred in inner-city areas. Among the semilocal crimes there is a marked difference between the cases occurring in and around the home and those occurring in the neighbourhood of one of the parties. The latter have to a much higher degree occurred in inner-city areas.

The distribution of crimes among the various classes of the distance typology is shown in Table 99.

Table 99. Distribution of the crimes according to the Distance Typology. Data from the 21 Police Districts Study

Distance Typology	Per cent	N
LOCAL CRIMES		
In and around the home of victim and offender	21.8	583
In and around home of offender, victim from neighbourhood	3.8	102
In and around home of victim, offender from neighbourhood	6.6	178
In the neighbourhood of both victim and offender	5.6	150
SEMILOCAL CRIMES		
In and around home of offender, victim from outside offender's neighbourhood	5.5	148
In and around home of victim, offender from outside victim's neighbourhood	12.2	327
In the neighbourhood of offender, but not of victim	6.3	171
In the neighbourhood of victim, but not of offender	6.4	172
NON—LOCAL CRIMES		
Both victim and offender outside their neighbourhoods	31.6	848

Of all crimes 38 % are local with a predominance of crimes in and around the home (58 %), 30 % are semilocal occurring in and around the home of victim with an offender from outside the neighbourhood as the most frequent subclass (40 %), and 32 % non-local.

10.2.4.7 Crime and Victim-Offender Characteristics in the Distance Typology

Victim-Offender Interpersonal Relationship (see Table 100)

Local Crimes

For natural reasons there is a heavy predominance of family violence among crimes occurring in and around the home of both victim and offender. The cases in the category "acquainted by recognition" refer e.g. to those occurring in hostels for university students (shared kitchen, but separate bedrooms).

Cases in and around the home of one of the parties and with the other party from the neighbourhood occur mainly between acquaintances, and a significant proportion are formerly married or fiancés, especially in cases occurring in the victim's home. Cases in which the victim-offender are acquainted by recognition refers often to quarrels between neighbours, not seldom with one party complaining or intervening.

The crimes occurring in the neighbourhood of both the victim and the offender differ mainly from the others in the smaller proportion of persons who are closely acquainted. However, in the majority of cases the victim-offender have some sort of acquaintanceship. This is the only type in which the majority of cases occur in the daytime (62 % between 08.00–19.59).

Semilocal Crimes

As regards semilocal crimes there is an apparent difference between those occurring in and around the home and those occurring in the neighbourhood of one of the parties. Of the former a significant proportion involves cases in which the parties had been formerly married (most of these cases) or are fiancés. The other significant proportion is cases between other close acquaintances – one of the parties visiting the other. These cases, together with local crimes that occurred in and around the home of the victim with offender from the neighbourhood, have the highest proportion of offenders who are unemployed and not students of all the subtypes.

Semilocal crimes occurring in the neighbourhood of one of the parties occur to a large degree between strangers and are much like the non-local crimes in distribution of victim-offender interpersonal relationships. It seems reasonable to hypothesize that a vast

Table 100. Distance Typology classes by victim-offender interpersonal relationship. Data from the 21 Police Districts Study. Per cent

Distance Typology	Married/ cohabiting Parent/ child*	Formerly married, fiancés	Close acquain- tance Rela- tives	Casual acquain- tance	Acquain- ted by recogni- tion	Stran- gers	Total
LOCAL CRIMES							
In and around home of victim and offender	70	3	13	0	14	0	100
In and around home of offender, victim from neighbourhood	1	7	52	3	18	20	101
In and around home of victim, offender from neighbourhood	3	15	42	1	20	18	99
In the neighbourhood of both victim and offender	7	2	26	1	28	36	100
SEMILOCAL CRIMES							
In and around home of offender, victim from outside offender's neighbourhood	3	20	45	7	11	14	100
In and around home of victim, offender from outside victim's neighbourhood	3	39	33	5	8	12	100
In the neighbourhood of offender, but not of victim	0	6	35	2	15	43	99
In the neighbourhood of victim, but not of offender	0	6	23	2	13	56	100
NON-LOCAL CRIMES							
Both victim and offender outside their neighbourhoods	3	3	23	3	15	52	99

* = or vice versa.

proportion of these crimes occur in the course of public entertainment and that it is mainly that the offender's or victim's place of residence happens to be located near areas of public entertainment that separates these cases from the non-local.

Non-Local Crimes

As already stated, the non-local crimes are, as regards the distribution of victim-offender interpersonal relationships, like semilocal

225

15

crimes occurring in the neighbourhood of one of the parties. As was shown in Figure 23, a vast proportion of the crimes occur in inner-city areas. They are strongly concentrated to weekends at nighttime (49 %), which is also the case for semilocal crimes that have occurred in the neighbourhood of one of the parties (40–42 %).

Scene of Crime (see Table 101)

Since scene of crime tends to covary with interpersonal relationship of victim-offender, the result of the comparison of the classes of the Distance Typology by scene of crime is fairly predictable. What may be commented upon is the differences that exist between non-local

Table 101. Distance Typology classes by scene of crime. Data from the 21 Police Districts Study. Per cent

Distance Typology	Street, square, park	Public enter- tain- ment	Public trans- port	Shop, service insti- tution	Apart- ment	Other	Total
LOCAL CRIMES							
In and around home of victim and offender	3	0	0	0	96	4	100
In and around home of offender, victim from neighbourhood	18	0	0	0	82	0	100
In and around home of victim, offender from neighbourhood	14	0	0	0	85	1	100
In the neighbourhood of both victim and offender	48	7	3	7	25	9	99
SEMILOCAL CRIMES							
In and around home of offender, victim from outside offender's neighbourhood	9	0	4	0	81	5	99
In and around home of victim, offender from outside victim's neighbourhood	5	1	1	1	89	2	99
In the neighbourhood of offender, but not of victim	36	26	4	6	22	6	100
In the neighbourhood of victim, but not of offender	36	27	4	6	20	6	99
NON–LOCAL CRIMES							
Both victim and offender outside their neighbourhoods	36	35	5	6	9	8	99

226

crimes and semilocal crimes occurring in one of the parties' neighbourhood. As suspected above, it turned out that not only a large proportion of non-local crimes but also of semilocal crimes occurred in the course of public entertainment. However, semilocal crimes in the neighbourhood of one of the parties occurred to a much higher degree in apartments – and may be hypothesized to be mainly heavy drinking parties in the apartments of others than those involved in the crimes.

Selected Victim-Offender Characteristics (see Table 102)

Table 102. Distance Typology classes by selected victim-offender demographic characteristics. Data from the 21 Police Districts Study. Per cent

Distance Typology	Both offender and victim less than 20 years old	Both offender and victim 40 years or older	Inter-male fights	Male-* female fights	Swede-** foreigner fights	Foreigers' internal fights
LOCAL CRIMES						
In and around home of victim and offender	0	21	24	68	14	18
In and around home of offender, victim from neighbourhood	5	7	59	29	12	14
In and around home of victim, offender from neighbourhood	2	15	59	34	18	14
In the neighbourhood of both victim and offender	21	7	69	23	26	9
SEMILOCAL CRIMES						
In and around home of offender, victim from outside offender's neighbourhood	2	10	58	37	17	9
In and around home of victim, offender from outside victim's neighbourhood	3	17	39	57	16	13
In the neighbourhood of offender, but not of victim	9	6	77	18	23	10
In the neighbourhood of victim, but not of offender	12	5	79	15	24	9
NON-LOCAL CRIMES						
Both victim and offender outside their neighbourhoods	8	4	78	15	23	9

* = Only cases with female victims.
** = Or vice versa.

Local Crimes

The crimes in and around the home of the victim and offender are, consistently with previously presented results, mostly cases in which males assault females. Fairly many of the cases involve persons 40 years and older. This is also the subtype with the highest proportion of internal fights between foreigners, well in accordance with what has been shown earlier.

Cases occurring in or around the home of one party with the other from the neighbourhood differ from those in and around the home of both victim and offender in that intermale fights predominate. Judging from my experience from reading the files, besides confrontations between neighbours and formerly married, this type also included a significant proportion of cases of socially loaded persons' drinking parties, an observation that may be of interest in the light of discussions concerning negative effects of concentrating socially loaded persons to certain wards.

The final type of local crimes shows some interesting results where selected victim-offender characteristics are concerned. This is a type of crime with a comparatively high proportion between victims and offenders less than 20 years (one fifth of the cases). Furthermore it is also the type with the highest proportion crimes between Swedes and foreigners. Although the analysis made in Section 10.2.3.1 did not indicate that friction between Swedes and foreigners would be the main "cause" of the higher rate of crimes of violence among foreigners, this result may indicate that the "ethnical friction hypothesis" may be of some relevance for outdoor local crimes in ethnical heterogen neighbourhoods of the victim and the offender.

In cases occurring in the neighbourhood of both victim and offender where both of the parties were less than 20 years old 35 % occurred between a Swede and a foreigner, which may be compared with that 19 % of the other cases occurring between two parties less than 20 years occurred between a Swede and a foreigner.

Semilocal Crimes

Regarding semilocal crimes, again there is an apparent difference between those occurring in and around the home and those occurring in the neighbourhood of one of the parties. The former, especially those occurring in and around the victim's home, are to a much higher degree cases in which males assault females, which of course is in line with the fact that these cases to a significant degree occur between formerly married couples.

The victim-offender characteristics of semilocal crimes occurring in the neighbourhood of one of the parties shows a nearly identical pattern to that of non-local crimes. However, as stated above, these

228

cases differs on one point in offender characteristics from non-local crimes, namely, the higher proportion of offenders unemployed and not being students.

Non-Local Crimes

Just as for semilocal crimes in the neighbourhood of one of the parties, non-local crimes are overwhelmingly intermale fights. Furthermore, a fairly large proportion involve foreigner-Swede fights. Partly this may be "explained" by the fact that many foreigners in these cases appear as offenders/victims during work, predominantly at restaurants.

10.2.4.8 The Distance Typology Related to Offender Rate of Ward

An interesting question is whether there are any marked differences between offenders from different wards according to offender rate of ward in patterns of crimes regarding their localness. Consideration first of the proportion of cases by class of Distance Typology (see Figure 23) that have occurred in high offender rate wards shows clear variations.

- Crimes in the neighbourhood of both victim and offender are the crimes most concentrated in high offender rate wards (40 % of these cases).

The least concentrated are those semilocal crimes in and around the home of one of the parties and the non-local crimes – between 22–24 % of these cases occurred in high offender rate wards. For the rest of the types the proportion of the other cases occurring in high offender rate wards varies between 30–34 %.

Crimes committed by offenders from high offender rate wards are clearly more local than crimes committed by offenders from other wards, as shown in Table 103.

- While 44 % of the crimes by offenders from high offender rate wards are local, the corresponding figure for offenders from low offender rate wards is 30 %. The difference between high and low offender rate wards has the same direction for all subtypes of local crimes. One plausible explanation of this is that crimes committed by offenders from low offender rate wards to a higher degree are those occurring in the course of public entertainment, while those by offenders from high offender rate wards to a higher degree are related to a socially loaded person's life style.

229

Table 103. Distance Typology classes by offenders home ward grouped according to offender rate. Per cent. Data from the 21 Police Districts Study

Distance Typology	Ward offender rate per 1,000 inhabitants		
	0—2.4	2.5—4.9	5.0—10.5
LOCAL CRIMES			
In and around home of victim and offender	20 (16)	21 (23)	23 (27)
In and around home of offender, victim from neighbourhood	2 (2)	4 (5)	5 (5)
In and around home of victim, offender from neighbourhood	4 (3)	7 (8)	8 (9)
In the neighbourhood of both victim and offender	4 (3)	5 (6)	8 (9)
SEMILOCAL CRIMES			
In and around home of offender, victim from outside offender's neighbourhood	7 (5)	5 (6)	5 (6)
In and around home of victim, offender from outside victim's neighbourhood	14 (12)	13 (12)	10 (13)
In the neighbourhood of offender, but not of victim	5 (5)	6 (7)	8 (8)
In the neighbourhood of victim, but not of offender	6 (7)	6 (6)	7 (6)
NON—LOCAL CRIMES			
Both victim and offender outside their neighbourhoods	37 (47)	33 (27)	27 (17)
Total	99	100	100
N	759	1,157	741

Note: Cases within brackets according to place of crime commission instead of by home ward of offender.

Considering place of crime commission rather than home ward of offender (figures within brackets in Table 103) shows clearly the localness of many of the crimes occurring in high offender rate wards. Note that most inner-city areas are likely to belong to the group of low offender rate wards.

230

10.2.5 Intracity Variations – a Summary and Discussion

In this Chapter some basic analyses have been made of the ecology of crimes of violence in medium-sized and smaller Swedish cities. A somewhat more detailed analysis has been made of crimes of violence and distance. A Distance Typology was developed. Wards were compared according to the offender rate of the ward.

In the next Chapter, with data from Stockholm, one major topic for research will be an analysis of the incidence and structure of crimes of violence on the basis of a classification of the wards from a factor analysis of population, housing and other ward characteristics. One reason for not adopting such an approach in the study of the 21 cities was the varying number of missing data for the studied variables. Many of the variables to be regarded as of greatest interest, such as "social security", were only available for a few of the cities. However, I made a series of factor analyses, varying the number of included wards and variables – either many wards and fewer variables or fewer wards and more variables (see Appendix 6).

The main results of the study of intracity variations of crimes of violence in Swedish medium-sized and smaller cities in 1978 may be summarized in the following points:

Overall Patterns

- The crimes are concentrated to inner-city areas. This is mainly a result of the localization of public entertainment to these parts of the city.

- The residences of offenders and victims also show a concentration in the urban area but to other parts than the crimes, mainly outer-city wards.

- High offender rate wards tend to be those that may be described as "Social Problem Areas". Low offender rate wards are predominantly single-family house wards with high social rank population.

- Excluding the inner-city areas, the crime distribution in the urban area is similar to that of victims and offenders. Hence the incidence of the crimes tends be highest in "Social Problem Areas".

Comparison of Wards Grouped according to Offender Rate

- No major difference in sex and age of offenders between the groups of wards, but an increasing proportion of foreign and socially loaded offenders with offender rate of ward. This is partly to be related to a higher proportion of foreigners and socially loaded persons residing in high offender rate wards (see further below).

231

- Considering differences in characteristics of the crimes committed, offenders from high offender rate wards tended to commit more of their crimes in apartments, and more crimes involved foreigners, while there were no marked differences in the intersex and interpersonal relationship between victims and offenders.

Ethnicity of Victim-Offender

- In all groups of wards according to offender rate there is a greater proportion of foreigners' internal fights (i.e. between two foreigners) than might be expected from their proportion of the population.

- There is some indication that the proportion of internal fights among foreigners increases with the offender rate of the ward, and more so than can be expected from the increase in their proportion of the population of the wards.

Basic Facts Concerning Crimes of Violence and Distance

- Comparison of offenders residing in the city with those not residing in the city shows that the former to a somewhat higher degree seem to be socially loaded persons and that they more often are involved in crimes occurring in apartments.

- Both the incidence of crimes committed (criminals' mobility) and victimization (victimization distance) show a J-shaped decrease with distance from the home of the offender and victim respectively.

- Not only do a fairly high proportion of the crimes tend to occur at or nearby the home of the offender and victim, but also in a significant proportion of the crimes the victim and offender reside nearby each other. Even after subtraction of the zero-distance cases the victim and offender live no more than 500 metres from each other in as many as one-fourth of the crimes.

Distance and Demographic Characteristics of Victim and Offender

- Contrary to the general finding in studies of criminals' mobility, older offenders in crimes of violence tend to "travel" a shorter distance than young. This is partly explained by the fact that younger offenders are seldom involved in crimes in their apartments. Excluding the zero-distance cases the age-distance relationship is reversed, with the exception of the oldest group of offenders (40 years and above) who still have the shortest distance "travelled" to the scene of the crime.

Females and foreigners tend to be victimezed closer to home than males and Swedes. Excluding the zero-distance cases the male-female difference in victimization distance disappears, but not the Swede-foreigner difference.

232

Different Types of Areas in Relation to Criminals' Mobility and Victimization Distance

- Crimes occurring in inner-city areas are much less local than crimes occurring elsewhere.

- Crimes occurring in high offender rate wards are more local than in other wards.

- Offenders from high offender rate wards commit more local crimes than from other wards.

- A smaller proportion of offenders from high offender rate wards have committed their crimes in inner-city areas.

- Crimes occurring in the neighbourhood of both the victim and the offender show a special concentration to high offender rate wards. These crimes occur to a significant extent between youths (less than 20 years of age) and there is some indication that to some degree they are a result of friction between Swedish and foreign youths. Further, these crimes occur mainly in the daytime.

The inner city is the main areas of occurrence of crimes of violence. It is clear from the results presented that the localization of public entertainment to the inner city is a major reason for this concentration. The question to be considered is what causes the high incidence of violence in the course of public entertainment?

Public entertainment is an activity in which it may be hypothesized that comparatively many of the contacts between people result in friction (i.e. irritation, conflicts, etc). Further, it may be a reasonable hypothesis that such friction results in violent actions to a much greater extent than in other contacts outside the home. This is likely to be so because public entertainment involves

A. the convergence of a disproportionate number of socially loaded and "conventional" people, the former of whom in general may be assumed to have a greater readiness to react to friction with violence.

B. the convergence of a disproportionate number of intoxicated strangers and the fact that intoxication may contribute to friction developing into violence which would otherwise not have done so.

To these two hypotheses may be added that

C. in the course of public entertainment a significant proportion of the participants are likely to experience frustration (see Section 4.5).

The results show that offenders are concentrated to outer-city wards that may be described as "Social Problem Areas" – according to such indicators as inhabitants receiving social security, in overcrowded dwellings, single working parents, etc. I wish to stress that this

233

labelling is done in a relative rather than in an absolute sense. For instance, the Social Problem Areas of Swedish cities are not to be compared with the Slum Areas of big US cities. In this perspective the use of the term Social Problem Area may even be disputed. What requirements are to be regarded as necessary for an area to qualify as a Social Problem Area is a complex but interesting issue which I, however, shall not go into here.

The question to be considered is why offenders are concentrated to some areas rather than others. Since many of the offenders are to be regarded as **socially loaded persons**, one reason is that these persons are **segregated to certain areas**. Walldén & Modig (1981:11) write in a discussion of residential segregation that problem tenant concentrations are mainly caused by the fact that "... *these are groups with weak resources, and little possibility to choose their area of residence. The availability of apartments for this group is restricted partly because private landlords do not always accept this kind of tenants and therefore they must resort to municipal housing."* (my translation). Of interest in this connection is also a study by Andersson-Brolin (1984) on **ethnical residential segregation** carried out in Stockholm at the parish level, which showed that "nearly all foreign nationalities show concentration to parishes with a greater number of unattractive apartments, which also may be assumed to reflect the low status of the parish." (p. 159, my translation). All in all, it seems reasonable to hypothesize that the segregation of socially loaded persons and foreigners[28] to certain wards is one reason for the concentration of offenders.

The distribution of the victims is very close to that of the offenders. One reason for that may be that

A. victims and offenders in crimes of violence are to a large extent recruited from the same groups.

The results presented in Part 2 give clear indications that this is so. Another factor that might make some contribution to the close correspondence between victim and offender distributions is that

B. the risk of victimization by violence in the neighbourhood may be related to the social problem level of the ward.

There are some indications in the results presented that 1) friction between neighbours resulting in violent actions is related to the problem level of the ward – crimes committed by offenders living in and crimes occurring in high offender rate wards are more local than in other wards, 2) some violence in ethnically heterogeneous neighbourhoods seem to be a result of friction between Swedish and foreign youth.

---

[28]Needless to say, foreigners may of course also be socially loaded.

234

11 Ecological and Situational Aspects of Crimes of Violence in Stockholm in 1982

There are three main topics to be dealt with in this Chapter. First, a comparison will be made of the basic patterns of crime, offender and victim distributions and their correlates in Stockholm with the results obtained in the study of the 21 medium-sized and smaller cities.

Second, the analysis based on simple zero-order correlations will be extended to encompass multivariate regression techniques, with the purpose of finding models that can best "explain" the ward variations in crime, offender and victim rates.

Third, on the basis of a factor analysis, the wards will be grouped into a smaller number of larger areal units. The structure of the crimes – including distance – and characteristics of persons involved in them will be compared.

A general point of departure for the analysis in this Chapter is the findings from previous Chapters and, in particular, Chapter 10.

The study is restricted to the municipality of Stockholm (see Section 1.1.3). This is somewhat troublesome, since some parts of the municipality have no clear demarcations from the rest of the Greater Stockholm Area. The number of wards in the municipality of Stockholm is 130. Five of these were excluded for the reason that there were very few inhabitants in those areas. One of them was Bromma Airport, another an industrial area (Lunda), and the remaining three consist mainly of woodland (Orhem, Flaten and Skrubba).

In the analysis a division of the municipalities into inner- and outer-city areas is often made. As mentioned in Chapter 10, what is understood as the inner city of Stockholm is a larger area than those defined as inner-city areas in the medium sized and smaller cities. It is largely the part of Stockholm that is traditionally defined as the inner city. In Map 6 the demarcation of the inner city and the location of the CBD is shown.

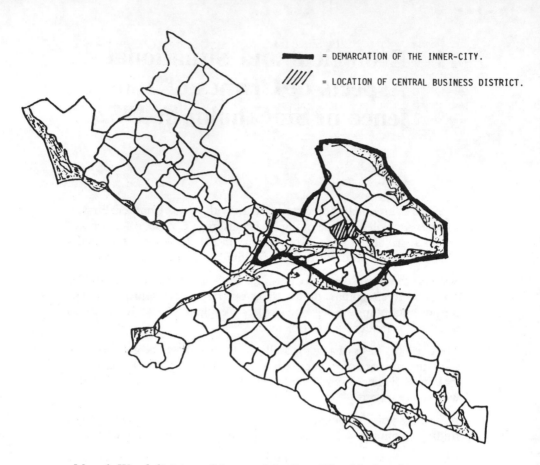

= DEMARCATION OF THE INNER-CITY.

///// = LOCATION OF CENTRAL BUSINESS DISTRICT.

Map 6. Ward division of the municipality of Stockholm, demarcation of inner city and location of CBD illustrated.

11.1 Crime, Victim and Offender Distributions and Their Basic Correlates

In this Section the relationship between the crime, victim and offender distributions, and their basic correlates, will be shown. A comparison will be made with the results from the study of the 21 medium-sized and smaller cities.

But before proceeding to that I shall say something about the validity of two of the variables which in previous analyses have turned out to be important namely "social security" and "foreigners".

Social security has been interpreted as a variable indicating variations among wards in the number of socially loaded persons. To be a socially loaded person (alcoholic, addict, criminal) is, of course, not the only reason why persons receive social security. Single females with children are, for instance, a significant group among those

236

receiving social security. Since information from the local police force was gathered about, e.g., the locations of pad rooms known to them (see Section 1.1.3) it was possible to obtain some validation of social security as a measure of the presence of socially loaded residents in a ward. As expected, social security among inhabitants was positively related to the relative existence of pad rooms (per 1,000 inhabitants). For the total municipality the correlation was (r.) 0.32. Excluding the inner city resulted in exactly the same correlation. Although statistically significant at the 5 % level the magnitude of the correlation is perhaps not overwhelming. But it is to be remembered that "pad rooms" are a rather crude indicator of the presence of socially loaded residents and that the relationship is clearly in the expected direction (see also Section 11.3.2 below).

The variable **"foreigners"** refers to foreign citizens. Since it is hardly the citizenship that is of interest, it may be questioned to what extent variations in foreign citizens measure variations in residents with a foreign background. There was some possibility to study this, since data about foreign born inhabitants were available in the Stockholm data for 118 of the 125 studied wards. The zero-order correlation between the two measures was very high (r.=0.96).

11.1.1   The Crime, Offender and Victim Distributions

Crimes of violence are highly concentrated in the urban area, as already reported in the introduction to Part 3 and in Chapter 10. In fact, the concentration may be described as extreme, as illustrated by Map 7, where the places of crime occurrence in the municipality of Stockholm have been plotted. There are several black spots in the inner-city area and especially in the CBD[29].

The most extreme concentrations appear in and around the railway station (Centralen) including the main underground station through which all underground lines pass. Other strong concentrations in the CBD are at the square Sergels torg, and at the crossing between two main streets (Kungsgatan–Sveavägen). In the south of the inner city there are concentrations to two places known as places of alcoholic gatherings – Slussen and Medborgarplatsen–Björns Trädgård – that former also known as a place of illegal alcohol sales. In the east of the inner-city area there is a concentration (only in summer time) in and around a large amusement park (Gröna Lund). In the north there is some concentration to a square (Odenplan) known as a place where alcoholics gather and also for illegal alcohol sales.

---

[29] The concentrations of these black spots are more extreme than the visual impression suggests, since many plots at these places are hidden.

Map 7. Map showing the places of occurrence of crimes of violence in Stockholm in 1982.
Note: The observations plotted are unweighted for differing sample fractions (see Section 1.1.3).

A detailed plot of the location of all restaurants with alcohol sales in the inner city (not shown) gave a strikingly similar pattern to that of crime occurrences. A result well in accordance with those referred to in the introduction to Part 3.

A plot of the victim and offender distributions (not shown) as well revealed concentrations. Mainly to some outer-city wards.

11.1.2 The Relationship between Crime, Victim and Offender Distributions

Just as in the study of the 21 cities (Section 10.2.1, Table 87) there are positive correlations between the crime, victim and offender distri-

238

butions and they are stronger when the inner city is excluded. However, in Stockholm there are not such marked differences between correlations of the different distributions for the total city – the correlation of the crime and victim distributions is not much lower than that of the offender and victim distributions (Table 104). This may partly be explained by the fact that a wider geographical definition of the inner city has been adopted for Stockholm. As shown above, not only the CBD but many residential areas in the central city are counted as inner city.

Table 104. Zero-order correlations of crime, victim and offender distributions (per 1,000 inhabitants). Total municipality and excluding inner city. Data from the Big City Crime Study

	Offenders Total	Excluding inner city	Victims Total	Excluding inner city
Crimes	24*	62*	50*	82*
Offenders			56*	67*

Note: Coefficients multiplied by 100. Correlations significant at 5 % level marked with an asterisk. N = 125; excluding inner city N = 90.

11.1.3 Basic Correlates of Crime, Victim and Offender Distributions

The basic correlates of the crime, victim and offender distributions between wards in Stockholm, to be compared with those for the 21 cities (Section 10.2.2, Table 88), show on the whole similar findings. But the correlations are generally stronger than for the medium-sized and smaller cities.

However, there are some differences that require comment. The variable "old dwellings" is negatively related to victim and offender distributions and to crime distribution excluding inner city. The variable "vacant dwellings" shows with one exception no positive association to victim and offender distributions in Stockholm. Further, there is rather strong correlation between vacant dwellings and crimes for total Stockholm. These differences may be related to differences in housing market and other differences between big and smaller cities and appear not to be of any great relevance for reconsideration of the conclusions drawn in Chapter 10. The same may also be argued concerning the variable "females, gainfully employed" which shows rather strong correlations with all distributions in Stockholm, but not so in the 21 cities.

Table 105. Zero-order correlations of ward characteristics with crimes, offenders and victims per 1,000 inhabitants. Total municipality of Stockholm and excluding the inner-city area. Data from the Big City Crime Study

Ward characteristics	Crimes Total	Excl. inner city	Offenders Total	Excl. inner city	Victims Total	Excl. inner city
Mean income	6	−38*	−36*	−45*	−40*	−43*
Income heterogeneity	28*	−38*	−39*	−46*	−30*	−44*
% aged 0—14 years	−16	− 2	1	− 2	− 7	− 6
% aged 60— years	4	−17	−16	−16	−17	−16
% females aged 15— years	−17	− 5	− 3	− 9	− 9	− 6
% foreign nationality	8	43*	32*	48*	41*	40*
Household size, mean	−13	− 8	−10	−16	−14	−15
% dwellings in one— and two—family houses	−11	−39*	−35*	−45*	−37*	−43*
% dwellings in municipal housing	− 6	51*	47*	56*	44*	50*
% small dwellings	32*	19	17	24*	23*	26*
% large dwellings	− 1	−35*	−36*	−42*	−38*	−39*
% old dwellings	13	−33*	−26*	−29*	−20*	−27*
% households with children/youth	−15	6	− 1	− 4	− 2	0
% children with single working parents	11	42*	36*	48*	40*	47*
% vacant dwellings	42*	31*	2	3	14	22*
% work places	36*	30*	− 4	6	14	14
Industrial work, number of employees	12	0	4	6	3	1
Commercial centre	87*	21*	− 8	16	5	3
Distance from city centre	−24*	13	8	11	2	7
% overcrowded	3	39*	28*	40*	33*	46*
% blue—collar workers	− 8	30*	43*	55*	32*	42*
% social security	7	46*	50*	59*	47*	49*
% females, gainfully employed	−25*	47*	32*	29*	29*	46*

Note: Total city (N = 125), excluding inner city (N = 90). Coefficients multiplied by 100. Correlations significant at the 5 % level marked with an asterisk.

The perhaps most interesting difference in substantial terms are the rather strong correlation of the variable "blue collar workers" with offender and victim distributions in Stockholm, which did not appear for the 21 cities. One speculation as to the reason for this difference may be that the segregation of blue collar workers in Stockholm (to Social Problem Areas) is stronger than in the medium-sized and smaller cities. It should be stressed that no efforts have been made to verify this speculation.

- The overall conclusion from the comparison is that the general pattern revealed for the medium-sized and smaller cities are largely replicated in the data from Stockholm.

11.2 The Factorial Social Ecology of Stockholm

In this Section a factor analysis of housing, population and other characteristics of wards in Stockholm is presented. The purpose of this analysis was

- to reduce the number of included variables to a smaller number of dimensions of urban structure to be used in correlational and regression analysis with the crime variables.

- to be the basis for grouping wards into larger aggregates in order to analyse crime structure, distance and characteristics of those involved in crimes of violence in various urban milieux.

Factorial social ecology is a well-established technique of research into the dimensions of urban structure. As Janson (1980:447) reports: *"Studies of urban spatial structure in modern Western society appear to have established fairly well the dominance of three classes of dimensions."* These dimensions are social rank, familism and ethnicity (see also Timms, 1971:85).

In a study of the factorial social ecology of 12 Swedish cities in 1960 with 44 variables, Janson (1971) extracts eight factors that together explain 83 % of the variation. The three most powerful factors are labelled Young Familism, Social Rank and Space. The latter are defined by high loadings on variables such as one-family houses and few persons per room (p. 253). The other factors are interpreted by Janson as Established Familism, Postfamilism, Residentialism (few work places) and two are concerned, respectively with, industrial areas and commercial centres (p. 254).

11.2.1 Factor Analysis

The choice of variables for the factor analysis is presented in Appendix 2. The Varimax-Promax strategy, earlier commented upon in Section 5.1, was used.

After the first factor analysis had been made, it was decided to drop the variable "population size". The reason was that, when the factor scores were plotted on maps, one factor that was interpreted as measuring Social Problems turned out to have high scores in inner-city areas of high social rank, with less social problems but with larger size of population, while in outer city areas this factor had high scores in areas with high rates of social security. This indicated that

241

this particular factor measured different things in inner- and outer-city areas. Before the population size variable was dropped, an analysis in which this variable was logged was carried out, but that did not change the result much.

Table 106 shows the result of the factor analysis. Five factors were extracted, using the criterion of inclusion of factors with an eigenvalue above one. Together they explained 80 % of the variance.

Table 106. Factor loadings and communalities. Varimax rotated factors. Stockholm 1980. N = 125

Variable	I	II	III	IV	V	h^2
Mean income	57*	−47*	56*	0	4	88
Income heterogeneity	29	−32	75*	2	−21	81
% aged 0—14 years	89*	15	− 1	−20	− 6	87
% aged 60— years	−80*	−42*	− 4	2	10	85
% females of those aged 15— years	−63*	−26	11	−11	46*	72
% foreign nationality	6	77*	8	5	−15	63
Household size, mean	96*	0	− 1	−16	− 5	96
% dwellings in one— and two—family houses	76*	−47*	− 7	−14	−28	92
% dwellings in municipal housing	− 2	69*	−29	− 9	32	68
% small dwellings	−92*	11	0	14	4	91
% large dwellings	75*	−42*	30	− 8	−11	86
% old dwellings	−48*	−54*	19	9	−45*	80
% households with children/youth	94*	16	− 4	−15	2	93
% children with single working parents	−69*	48*	5	10	29	82
% vacant dwellings	−24	19	52*	0	0	37
% work places	−26	3	31	82*	0	83
Industrial work places	−12	− 6	−15	89*	9	85
Commercial centre	−20	23	54*	41*	−29	64
Distance from city centre	68*	21	−40*	−25	21	78
% overcrowded	−72*	32	− 4	− 3	−19	66
% blue collar workers	− 6	47*	−74*	0	− 4	80
% social security	0	92*	−11	0	7	86
% females, gainfully employed	−14	10	−12	10	84*	76
Contribution %	37	21	10	6	6	

Note: Coefficients have been multiplied by 100. Loadings 40 and higher marked with an asterisk.

Interpretation and labelling of factors are always somewhat arbitrary. The first factor was interpreted as **familism** with high positive loadings on the variables "household size" (96), "household with children/youth" (94), "persons aged 0–14 years" (89), "dwellings in

242

one- and two-family houses" (76), "large dwellings" (75), "distance from city centre" (68), and "mean income" (57), and with high negative loadings on the variables "small dwellings" (–92), "persons aged 60– years" (–80), "overcrowded dwellings" (-71), "children with single working parents" (–69), "females of those aged 15– years (–63) and "old dwellings" (–48). An alternative labelling of this factor may be *familism-space*, since obviously some of the high loading variables are of relevance for space. The plotting of the factor scores in five classes is shown in Map 8. Most of the inner-city areas show negative scores for this factor, while the highest scores are to be found among outer-city areas in the western, and especially in the northwest, parts of Stockholm.

The second factor was interpreted as a factor measuring **social problems** with high positive loadings on "social security" (92), "foreigners" (77), "municipal housing" (69), "children with single working parents" (48) and "blue-collar workers" (47), and high negative loadings on "old dwellings (–54), "mean income" (–47), "dwellings in one- and two-family houses" (–47), "large dwellings"

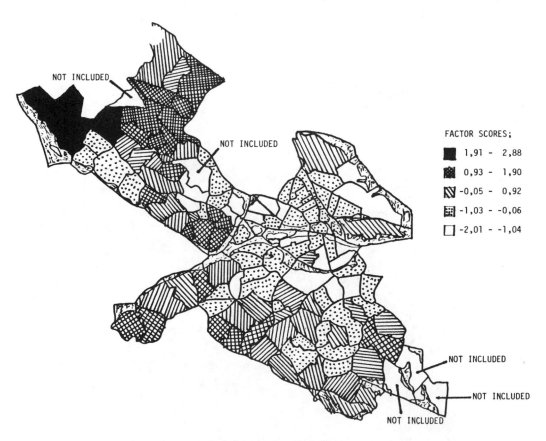

FACTOR SCORES;

◼ 1,91 – 2,88
▨ 0,93 – 1,90
◩ -0,05 – 0,92
▦ -1,03 – -0,06
☐ -2,01 – -1,04

Map 8. Plot of scores for Factor 1 – Familism.

243

(–42) and "aged 60– years" (–42). Alternative labellings of this factor are of course possible, but the labelling "social problems" was chosen because of the special interest of this aspect in relation to the crime variables and since this appears to be a label not inadequate with regard to the defining variables of the factor. A plot of the scores for Factor II in five classes is shown in Map 9. High positive scores for this factor appear in groups of wards in the north-west, west and south parts of Stockholm. These wards tend to be located on the outskirts of the municipality. In the inner city the CBD and the ward containing the University of Stockholm have higher positive scores.

The third factor was interpreted as **social rank** with high positive loadings on the variables "income heterogeneity" (75), "mean income" (56), "commercial centre" (54) and "vacant dwellings" (52), and high negative loadings on the variables "blue-collar workers" (–74) and "distance from city centre" (–40). The plot of the scores in five classes for this factor is shown in Map 10. It is apparent that it is mainly two groups of wards that have a high social rank, the wards around and including the CBD and a group of wards west of the inner city. This is well in accordance with "everyday knowledge" of high status areas in the municipality of Stockholm.

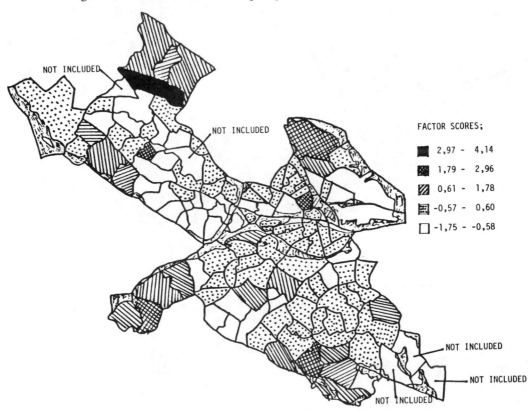

Map 9. Plot of scores for Factor II – Social Problems.

244

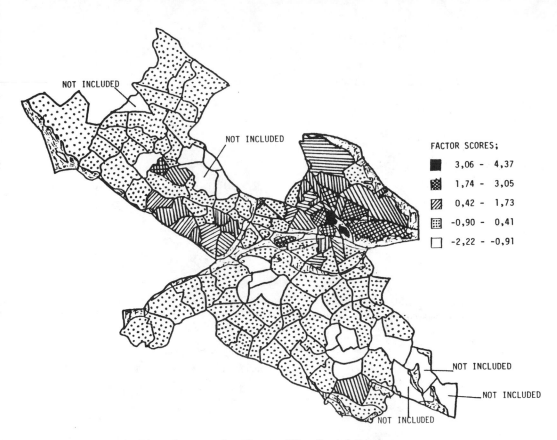

NOT INCLUDED

NOT INCLUDED

NOT INCLUDED

NOT INCLUDED

NOT INCLUDED

FACTOR SCORES;

■   3,06 - 4,37

▨   1,74 - 3,05

▨   0,42 - 1,73

▦   -0,90 - 0,41

☐   -2,22 - -0,91

Map 10. Plot of scores for Factor III – Social Rank.

The fourth factor expresses clearly the work place area – residential area differentiation and was labelled **work place areas.** The variables with high positive loadings were "work places" (82), "industrial work places" (89) and "commercial centre" (41). The plot of the scores for this factor in five classes is shown in Map 11. Note that one work place area in the north-west of Stockholm has been omitted from the analysis and, further, that Bromma Airport is also omitted.

The final and fifth was the perhaps most difficult factor to give a meaningful interpretation. Two variables concerned with females; "females of those aged 15– years" (46) and "females, gainfully employed" (84) with high positive loadings, were, together with "old dwellings" (–45) with a higher negative loading, the defining variables of the factor.

Also an **oblique solution** (Promax) was carried out. This resulted in the same factor structures as in the orthogonal solution, but factor three was more clearly a social rank factor in the oblique solution, the loadings on "mean income" (64) and "blue-collar workers (–80) being higher.

245

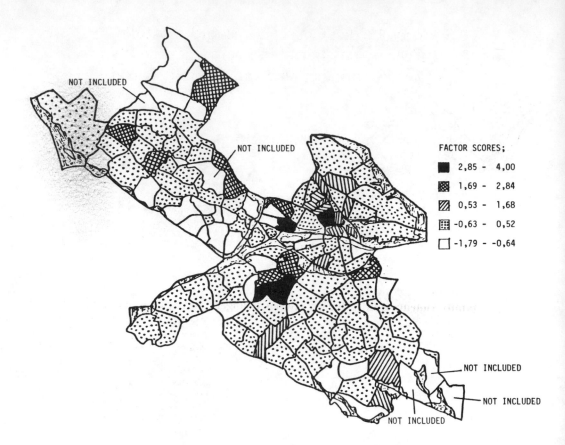

Map 11. Plot of scores for Factor IV – Work Place Areas.

As regards the **interfactor correlations** none were above 0.31. Familism (F I) was negatively related (–0.31) to work place area (F IV), social problems (F II) negatively related (–0.28) to social rank (F III), while social rank was negatively related (–0.26) to "the female factor" (F V). All in all, the interfactor correlations do not appear to be as strong as to warrant the use of an oblique rather than an orthogonal solution, especially in the light of the more complex interpretations that result when using correlated factors.

11.3 Zero-Order Correlations and Multiple Regressions between Factors, Some Additional Variables and Crime Variables

11.3.1 Zero-Order Correlations between Factors and Crime Variables

Having reduced the included variables to a fewer dimensions describing main variations of ward characteristics in Stockholm in terms of Familism, Social Problems, Social Rank and Work Place – Residential Differentiation[30], now the crime variables will be related to the dimensions. In addition to previously used crime variables, one variable measuring variations in **young offenders** (less than 25 years), and two measuring variations in the extreme forms of crimes according to victim-offender interpersonal relationship, namely **family violence** and **violence between strangers**, have been included. The results for the total city are shown in Table 107 and separately for inner- and outer-city areas in Table 108.

The **Familism** factor shows generally weak negative associations with all crime variables. Only in the case of victim distribution is the negative association so strong as to reach statistical significance (Table 107). Separating between inner- and outer-city areas, the associations are weakly positive in some instances in the inner-city (Table 108). For the outer-city areas the pattern is the same as for the total city, although most correlations are somewhat stronger.

The **Social Problem** factor is rather strongly related to most crime variables, and especially so for the victim and offender distributions and the distribution of family violence cases (Table 107). As regards the difference between inner- and outer-city areas, the associations are with one exception much stronger in the outer-city (Table 108). It is only in the case of crimes between strangers that inner-city areas have a stronger correlation with the Social Problem factor. Further, in the inner-city areas the offender variables show no association with the Social Problem factor, and the same is largely true for the family violence cases.

The **Social Rank** factor shows negative association with offender and victim distributions, although non-significant in the latter case (Table 107). The distribution of the crimes, and restriction to crimes between strangers, shows rather strong positive correlations with Social Rank. This is, however, likely to be explained mainly by the location of many of the high Social Rank wards around the CBD. This

---

[30]The so-called "female factor" will not be commented upon here, although the correlations with that factor will be shown.

is also well illustrated by separating inner- and outer-city areas (Table 108). In inner-city areas Social Rank is strongly correlated to total crimes and crimes between strangers, while in outer-city areas it is negatively or weakly positively correlated.

The **Work Place Area** factor, just as the Social Rank factor, is rather strongly positively associated with total crimes and crimes between strangers (Table 107). The reason for that is mainly the concentration of work place areas in and around the CBD, and consequently this association persists for inner- but vanishes for outer-city areas (Table 108).

Table 107. Zero-order correlation of factor scores (see Table 106) with crime variables. Total municipality. Data from the Big City Crime Study. N = 123

Crime variables	Factors Familism	Social problems	Social rank	Work place areas	"Female factor"
Offenders per 1,000 inhabitants	−15	50*	−23*	0	15
Young offenders per young in- habitants**	− 3	38*	−31*	8	8
Victims per 1,000 inhabitants	−23*	56*	−13	7	0
Crimes per 1,000 inhabitants	− 8	21*	46*	31*	−33*
Crimes within the family per 1,000 inhabitants	−13	47*	− 4	8	6
Crimes between strangers per 1,000 inhabitants	− 8	19*	46*	31*	−32*

Note: Coefficients have been multiplied by 100. Correlations significant at the 5 % level marked with an asterisk.
** = offenders below the age of 25 per inhabitants aged 10—24 years.

248

Table 108. Zero-order correlation of factor scores (see Table 106) with crime variables. Separately for inner- and outer-city areas. N is 35 and 88 respectively

| Crime variables | Factors | | | | | | | | | |
| | Familism | | Social problems | | Social rank | | Work place areas | | "Female factor" | |
	Inner	Outer	Inner	Outer	Inner	Outer	Inner	Outer	Inner	Outer
Offenders per 1,000 inhabitants	−10	−21	− 7	66*	−22	−31*	−14	6	26	10
Young offenders per young inhabitants**	− 4	−18	2	45*	− 8	−34*	−13	20	0	10
Victims per 1,000 inhabitants	4	−27*	45*	60*	−12	−30*	16	3	−38*	17
Crimes per 1,000 inhabitants	13	−18	51*	62*	59*	−22*	48*	9	−52*	19
Crimes within the family per 1,000 inhabitants	− 8	−11	14	60*	2	−17	23	− 2	− 2	15
Crimes between strangers per 1,000 inhabitants	14	− 8	51*	27*	60*	9	48*	13	−52	21*

Note: Coefficients multiplied by 100. Correlations significant at the 5 % level marked with an asterisk.
** = see Table 107 for definition

11.3.2 Some Additional Variables – Residential Mobility, Public Entertainment and an Index of Socially Loaded Persons

Although the variables used in the factor analysis are believed to grasp the essential aspects of variations in urban milieux, it was decided to add three more variables to the analysis because of their special interest in relation to the crime variables.

As mentioned in the introduction to Part 3, social instability of an area is one "classical" explanation of, in the first instance, variations in juvenile delinquency rates. Two prime measures of social instability that have been advanced are a) residential mobility, and b) ethnically heterogeneous neighbourhood. Since wards with a large foreign population tend also to be ethnically heterogeneous, this variable may also be regarded as a crude measure of ethnical heterogeneity. However, no data concerned with residential mobility have so far been considered.

Data about population movements were available for the year 1979 for 118 of the 125 studied wards. For these wards a measure of **residential mobility** was created by totalling the number of residents moving into and out of the ward and dividing it by the population of the ward. Closer examination of the data showed that there were two wards which were "problematic" vis-a-vis the measure of residential mobility. These were two areas in the inner city where quite a large proportion of the inhabitants were living in students' hostels, which have restrictions as to the number of years the apartments are at their disposal. Hence for "natural reasons" there will be a quite high residential mobility in these areas. These two wards were omitted when calculations involving the variable "residential mobility" were made. In this context it may be mentioned that the residential mobility was overall higher in the inner-city than in the outer-city areas, which may be partly related to the area clearance schemes in the inner city.

On the basis of earlier presented results, public entertainment is likely to be a key variable in predicting ward variations in total crimes of violence and violence between strangers. As a measure of **public entertainment** I have used licensed restaurants (excluding those not open to the public). The addresses of the restaurants were plotted on a map, with the incidence of restaurants in each ward. As mentioned in Section 11.1.1, a visual inspection of the plots of crimes and restaurants showed a strikingly similar pattern. Restaurants were also subdivided into groups according to the time of the day when they were permitted to be open. This was done since it was believed that restaurants with a late closing time would provide a better measure of public entertainment than those with an earlier closing time. A special variable was created for those restaurants permitted to be open until at least 01.00.

Although "social security" may be regarded as a variable indicating the variations in socially loaded residents among wards (see Section 11.1), it was decided to try to create a measure of the presence of socially loaded persons in the wards. This is, of course, a very difficult task and it should be stressed that the resulting variable is to be regarded as no more than a highly crude measure. The basis for the **Index of Socially Loaded Persons** was information gathered by the local police authorities about the presence of certain illegal and asocial activities that occurred at given places with some persistence (see Section 1.1.3). These addresses were plotted in maps, with the incidence in each ward. The incidences of the various activities were simply totalled, since there seemed to be no obvious criteria for weighting of the different activities. Places of illegal sales of narcotics were not used in the index due to the non-specific information given. Apartments known as places where prostitution occurs were also omitted from the index. Correlation of the various activities with the index showed that the existence of pad rooms and receiving of stolen

250

goods were those of the included activities most strongly correlated to the index.

The zero-order correlation between the additional variables and the factors (scores) is shown in Table 109. **Public Entertainment** (number of restaurants in ward) shows a positive relationship with Social Rank and Work Place Areas and negative with Familism. The association with Social Rank is due to the high Social Rank of the CBD and adjacent areas, as illustrated by the separation of Stockholm into inner- and outer-city areas. The fact that work place areas show an association both in inner- and outer-city areas is likely to be a result of restaurants in outer-city areas tending to be located in commercial centres.

Table 109 Zero-order correlations between residential mobility, public entertainment, index of socially loaded persons and urban structure factors (see Table 106). Total municipality and separately for inner- and outer-city areas

Factors	Public entertainment			Residential mobility			Index of socially loaded persons		
	Total city	Outer– city	Inner– city	Total city	Outer– city	Inner– city	Total city	Outer city	Inner– city
Familism	−27*	−19	35*	−36*	−25*	11	−31*	−35*	− 4
Social Problems	9	17	33*	51*	59*	68*	37*	42*	45*
Social Rank	64*	−16	70*	28	− 4	34	9	−29*	19
Work Place Area	39*	41*	53*	38*	25*	55*	14	− 5	29
"Female factor"	−21*	3	−31	− 8	13	−52*	−14	16	45*

Note: Coefficients multiplied by 100. Correlations significant at 5 % level marked with an asterisk. Number of observations used in correlations with Public Entertainment and Index of Socially Loaded Persons, N = 125, Outer = 90, Inner = 35. Number of observations used in correlations with Residential Mobility: N = 116, Outer = 87, Inner = 29.

The strongest positive correlation of **Residential Mobility** is with the Social Problems factor. This is so both for the total city and for a separation into inner- and outer-city areas. Residential Mobility is hence to be regarded as an additional characteristic of Social Problem Areas. Familism, on the other hand, with the exclusion of the inner city, is considered separately, being negatively related to Residential Mobility. Finally Social Rank and Work Place Area are positively related to Residential Mobility, which partly is caused by the overall higher residential mobility in inner-city (as mentioned in Section 11.3.2) than in outer-city areas.

Just as for Residential Mobility, **the Index of Socially Loaded Persons** (number of places) shows a clear positive correlation with the Social Problems factor and a negative with Social Rank for the total city and outer city.

251

11.3.3 Strategies Applied to Deal with the Problem of Measuring the Relative Incidence of Crimes of Violence in a Study of Intracity Variations

The problem of measuring the relative incidence of crimes of violence was discussed in the introduction to Part 3. It was concluded that using "per inhabitant" as denominator was "problematic" considering the distribution of all crimes or restriction to outdoor crimes. Further, that it was the inner-city areas that caused the problem, since crimes in these areas have very little to do with the residents. To deal with this problem I have so far used the strategy of showing the results both when inner-city areas are included and when they are excluded from the calculations. In addition to this strategy, I shall here also consider the use of alternative denominators to "per inhabitant". Since the inner-city area represents a wider geographical unit in Stockholm than the area in and around the CBD, I shall also make calculations excluding only the CBD in addition to those excluding the whole inner city.

In order to try to improve the measure of relative incidence of crimes of violence I experimented with several different denominators, including both residential and day population, the latter in order to have some indication of the number of people present in the areas area in addition to those resident in them. These efforts were, however, less successful since it was not possible to construct a denominator including total day population or day population in certain work that made sense as a measure of "residents + persons present in the area at nighttime" (the latter because most outdoor crimes of violence occur at nighttime).

As an alternative to "per inhabitant" I shall instead use "per acre". It was believed that this denominator more adequately represents crime variation in most inner-city areas, and in particular the CBD, than "per inhabitant". Further, "per acre" as denominator has the advantage of not producing such extreme values for the CBD as when using "per inhabitant" as denominator. The zero-order correlations of the absolute incidence and the relative of crimes of violence measured "per inhabitant" and "per acre", respectively, are shown in Table 110. All measures are fairly strongly correlated, least so in the case of "per inhabitant" correlated with "per acre". Excluding the inner-city area, the correlation of crimes per inhabitant with the other two measures is markedly lower than when these two measures are correlated.

Table 110. Zero-order correlations of alternative measures of crimes of violence. Data from the Big City Crime Study. Total municipality of Stockholm

	Crimes per acre	Crimes per inhabitant
Number of crimes	82* (91)*	83* (52*)
Crimes per acre		71* (55*)

Note: Coefficients multiplied by 100. Coefficients significant at 5 % level marked with an asterisk. N = 125. Figures in brackets excluding inner–city area. N = 90.

In the calculation to be made in Section 11.3.5 I shall both alter the denominator used and the area of the city included. This results in six calculations for each regression model as illustrated below;

	Total city	Excluding the CBD	Excluding the inner city
Per inhabitant	1	2	3
Per acre	4	5	6

Before proceeding to the regression analysis of crime, victim and offender distributions, it should be stated that **two additional wards have been excluded** from these calculations. One was a ward with a large institution for alcoholics and one with a large mental hospital. The reason for excluding these wards was that it was found that the crimes occurring in these areas, and the victims and offenders, almost without exception were related to these institutions. Hence it made little sense to relate the crimes (offenders, victims) in these areas to their population and housing.

11.3.4 Multiple Regression Predicting Victim and Offender Distributions

As shown in Section 11.3.1, Social Problems were positively, and Social Rank and Familism negatively, related to the victim and offender distributions. In this Section the question will be raised as to how much of the variations in the victim and offender distributions can be accounted for by the factors Social Problems, Social Rank and Familism together. Also the variable Residential Mobility was first included in the multiple regression but, since it did not add much in explained variance (at best one or two per cent), only the results including the three factors will be shown (Table 111).

253

Table 111. Multiple regressions (R^2) between factor scores (Factor I – Factor III) and victim and offender distributions. Total municipality, separately for inner and outer city. N = 123 (Inner = 35; Outer = 88)

Variables in model	Dependent variable	Total city. R^2	Outer city. R^2	Inner city. R^2
Social problems	Offenders per 1,000 inhabitants	25	43	1
Social problems + Social rank	Offenders per 1,000 inhabitants	33	46	5
Social problems + Social rank + Familism	Offenders per 1,000 inhabitants	38	48	5
Social problems	Young offenders per young in– habitant**	14	21	0
Social problems + Social rank	Young offenders per young in– habitant**	23	28	1
Social problems + Social rank + Familism	Young offenders per young in– habitant**	23	28	1
Social problems	Victims per 1,000 inhabitants	32	36	21
Social problems + Familism	Victims per 1,000 inhabitants	37	42	21
Social problems + Familism + Social Rank	Victims per 1,000 inhabitants	38	43	28

Note: Coefficients have been multiplied by 100.
** = Victims less than 25 years per inhabitants aged 10—24.

The overall result is that addition of either or both Social Rank and Familism to Social Problems causes a substantial increase in the proportion of variance explained. In the case of offender distribution it is Social Rank, and in the case of victim distribution Familism, that makes the most significant contribution when added to Social Problems (see also Appendix 7).

The variance explained is less in the case of the distribution of young offenders than for all offenders, and higher when considering the outer-city areas separately compared to the whole city, while in inner-city areas the included variables are poor in predicting variations in offender rates. However, for the victim distribution in

254

the inner city the result is different. This difference in proportion of variance explained is due mainly to the fact that the CBD and the ward including the University of Stockholm, each with higher scores for the Social Problems factor[31], have no offenders. Exclusion of the CBD and the ward with the University of Stockholm results in a proportion of explained variance of about the same magnitude as for the victim distribution. I wish to stress that this recalculation was made merely in order to point to the reason for the lack of stronger association and not because there is any apparent reason for excluding these two wards from the calculations.

Plots of residuals were made for the full model (Social Problems + Social Rank + Familism) predicting the offender and victim distributions (not shown). Visual inspection did not reveal any apparent patterning of these residuals.

11.3.5 Multiple Regression Predicting the Crime Distribution

Three variables were chosen on the basis of previous results for inclusion in regression models predicting the distribution of crimes totally and restricted to crimes between strangers.

One major reason for the strong concentration of crimes of violence to the inner-city areas (see Map 7) is the concentration of public entertainment to these areas. This is well illustrated by Map 12 (compared with Map 7) showing the distribution of the number of licensed restaurants in classes among the wards. As stated in Section 11.1.1, a comparison of detailed plots of crime and restaurant distribution in the inner city aslo showed this close association. Hence it was natural to include a measure of Public Entertainment.

As discussed in Chapter 10, the presence of socially loaded persons in the wards may be hypothesized to be a factor of importance for variations in crimes of violence. For this reason the Index of Socially Loaded Persons was included. This variable is likely predominantly to measure variations in socially loaded persons present in wards.

Finally, the Social Problems factor was included. There are good reasons to believe that this variable is, in the first instance, of importance for crime variations in the outer-city areas (concentration to Problem Areas).

In the results presented (Table 112) I have varied denominators and areas of city included, as discussed in Section 11.3.3 above.

---

[31] The extreme values for the inner-city area.

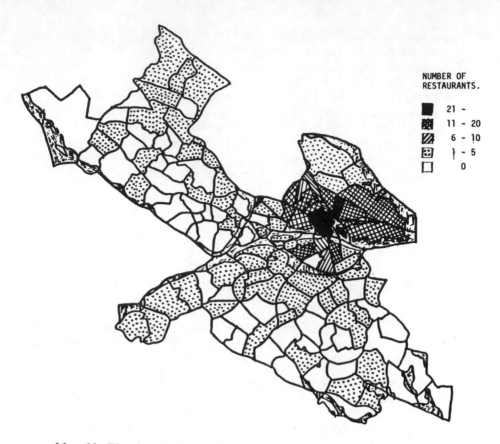

NUMBER OF
RESTAURANTS.

■   21 –
▓   11 – 20
▨   6 – 10
⊡   1 – 5
□   0

Map 12. The distribution of licensed restaurants among the wards of Stockholm in 1982.

The Index of Socially Loaded Persons is the single most powerful predictor of both total crime rate and rate of crimes between strangers when considering the **total city**. However, if the CBD is excluded (figures within brackets. Table 112) the predictive power of the index vanishes totally (in calculations per inhabitant) or is markedly reduced (in calculations per acre) and Public Entertainment instead turns out to be the most powerful predictor. This is a result of extreme extreme-values for the index variable in the CBD, especially when using "per inhabitant" as denominator.

As regards models including two predictors, the predictive power increases considerably if both Public Entertainment and the Index of Socially Loaded Persons are included. However, in the case based on crimes "per inhabitant" there is not much room left for an increase when adding one of these predictors to the other since the zero-order relationships of both are already so strong. However, if the CBD is excluded from the calculations, addition of the Index of Socially

256

Table 112. R^2 of correlations and multiple regression of Public Entertainment, Index of Socially Load Persons and Social Problems factor with total crime distribution and distribution of crimes between strangers. Separately for total city and outer city. Figures within brackets excluding the CBD (Klara, Jakob). Data from the Big City Crime Study

Variables in model	ALL CRIMES (R^2) Denominator used				CRIMES BETWEEN STRANGERS (R^2) Denominator used			
	Per acre		Per inhabitant		Per acre		Per inhabitant	
	Total city	Outer city	Total city	Outer city	Total city	Outer city	Total city	Outer city
Public Entertainment	50 (40)	0	86 (71)	2	49 (40)	2	86 (68)	5
Index of Socially Loaded Persons	59 (35)	22	93 (0)	17	53 (25)	28	92 (0)	5
Social Problems Factor (scores)	5 (2)	56	4 (0)	38	2 (0)	28	4 (0)	7
Public Entertainment + Index of Socially Loaded Persons	70 (52)	22	98 (71)	20	66 (47)	30	98 (68)	11
Public Entertainment + Social Problems Factor	53 (43)	56	86 (71)	44	53 (41)	31	86 (68)	15
Index of Socially Loaded Persons + Social Problems Factor	59 (35)	61	93 (0)	47	50 (26)	42	92 (0)	10
Public Entertainment + Index of Socially Loaded Persons + Social Problems Factor	71 (53)	61	98 (72)	53	66 (47)	44	98 (68)	18

Note: Coefficients multiplied by 100. When acre or inhabitants is used as denominator for the crime variables, the same denominator is used for the variables Public Entertainment and Index of Socially Loaded Persons. Social Problems are in all calculations factor scores.

Loaded Persons to Public Entertainment does not make any contribution to the explained variance.

Finally, in models including all three predictors, addition of the Social Problem Factor to the other two predictors does not increase the proportion of variance explained or does so only marginally.

With restriction to **outer-city areas**, the single most powerful predictor is the Social Problems factor. The proportion of explained variance is much less with restriction to crimes between strangers, and lower when using "per inhabitant" as denominator. In outer-city

257

wards the Social Problems factor predicts much better variations in crimes of violence in the family than between strangers (see Table 108).

As regards two-predcitor models, inclusion of the Index of Socially Loaded Persons leads to an increase from 3 to 14 % in the proportion of variance explained. In the three-predictor models there is in three out of four calculations a further increase, mostly so in cases between strangers calculated per inhabitant.

Furthermore it may be mentioned that substitution of all restaurants by only those permitted to be open at least to 01.00 as measure of public entertainment increased the R^2 until the Public Entertainment variable somewhat, in line with the expectations stated in Section 11.3.2.

Plots of the residuals were made (not shown) for the full regression model (Public Entertainment + Index of Socially Loaded Persons + Social Problems factor) for the total city, both when using "per inhabitant" and "per acre" as denominator. No consistently interpretable patterns of the residuals could be identified.

The overall interpretation of the findings presented in this Section is that

- crimes of violence are strongly concentrated to areas of Public Entertainment (predominantly in the inner city) but also to Social Problem areas (in the outer city) and to areas with concentrations of Socially Loaded Persons (predominantly the CBD).

As discussed in Chapter 10, there are good reasons to believe that a disproportionate number of socially loaded persons participate in public entertainment and hence some correspondence between concentrations of socially loaded persons and public entertainment is to be expected. In this connection it may be mentioned that in the Stockholm Violent Crime Study (see Wikström, 1981a) I found that the areas with the greatest number of outdoor crimes of violence also were the areas which had the highest incidence of intervention by the police due to drunkenness and because of illegal handling of alcohol and narcotics.

11.4 Structure of the Crimes and Characteristics of the Persons Involved in Different Urban Environments

After the correlational and regression analyses of ward variations in crimes, victims and offenders and their correlates, the next step in the analysis will be to group the wards into larger aggregates sharing similar characteristics, then to compare the characteristics of the crimes and of persons involved in the groups of wards. The point of departure for the grouping of the wards is the factor analysis presented in Section 11.2.1.

11.4.1 Grouping of the Wards

As already mentioned, only 125 of the 130 wards of Stockholm were included in the factor analysis. The five wards excluded will therefore also be excluded now. The two wards where nearly all crimes were related to the presence of large institutions (mental hospital, institution for alcoholics) have also been excluded (see Section 11.3.3).

All grouping may, of course, be disputed. Some more or less arbitrary decisions are involved in making the grouping. However, I shall argue that the grouping that finally resulted is fairly adequate in relation to the purpose of describing variations in crime, victim and offender characteristics in different urban environments. This type of analysis may also be regarded as having clear implications for **relating situational and ecological aspects** of crimes of violence.

The three main principles used for the grouping are stated below

- To separate inner- and outer city groups of wards,
- To try as far as possible to have geographically coherent groups of wards,
- To use the scores for the Social Problems and Social Rank factors as the main criteria for the grouping.

The resulting grouping is shown in Map 13. Selected mean characteristics of the wards in the various groups are shown in Table 113.

Table 113. Some mean characteristics of wards in different groups (see Map 13)

Ward group**	% social security	% foreig- ners	% munici- pal housing	Mean income*	% blue- collar workers	% house- holds with children/ youth
INNER CITY						
CBD (1)	5.4	11.5	7.6	61	9.8	5.7
High Social Rank, Low Social Problems (3)	1.2	4.6	6.2	72	4.8	13.8
Medium Social Rank, Low Social Problems (2)	3.3	7.2	12.7	56	8.6	11.5
Medium Social Rank, High Social Problems (4)	4.7	22.4	37.7	47	12.9	17.5
Low Social Rank, Low Social Problems (5)	2.4	5.9	14.4	50	11.4	7.0
OUTER CITY						
High Social Rank, Low Social Problems (11)	0.5	2.7	2.7	78	3.9	33.4
Medium Social Rank, Low Social Problems						
North-west (12)	1.0	4.4	4.5	64	12.7	50.0
South-west (13)	0.9	3.8	0.0	62	13.3	35.5
Low Social Rank, Low Social Problems						
West (14)	2.4	4.8	21.7	54	14.8	17.7
South (15)	3.0	5.6	30.2	53	17.4	17.9
Low Social Rank, High Social Problems						
North-west (6)	10.7	26.7	54.9	51	18.4	40.3
West (7)	5.4	6.1	86.1	51	19.4	17.4
South-west (8)	8.2	12.3	40.1	53	16.8	41.9
Middle-south (9)	8.9	9.9	72.4	51	20.9	34.8
South (10)	8.8	6.8	74.6	50	20.6	27.6

* = In thousands of Swedish crowns. ** = Figures within brackets show numbering of group in map 13.

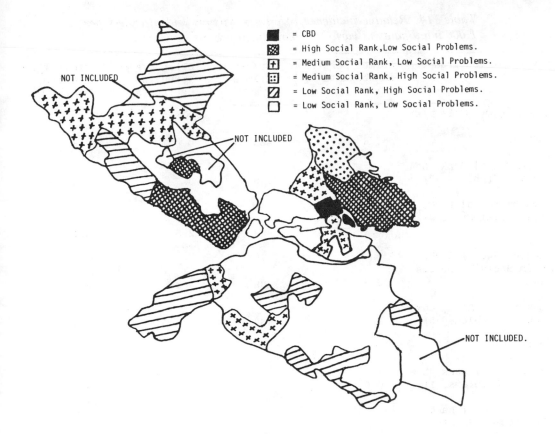

NOT INCLUDED

NOT INCLUDED

NOT INCLUDED.

Map 13. Grouping of wards into areas of different urban milieux illustrated.

11.4.2 Relative Incidence of Crimes, Offenders and Victims

The relative incidence of crimes, offenders and victims for the various groups of wards defined in Map 13 are shown in Table 114. The overall results are as could be expected by reason of the previous analysis. The pattern is very clear in the outer-city areas. For instance, the highest relative incidences for all crime variables are among the Low Social Rank, High Social Problem wards, while the reverse is true for the High Social Rank, Low Social Problem wards. In fact the latter area may be described as nearly free of crimes from violence. This means, of course, that there are not many crimes from which to analyse the crime structure.

Table 114. Relative incidence of crimes, victims and offenders per 1,000 inhabitants in various urban milieu groups

Urban milieu group	Crimes per 1,000 inhabitants	Number of crimes	Offenders per 1,000 in-habitants	Victims per 1,000 in-habitants
INNER CITY				
CBD (1)	557.4	432	0.0	3.8
High Social Rank, Low Social Problems (3)	3.6	175	0.7	1.3
Medium Social Rank, Low Social Problems (2)	6.1	494	2.5	3.1
Medium Social Rank, High Social Problems (4)	8.9	39	0.0	5.7
Low Social Rank, Low Social Problems (5)	2.8	262	1.6	2.7
OUTER CITY				
High Social Rank, Low Social Problems (11)	0.0	0	0.2	0.0
Medium Social Rank, Low Social Problems				
North–west (12)	0.8	28	0.5	1.2
South–west (13)	1.3	12	0.6	0.6
Low Social Rank, Low Social Problems				
West (14)	2.1	87	1.5	2.5
South (15)	2.1	338	1.7	2.3
Low Social Rank, High Social Problems				
North–west (6)	4.1	225	3.6	3.9
West (7)	2.3	39	2.7	2.5
South–west (8)	3.4	105	2.4	3.4
Middle–south (9)	3.0	29	3.3	5.1
South (10)	4.0	130	3.3	5.8

Note: Figures within brackets show numbering of groups in Map 13.

The patterns for the inner city are more complex. However, the High Social Rank, Low Social Problem group of wards has with one exception the lowest rate of offenders and victims. As regards crimes, we know by now that these generally may not be related to the population of the inner city. For example, the vast majority of crimes committed in the High Social Rank, Low Social Problems area of the inner city have occurred in and around a large amusement park (Gröna Lund) or in parts with many restaurants adjacent to the CBD. In the inner city it is only in the Low Social Rank, Low Social Problem areas of the inner city that any major proportion of crimes occur in apartments (see Table 115).

In the following analysis I shall first consider the crime structure in different urban environments, secondly the characteristics of offenders and their crimes from different urban environments. The results to be presented below will not be shown in as great detail as has been done so far, although I shall comment upon differences between subtotalled groups of wards if it seems warrant.

I shall only separate between the CBD and other areas of the inner city. In the outer city the areas with High and Medium Social Rank will be lumped together; all areas with High Social Problems will regardless of their geographical location, be lumped together. Finally, the remaining wards in the west and the south will be treated as one group.

Table 115. Scenes of crimes in different urban environments (see Map 13). Data from the Big City Crime Study. Per cent

Urban milieu group	Street, square, park	Public entertainment	Public transport	Shop, service institution	Apartment	Other	Total
INNER CITY							
CBD (1)	30	33	23	1	3	9	99
High Social Rank, Low Social Problems (3)	36	34	9	3	14	3	99
Medium Social Rank, Low Social Problems (2)	25	26	13	7	23	6	100
Medium Social Rank, High Social Problems (4)	(31)	(38)	(23)	(0)	(0)	(8)	(100)
Low Social Rank, Low Social Problems (5)	20	9	16	2	48	5	100
OUTER CITY							
High Social Rank, Low Social Problems (11)	–	–	–	–	–	–	–
Medium Social Rank, Low Social Problems							
North–west (12)	–	–	–	–	–	–	–
South–west (13)	–	–	–	–	–	–	–
Low Social Rank, Low Social Problems							
West (14)	15	4	7	0	74	0	100
South (15)	15	7	13	3	50	12	100
Low Social Rank, High Social Problems							
North–west (6)	19	2	3	1	70	5	100
West (7)	(23)	(8)	(0)	(0)	(69)	(0)	100
South–west (8)	26	0	18	3	52	1	100
Middle–south (9)	–	–	–	–	–	–	–
South (10)	9	0	5	2	81	3	100

Note: Figures within brackets in the left column show numbering of groups of wards. Figures in brackets in the table calculated on between 30—50 cases. No figures shown if less than 30 cases.

11.4.3 Crimes of Violence in Different Urban Environments

That there is a major difference in crime structure between inner and outer city areas was shown already in Section 3.1. In the exploration below I shall concentrate on differences between the CBD and other inner-city areas and between Social Problems and other areas in the outer city. The High-Medium Social Rank wards are difficult to include in a comparison since, even when lumped together, they have so few crimes. Data for this group of wards will nevertheless be shown in some instances.

Crimes occurring in the inner city, and in particular the CBD, involve in the majority of the cases either or both an offender and a victim residing outside the municipality of Stockholm (see Table 116). In fact, as many as 63 % of those victimized, and 33 % of the offenders, were living outside Stockholm. However, of these offenders 53 % were residing in the Greater Stockholm Area, and the corresponding figure for victims from outside Stockholm was 82 %. In the outer-city areas the vast majority of both offenders and victims were residents of Stockholm.

Table 116. Proportion of offenders and victims residing in or outside various parts (urban environments) of the municipality of Stockholm. Per cent

Urban milieu group	Both from within city	Both from outside city	Offenders from out-side city	Victims from outside city	Total	N
INNER CITY						
CBD (1)	16	12	21	51	100	289
Other inner city (2—5)	48	10	19	23	100	718
OUTER CITY						
High—Medium Social Rank, Low Social Problems (11—13)	(80)	(0)	(20)	(0)	100	30
High Social Problems, Low Social Rank (6—10)	79	3	11	7	100	408
Other outer city (14—15)	63	10	13	15	100	380

Note: Figures within brackets in left column refer to areas shown in Map 13. Figures within brackets in the table are calculated on between 30—50 cases.

265

Restriction to cases between residents in Stockholm, according to the Distance Typology (see Section 10.2.4.6), illustrates further the non-localness of crimes in the CBD, and the lesser localness of crimes occurring in the inner as compared to the outer city. In line with the results from medium-sized and smaller cities presented in Chapter 10, it turns out that crimes occurring in Social Problem areas are the most local (Table 117). In this connection it may be of interest to mention that, when separating between the different Social Problem areas, the proportion of cases occurring in the neighbourhood of both victims and offenders is markedly higher (15 %) in the north-west of the High Social Problem, Low Social Rank area (see Map 13), which is also the area with the highest foreign population (see Table 113).

Table 117. Distance Typology, main and selected subclasses, for crimes occurring in different urban environments. Per cent. Data from the Big City Crime Study

Urban milieu group	LOCAL CRIMES	thereof in and around home of both parties	thereof in neigh- bourhood of both parties	SEMILOCAL CRIMES	thereof in one of the parties' home	NON—LOCAL CRIMES	Total	N
INNER CITY								
CBD (1)	(0)	(0)	(0)	(0)	(0)	(100)	100	45
Other inner city (2—5)	37	32	0	26	17	36	99	348
OUTER CITY								
High–Medium Social Rank, Low Social Problems (11—13)	–	–	–	–	–	–	–	24
High Social Problems, Low Social Rank (6—10)	65	46	6	28	25	7	100	317
Other outer city (14—15)	42	32	2	39	27	18	99	225

Note: Figures within brackets in left column refer to areas shown in Map 13.

Fairly many of those victimized by violence become involved in the crimes during their work (see Section 5.7). Adding those who commit their crimes during work (almost no cases are between two persons at work) makes this an important part of the violent crimes. Most people who become involved in crimes of violence during work have a type of work that puts them into close contact with public entertainment or are employed at places of public entertainment. Hence it is to be expected that the proportion of cases involving persons at work may be quite high in the inner-city area and in particular in the CBD. This is in fact so (Table 118).

- In nearly 4 out of 10 (38 %) of the crimes occurring in the CBD either the victim or the offender was involved in the crime during work.

With restriction to those involved during work in crimes occurring in the CBD, most of the offenders were policemen (48 %), watch-guards, mainly at restaurants (31 %), or employees in restaurants excluding watch-guards (10 %). The corresponding figures for the

Table 118. Proportion of cases in different urban environments where either offender or victim was involved in the crime during work. Per cent. Data from the Big City Crime Study

Urban milieu group	Victim or offender involved in crime during work. %	N
INNER CITY		
CBD (1)	38	361
Other inner city (2—5)	24	921
OUTER CITY		
High—Medium Social Rank, Low Social Problems (11—13)	(0)	36
High Social Problems, Low Social Rank (6—10)	8	481
Other outer city (14—15)	18	490

Note: Figures within brackets in left column refer to areas shown in Map 13.

victims were 45 % watch-guards, 16 % restaurant employees and 11 % policemen[32].

In the discussion of the results of the study of intracity variations in the 21 medium-sized and smaller cities (see Section 10.2.5) one of the hypotheses advanced to account for the high incidence of crimes in the course of public entertainment was the convergence of socially loaded and "conventional" people. It was believed that this would lead to friction that at times could turn into violence. The results presented in Section 11.3.5 showed also the strong concentration of public entertainment, a strong concentration of the presence of socially loaded persons, as well as the extremely high rate of crimes of violence, in the CBD. As a further test of this hypothesis the proportion of crimes in various urban environments where one, but not both, of the parties was previously recorded for criminality was calculated (Table 119). The result shows that the proportion of such cases dominates in the CBD and is much higher there than in any other of the areas.

Table 119. Previous criminality of victim and offender in crimes of violence occurring in different urban environments. Data from the Big City Crime Study. Per cent

Urban milieu group	Previous criminality	
	One of the parties	Both of the parties
INNER CITY		
CBD (1)	63	20
Other inner city (2—5)	43	25
OUTER CITY		
High–Medium Social Rank, Low Social Problems (11—13)	–	–
High Social Problems, Low Social Rank (6—10)	48	29
Other outer city (14—15)	46	22

Note: Figures within brackets in left column refer to areas shown in Map 13.

---

[32] Note that crimes of violence against officials are not included in the study. That explains the lower proportion of policemen among victims compared with offenders.

268

However, as shown above, since many cases in the CBD involve persons at work, this might be the reason for the high proportion of cases in which one but not both of the parties was previously recorded for crimes. To explore this, a crosstable between victim's and offender's previous criminality and their involvement in crime during work, with restriction to crimes occurring in the CBD, was produced (Table 120). The result shows (per cent within brackets in the table), that even if the cases where either of the parties was involved in the crime during work were excluded, this would only marginally affect the result. Table 120 indicates further that most of the crimes involving a person at work are due to confrontation between that person and a socially loaded person, since the former in most cases is not recorded for previous criminality.

Table 120. Crimes occurring in the CBD by previous criminal record of victim and offender and by involvement of victim or offender in crime during work. Per cent. Data from the Big City Crime Study

INVOLVEMENT IN CRIME DURING WORK	PREVIOUS CRIMINAL RECORD			Total
	Both parties unrecorded	One party recorded	Both parties recorded	
Neither of the parties	11 (18)	37 (61)	13 (21)	61 (100)
One of the parties *	6 (15)	25 (64)	8 (21)	39 (100)
Total	17	62	21	100

Note: * = In almost no case were both of the parties involved in the crime during work. N = 191. Total per cent and row per cent (within brackets) given.

As regards sex and nationality of victim-offender the results are in accordance with previous findings. What may be commented upon is that the proportion of male-female crimes is highest in the Social Problem areas and that the proportion of fights between Swedes and foreigners is very high in the CBD compared to other areas. Although not more closely investigated here, this may indicate that friction between Swedes and foreigners is likely to occur especially in the course of public entertainment (Table 121).

Table 121. Selected victim-offender characteristics in crimes occurring in different urban environments. Per cent. Data from the Big City Crime Study

Urban milieu group	Male–male fights*	Male–female fights	Swede–foreigner fights**	Foreigners' internal fights
INNER CITY				
CBD (1)	82	13	42	6
Other inner city (2—5)	67	26	23	12
OUTER CITY				
High–Medium Social Rank, Low Social Problems (11—13)	(58)	(42)	(0)	(10)
High Social Problems, Low Social Rank (6—10)	39	55	20	25
Other outer city (14—15)	50	42	18	10

Note: Figures within brackets in left column refer to areas shown in Map 14. Figures within brackets in the table are calculated on between 30—50 cases.
* = Female victims.
** = Or vice versa.

11.4.4 Violent Offenders in Different Urban Environments

Most offenders living in Social Problem areas commit their crimes locally (Table 122) and much more so than offenders from other types of residential areas

Table 122. Distance Typology, main and selected subclasses, for offenders from different urban environments. Per cent. Data from the Big City Crime Study.

Urban milieu group	LOCAL CRIMES	thereof in and around home of both parties	thereof in neigh-bourhood of both parties	SEMILOCAL CRIMES	thereof in one of the parties home	NON-LOCAL CRIMES	Total	N
INNER CITY								
CBD (1)	−	−	−	−	−	−	−	0
Other inner city (2—5)	43	37	3	31	22	26	100	300
OUTER CITY								
High–Medium Social Rank, Low Social Problems (11–13)	−	−	−	−	−	−	−	19
High Social Problems, Low Social Rank (6—10)	57	40	8	24	19	19	100	370
Other outer city (14—15)	35	27	1	36	26	29	100	237

Note: Figures within brackets in the left column refer to areas shown in Map 13.

To a large extent, this is explained by the fact that much more of the crimes of offenders from Social Problem areas are family violence (Table 123). Comparatively few of the crimes committed by these offenders occur between strangers.

It is worth noting in light of the results presented in Chapter 10 that the proportion cases occurring in neighbourhood of both victim and offender is highest in Social Problem areas.

Table 123. Victim-offender interpersonal relationship in crimes committed by offenders from different urban environments. Data from the Big City Crime Study. Per cent

Urban milieu group	Family and like	Acquain-tances	Strangers	Total	N
INNER CITY					
CBD (1)	–	–	–	–	0
Other inner city (2—5)	34	27	39	100	380
OUTER CITY					
High–Medium Social Rank, Low Social Problems (11—13)	–	–	–	–	24
High Social Problems, Low Social Rank (6—10)	45	27	28	100	440
Other outer city (14—15)	29	28	43	100	324

Note: Figures within brackets in the left column refer to areas shown in Map 13.

Regarding offender characteristics, a comparatively high proportion of these are under the age of 20 (Table 124). In fact, of all offenders under the age of 20 residing in the municipality as much as 59 % had their home address in any of the Social Problem areas.

Table 124. Selected offender characteristics for offenders from different urban environments. Per cent

| | INNER CITY | | OUTER CITY | | |
	CBD	Other inner city	High–medium social rank, low social problems	High social problems, low social rank	Other outer city
OFFENDERS' SEX					
Male	–	90	–	95	93
Female	–	10	–	5	7
OFFENDERS' AGE					
0—19	–	4	–	13	7
20—29	–	33	–	25	33
30—39	–	32	–	32	37
40—	–	31	–	30	23
OFFENDERS' NATIONALITY					
Swedish	–	75	–	65	79
Other Scandinavian	–	10	–	12	8
Outside Scandinavia	–	15	–	23	13

273

18

There are clear indication that a greater proportion of the offenders from Social Problem areas are socially loaded persons. The mean years of previous recorded criminality, and the proportion offenders recorded for needle-marks (hard drug use) is clearly higher in the Social Problem areas than in other types of areas.

Table 125. Mean years with a previous criminal record and proportion with a recorded needle mark (1981 – June 1982) for offenders from different urban environments. Data from the Big City Crime Study

Urban milieu group	Mean years with a previous criminal record	Proportion recorded for needle marks
INNER CITY		
CBD (1)	–	–
Other inner city (2—5)	2.2	6
OUTER CITY		
High–Medium Social Rank, Low Social Problems (11—13)	–	–
High Social Problems, Low Social Rank (6—10)	4.0	11
Outer outer city (14—15)	3.6	7

Note: Figures within brackets in the left column refer to areas shown in Map 13.

PART 4

Summary and Integration of Main Findings

Theoretical Implications

In this fourth and final Part, I shall summarize and interpret some of the main findings in the previous parts and discuss the theoretical implications of the results obtained[1].

Since the results presented in this dissertation are based on data from police-recorded crimes, it was natural to first consider the adequacy of using police-recorded crimes of violence for a description of actual crimes of violence (Part 1). The problem to be dealt with was defined in relation to the research objects (situational and ecological aspects) as one of possible bias due to differential dark figures and clearance.

Swedish research of relevance for the problem and some analyses of police-recorded crimes thought to be of value in this respect, e.g. concerning variations between different kinds of crimes as regards who notified the police, have been reviewed and discussed.

On the basis thereof, calculations involving "estimated" differential dark figures were made in order to have some rough indication as to how these would affect descriptions of crime structure and characteristics of persons involved in the crimes. A similar analysis was made with reference to spatial variations of the incidence of crimes, offenders and victims, and the characteristics of crimes.

Also the possible bias caused by differential clearance was considered and some analyses of the police-recorded crimes of relevance for that topic were made, e.g. selected offender characteristics estimated by victim and witnesses in uncleared cases were compared with the corresponding data in cleared cases.

The overall conclusion from the analysis of bias caused by differential dark figures and clearance was that

● data of police recorded crimes of violence give regarding crime structure, characteristics of persons involved in the crimes and spatial variations, probably a fairly good or at least not a seriously misleading picture of actual crimes of violence.

Characteristics of the persons involved in and the circumstances of the crimes were the next main topic to be dealt with (Part 2). The actor's definition of the situation, the offender's motive, actions preceding the violence and structural aspects of the situation in terms of victim-offender interpersonal relationship and characteristics were all judged to be interesting aspects of the violent event. It was, however, concluded that, with the kind of data used (police records), it was difficult to study motives and actor's definitions of the situation.

---

[1] However, I shall make no extensive review of the findings. For detailed results the reader is referred to the summaries in the various chapters.

Classifications of the violent event were discussed and a classification based on the parties' actions preceding the violence was proposed, applied empirically and related to victim-offender and crime characteristics. A more direct analysis of structural aspects was also made by means of factor analysis. The defining variables of extracted factors were used to create subgroups of cases that were further analysed. Finally, and focusing on the offenders, cohort data were used to study such aspects as persistence and specialization in crimes of violence.

One of the most striking findings concerning the persons involved in the crimes was that

- most of the offenders and many of the victims were to be regarded as socially loaded persons (alcoholics, criminals, addicts). Further, that most of the crimes occurred either between two socially loaded persons or between a socially loaded and a "conventional" person, while crimes involving two "conventional" persons were comparatively rare.

One plausible interpretation of the reason for the great involvement of socially loaded persons in crimes of violence is that it is

- partly a consequence of a way of living that often leads to confrontation with others, partly because socially loaded persons in general have a greater readiness than "conventional" people to react to friction with violence.

Most crimes of violence develop out of a conflict between the parties involved, although there is a non-negligible proportion of the crimes that are preceded by molestation or constitute a sudden attack. Regarding the setting of the crime

- most cases occur in the home or in the course of public entertainment, while few cases occur in the course of work.

Of those that get involved in crimes of violence during work most have work either in the public entertainment sector or which brings them into close contact with public entertainment or with socially loaded persons.

Of the crimes occurring in the home there are two main types: a) relationship conflicts within the family, and b) heavy drinking parties.

In the "family violence cases" it is mostly males, often socially loaded males, that assault their females. Those involved in these cases tend to be older than in other types of violence and especially in relation to violence occurring outside the home. Those involved are likely to be of the same age and nationality. A non-negligible proportion of these cases occur after a relationship has been broken or is under strain. There is much to indicate that

278

- it is in male-female relationships under socially unstable conditions that most male-female violence occurs.

This hypothesis is likely to be more true for severe and repeated than for occasional and less severe cases of male-female violence.

In the "heavy drinking party cases" it is generally males assaulting males; often both are to be regarded as socially loaded persons. Situational conflicts and intervention preceding the violence are common. These cases appear to be highly related to a socially loaded person's style of living.

Contrasting crimes in apartments with other crimes of violence

- there is some tendency that crimes in apartments involve people of a similar kind, while there is a tendency that outdoor crimes occur between people of different kinds.

In the "apartment cases" this may be regarded as a natural consequence of the fact that people associating in apartments are generally acquainted with each other. Further, one is likely to be acquainted with people of a similar kind to oneself. However, in the outdoor crimes, and especially those occurring in the course of public entertainment, many of the violent actions seem to have a background in friction between people of different kinds, often socially loaded persons confronted with "conventional" people. These conflicts are often of a trivial kind.

Although alcohol intoxication has a great role in all kinds of violence, this is particularly so in situational conflicts arising in the course of public entertainment. In the vast majority of such cases both parties are intoxicated, often highly intoxicated. It seems reasonable that the convergence of intoxicated strangers contributes to the occurrence of friction and facilitates its development into violence. All in all, the high incidence of violence in the course of public entertainment is likely to be a result of a high incidence of friction due to

- the convergence of different kinds of intoxicated persons who are strangers to each other, and the fact that most friction producing convergence is that between socially loaded and "conventional" persons.

In more general terms it may be hypothesized that it is the social instability of public entertainment that causes the high incidence of crimes of violence: a large number of interacting intoxicated strangers of different kinds, making it sometimes difficult to anticipate the reactions and behaviour of others, etc.

In the third Part ecological aspects of crimes of violence were the point of focus. Although various studies of regional variations, urban-rural differences, intercity variations and temporal variations of crimes of violence are presented in the third Part, I shall here

279

concentrate on the ecology of crimes of violence in the city. Partly because, as stated in the introduction to the dissertation, it is believed that this is the most fruitful level when the concern is possible milieu effects on violent behaviour.

The three main strategies used to analyse intracity variations was 1) correlational and regression analysis of ward characteristics and the incidence of crimes, offenders and victims, 2) the grouping of wards into larger aggregates either by offender rate of ward or by characteristics of wards which were then compared regarding characteristics of the offenders living in the ward and of their crimes and of crimes occurring in the ward and 3) exploring crime and distance by offender, crime and ward characteristics. A Distance Typology was developed for this purpose.

In somewhat simplified terms it may be stated that it is mainly two types of areas in the city that are of interest when the concern is crimes of violence.

- The city centre is the major crime area. In fact crimes between strangers are extremely concentrated here.

- Social Problem areas are the major areas of residence for both offenders and victims in crimes of violence. They are also the first ranking crime areas among the outer city areas.

The character of the crimes occurring in these two types of areas differs a lot. In the city centre it is mainly crimes that occur in the course of public entertainment (see above). Hence,

- the localization of public entertainment to central city areas is a major reason for the high incidence of crimes of violence in these areas.

In the Social Problems areas a vast proportion of the crimes occurs in apartments. They differ from other residential areas in that crimes occurring there tend to be much more local. Offenders living in these areas are also much more local in their crimes than offenders from other types of areas. Crimes in the neighbourhood of both victim and offender are most common in Social Problem areas. Compared with other areas, offenders from Social Problem Areas are to a much higher degree socially loaded persons. There is much that indicates that the higher rate of crimes among the outer city areas for the Social Problem area is a consequence of

- a high proportion "problem tenants" that fights internally or gets into conflict with neighbours.

There seems to be much pointing in the direction that the degree of social instability of residential area is positively related to crimes of violence in the area.

280

Regarding the concentration of offenders and victims it appears mainly to be a consequence of that

- socially loaded persons are segregated to certain wards.

There are also some results indicating that the segregation of foreigners may be of relevance for explanations of the victim and offender distributions. An intersting field of study in this connection is the comparison, of the crime structure and persons involved in the crimes, between ethnical heterogen and other Social Problem Area.

On the basis of the data presented, there are much that indicates that future research on crime of violence from an ecological-situational perspective should consider more carefully how a) social characteristics of persons staying and/or living in an area, and b) types of activities occurring in an area, affects the social stability of the area (totally or at certain times of the day) and how that in turn affects the rate of frictions between people that at times develops into violence.

Police reports/investigation records. An overview of variables coded in the Gävle Study, the 21 Police Districts Study and the Big City Crime Study

The police report is a data-sheet filled in when a crime is reported. It is mainly based on the victim's statement. A short description of the crime, date, time and place of occurrence, and some data about the victim and, if known, about the offender, such as sex, age and home address, are the main contents of the police report.

For the majority, but not all, of violent crimes there is an investigation record which contains the interrogations of the victim and possibly of the offender and witnesses, personalia of the offender, technical investigation of the scene of the crime, medical examination of the injury to the victim, etc.

The data in the police files may vary between the extremes of a mere police report up to investigation records covering hundreds of pages. A usual example of the first is reported family violence cases in which the victim, soon after the report of the crime, withdrew the report, while the most frequent example of the latter is cases of killing and aggravated assault.

The Table shows an overview of the variables coded in the three studies concerned.

Table. An overview of variables coded from police reports/investigation records in the Gävle Study, the 21 Police Districts Study and the Big City Crime Study

Variable	Variable included (=X) in;		
	Gävle	21 Police Districts	Big City
Crime (written classification)	X	X	X
Police Crime Code (digits)		X	
Counting of crimes		X	
Person notifying the police		X	
Eye witnesses	X		X
Month of crime	X	X	X
Day of crime	X	X	X
Hour of crime	X	X	X
Place of occurrence	X	X	X
Type of violence/weapons	X	X	X
Reciprocal violence	X		
Preceding actions	X		
Victim–offender relationship	X	X	X
Sex of offender	X	X	X
Age of offender	X	X	X
Nationality of offender	X	X	X
Occupation of offender	X	X	X
Offender at work at the time of the crime	X	X	X
Alcoholic intoxication of offender	X		
Offender in youth gang at the time of the crime			X
Number of offenders	X		
Sex of victim	X	X	X
Age of victim	X	X	X
Nationality of victim	X	X	X
Occupation of victim	X		
Victim at work at the time of the crime	X	X	X
Alcoholic intoxication of victim	X		
Victim in youth gang at the time of the crime			X
Number of victims	X		
Injury to the victim	X		X
Place of occurrence, address	X	X	X
Offender's residence, address	X	X	X
Victim's residence, address	X	X	X

Data of population and other characteristics of the wards of cities. Data used in the Big City Crime Study and the 21 Police Districts Study

The purpose of the data presented in this Appendix is to describe the city structure. It is therefore of utmost importance that the variables grasp the essential variations that exist between different areal units. The variables have been chosen in the light of the results of urban sociological studies (see, e.g., Janson, 1980; Timms, 1971). Twenty four variables were selected from a large number of possible variables (see Table).

The first group of variables was primarily chosen to measure characteristics of the wards: location in relation to city centre, mainly work place or residential area, the occurrence of manufacture, shops and service institutions in the ward, and the size of the population.

The work-place area variable has been calculated as the day population divided by the sum of the day population and the residential population. Then we have a measure that will be 100 % if the area only has a day population and 0 % if the area only has a residential population. The occurrence of manufacture (number of persons working in) and shops and service institutions (number of persons working in) is counted as incidence. The latter is thought to be a measure of the existence of commercial centres, and their size, in the wards.

The second group of variables was selected to measure the demographic characteristics of the population: age, sex and nationality. Ethnical status has proved to be an important variable in residential segregation especially in ethnically heterogeneous communities.

The third group of variables focuses on household characteristics: Size of family, families with children, children with single working parents, and crowding (number of households in which the members of the household number more than 2 per room, the kitchen and one room not counted). Family status is a variable that is usually important in residential segregation.

WARD CHARACTERISTICS	Comment:
a) Distance from city centre	In hundreds of metres
b) Commercial centre	Persons working in shops, service institutions, hotels, restaurants, etc. (Day population)
c) Manufacture, work–places	Persons working in manufacture. (Day population)
d) Work–places, %	Per cent day population of the sum of day and residential population
e) Residential population	Number
DEMOGRAPHIC CHARACTERISTICS	
f) Young persons, %	Aged 0—14 years
g) Old persons, %	Aged 60— years
h) Females aged 15— years	Of all aged 15— years
i) Foreigners, %	Persons with foreign citizenship
HOUSEHOLD CHARACTERISTICS	
j) Household size, mean	
k) Overcrowded households, %	According to norm 2
l) Households with children/ youth, %	Households with members aged 0—17 years
m) Children with single working parents, %	Children aged 0—12 years living in household with single working parents
HOUSING CHARACTERISTICS	
n) One– and two–family houses, %	Dwellings in one– and two–family houses
o) Municipal housing, %	Dwellings in municipal housing
p) Small dwellings, %	2 rooms and kitchen or less
q) Large dwellings, %	5 rooms and kitchen or more
r) Old dwellings, %	Built before 1951
s) Vacant dwellings, %	
SOCIO–ECONOMIC CHARACTERISTICS	
t) Income, mean	
u) Income heterogeneity	Mean — median
v) Workers, %	Residential population employed in manufacture
x) Females, gainfully employed	Females with an income of 20,000 Sw.Cr. — of all females 15— years
y) Social security, %	Persons receiving social security

The fourth group of variables concerned housing characteristics, and the fifth and final group the socio-economic characteristics of the populations. Socio-economic status is generally the most important factor in residential segregation.

In the Big City Crime Study there were no problems in collecting the information listed in the Table for the wards. However, in the 21 Police Districts Study such problems arose. For some cities the local authorities did not possess the requested information, notably for socio-economic status indicators such as social security and income.

This means that it was not possible[1] to include all the wanted indicators for all of the studied cities in the 21 Police District Study.

The research year in the Big City Crime Study is 1982 and most data of city structure stems from that year or the census made in 1980. Only income data are taken from another year (1979).

In the 21 Police Districts Study the research year is 1978 and the data not available for that year are mainly taken from the censuses made in 1975 and 1980[2]. The divergence of some years from the research year for certain variables relating to city structure is, of course, not satisfactory, but on the whole not judged to involve any serious errors. Population and other characteristics of wards generally change slowly. The main problem is newly-built areas, but that has been overcome by asking for information about production of buildings just before and after the year 1978. This is no great problem. Looking at single indicators, one is troublesome in that it is likely to be sensitive for the year chosen, namely income. If wages rise, which they usually do, from one year to another, and income data are selected for different years for different cities, this disturbs a comparative analysis of the cities with this indicator. As mentioned, this was an indicator which could not be obtained on the ward level for all cities and, if such information was available, only the data for 1978 and, in cases when no such data existed, for the years 1977 and 1979 were used. In some cities only data for, e.g., 1980 were available, but in these cases they were not used.

---

[1] For practical-economical reasons.

[2] Besides the censuses the other main sources of data are DEMOPAK and INKOPAK.

*Coding of variables used in factor analysis of victim–offender
relationships and correlation between factor scores and crime
characteristic*

Variable	Coding
A) Apartment/proximity area	1 = Apartment/proximity area 0 = Other places
B) Weekend	1 = 16.00 Friday to 08.00 Monday 0 = Others hours
C) Daily rhythm	0 = 04.00—07.59 hours 1 = 08.00—11.59 hours 2 = 12.00—15.59 hours 3 = 16.00—19.59 hours 4 = 20.00—23.59 hours 5 = 24.00—03.59 hours
D) Acquaintanceship	0 = Strangers 1 = Casual acquaintances 2 = Acquaintances (non–family) 3 = Family relationships
E) Weapons	1 = Weapons present 0 = No weapons present
F) Victim's injury	0 = No injury 1 = Bruises or less injuries 2 = Minor fractures, bleeding 3 = Severe injury, e.g. broken bones, unconsciousness 4 = Death
g) Sex of victim H) Sex of offender	0 = Male 1 = Female
I) Age of victim J) Age of offender	Age
K) Victim of foreign nationality L) Offender of foreign nationality	0 = Swedish 1 = Non–Swedish
M) Victim's previous criminality N) Offender's previous criminality	Number of years with at least one record in the police register
O) Victim's previous crimes of P) violence, offender's pre- vious crimes of violence	Number of recorded crimes of violence in the police register
Q) Victim hard drug user R) Offender hard drug user	0 = No recorded needle–marks in last one and a half years 1 = Recorded needle–marks during at least one and a half years
S) Victim in youth gang T) Offender in youth gang	0 = Not in youth gang 1 = In youth gang
U) Victim at work V) Offender at work	0 = Not at work 1 = At work

Number of wards for which information concerning the ward characteristic variables in the 21 Police Districts Study was available. Totally and excluding inner-city areas

Ward characteristic	Total city	Number of wards Excluding inner-city areas
Mean income	280	265
Income heterogeneity	143	137
% aged 0—14 years	397	374
% aged 60— years	365	343
% females aged 15— years	396	373
% foreign nationality	396	328
Household size, mean	396	373
% dwellings in one— and two family houses	395	373
% dwellings in municipal housing	395	372
% small dwellings	396	373
% large dwellings	396	373
% old dwellings	396	373
% households with children/youth	387	365
% children with single working parents	368	347
% vacant dwellings	387	365
% workplaces	394	371
Industrial work, number of employees	385	363
Commercial centre	385	363
Distance from city centre	399	376
% overcrowded	396	373
% blue—collar workers	345	324
% social security	47	45
% females, gainfully employed	189	179

Note: Wards with less than 481 inhabitants have been excluded. With this exclusion the total number of studied wards is 399.

289

Appendix 5

Number of wards, range of and mean population for the 21 cities studied in the 21 Police Districts Study

City	Number of wards	Range of population in wards	Mean population of wards
Boden	10	695— 3275	1798
Luleå	14	660— 8153	3760
Umeå	22	623— 5165	2415
Östersund	9	532—10813	4529
Sundsvall	13	965— 6116	4194
Gävle	13	628— 9259	4753
Uppsala	18	2123—10187	5807
Västerås	24	677—11510	4050
Södertälje	15	907— 8042	3918
Eskilstuna	15	744— 8510	4228
Falun	9	1142— 6372	3491
Sandviken	18	494— 5541	1486
Karlstad	26	635— 5246	1978
Örebro	25	696— 6469	3293
Norrköping	23	1191—10127	3830
Linköping	18	831— 7800	4507
Jönköping	30	566— 5493	2377
Borås	22	488— 7993	2899
Halmstad	16	519—10014	2988
Helsingborg	31	875— 5104	2498
Kalmar	28	533— 2851	1041

Note: Wards with less than 481 inhabitants excluded.

Appendix 6

Some results from a series of factor analyses of the 21 cities' varying numbers of wards and variables (data from the 21 Police Districts Study)

As is evident from Table 89 in Section 10.2.2, several of the variables correlated with the crime variables were more or less strongly associated. There is good reason to believe that many of the variables included measures of more or less the same thing. To have some further indication of the correctness of that belief a series of factor analyses was made. The reason for making this series of analyses was the marked differences in the number of variables available for different numbers of wards. Hence, making several factor analyses with varying numbers of variables and wards made it, so to speak, possible to avoid the choice between few variables and many wards or the reverse.

Six factor analyses were made. The variation was between inclusion of 22 variables and 128 wards to inclusion of 365 wards and 10 variables. Two variables were totally excluded from the social security and income heterogeneity analyses due to the very high number of missing cases. On the other hand, in contrast to the factor analysis of Stockholm (see Section 11.2.1), the variable "population size" was included.

The number of extracted (Varimax rotated) factors varied between 6 in the case of 22 variables to 3 in the case of 10. Comparing the results with those from the analysis of Stockholm, the first four factors from the Stockholm analysis seemed also to be identifiable for the 21 medium sized and smaller cities namely, Familism, Social Problems, Social Rank and Work Place Area, although the interpretation of a factor as a Social Problem factor was less straightforward. Note that the variable "social security" was not included.

In the four following tables I have shown the structure for each of the four discussed factors as they turned out in each of the various factor analyses. The factors are presented from left to right in order of number of wards included – least in the left column and most in the right. The Work Place Area factor appeared only in five of the factor analyses. In the analysis with 10 variables only three factors were extracted, and in that factor analysis two of the defining variables of the Work Place factor were not included. This factor did not appear in that analysis.

	Factor 1, Familism					
Population size	−13	− 6	− 5	− 4	− 3	0
Mean income	38*	60*	NI	NI	NI	NI
% aged 0—14	67*	70*	75*	81*	79*	82*
% aged 60—	−38*	−48*	−56*	−65*	NI	NI
% females aged 15—	11	9	5	3	− 1	− 5
% foreign nationality	− 3	− 3	4	NI	NI	NI
Household size	94*	92*	95*	96*	97*	97*
% dwellings in one— and two family houses	82*	85*	81*	77*	78*	75*
% dwellings in municipal housing	−14	−19	−14	− 8	− 6	0
% small dwellings	−89*	−86*	−88*	−87*	−88*	−87*
% large dwellings	79*	84*	80*	77*	77*	72
% old dwellings	−40*	−34*	−39*	−46*	−47*	−56*
% households with children 0—17	86*	82*	87*	92*	92*	95*
% children with single working parents	−41*	−56*	−52*	−50*	−51*	NI
% vacant dwellings	− 7	1	0	4	2	NI
% work places	−28	−23	−29	−32	−32	−53*
Industrial work places	− 7	− 8	− 9	− 9	− 7	NI
Commercial centre	−21	−15	−22	−20	−21	NI
Distance from city centre	75*	71*	74*	71*	72*	75*
% overcrowded	−32	−30	−22	−24	−27	−26
% blue—collar workers	4	3	5	NI	NI	NI
% females with an income 20,000 — Sw.Cr.	14	NI	NI	NI	NI	NI
Contribution %	32	32	32	38	37	45

Note: Coefficients multiplied by 100. NI = variable not included.
Correlations marked with an asterisk significant at 5 % level.

Factor 2, Social Problems

Population size	80*	80*	77*	74*	70*	71*
Mean income	− 2	11	NI	NI	NI	NI
% aged 0—14	30	38*	37*	30	36	34
% aged 60—	−28	−35*	−35	−32	NI	NI
% females aged 15—	8	11	12	9	22	11
% foreign nationality	11	25	36*	NI	NI	NI
Household size	12	15	11	0	0	3
% dwellings in one− and two family houses	−32	−32	−39*	−47*	−50*	−44*
% dwellings in municipal housing	58*	57*	66*	71*	75*	76*
% small dwellings	2	− 2	2	13	17	17
% large dwellings	−24	−24	−30	−37	−40	−40
% old dwellings	−74*	−75*	−75*	−70*	−65*	−60*
% households with children 0—17	31	37*	33	22	22	26
% children with single working parents	29	33	44*	48*	46*	NI
% vacant dwellings	− 8	− 2	1	3	19	NI
% work places	−53*	−48*	−40*	−33	−28	−42
Industrial work places	−10	− 5	− 2	0	1	NI
Commercial centre	14	12	13	11	6	NI
Distance from city centre	9	10	2	1	6	13
% overcrowded	12	5	7	16	27	36
% blue−collar workers	2	3	7	NI	NI	NI
% females with an income 20,000 — Sw.Cr.	24	NI	NI	NI	NI	NI
Contribution %	16	17	16	16	16	18

Note: Coefficients multiplied by 100. NI = variable not included.
Correlations marked with an asterisk significant at 5 % level.

293

	Factor 3, Social Rank					
Population size	− 1	− 3	4	0	2	3
Mean income	0	− 6	NI	NI	NI	NI
% aged 0—14	−14	− 3	2	5	21	28
% aged 60—	− 4	−10	−13	− 2	NI	NI
% females aged 15—	−23	−24	−22	− 6	76*	85*
% foreign nationality	0	− 2	42*	NI	NI	NI
Household size	1	8	3	− 3	− 3	− 1
% dwellings in one— and two family houses	−19	−10	−18	−20	9	6
% dwellings in municipal housing	44*	30	19	32	−17	− 8
% small dwellings	29	24	28	30	−22	−19
% large dwellings	−33	−26	−31	−28	21	19
% old dwellings	− 3	− 2	2	15	−14	−16
% households with children 0—17	5	10	7	1	− 5	− 2
% children with single working parents	38*	32	7	13	−19	NI
% vacant dwellings	51*	11	5	75*	−39	NI
% work places	8	4	5	21	−13	−15
Industrial work places	37*	32	32	14	−16	NI
Commercial centre	−13	−15	−20	− 6	13	NI
Distance from city centre	25	39*	27	13	−11	− 8
% overcrowded	76*	71*	75*	71*	−70*	−66*
% blue—collar workers	84*	81*	82*	NI	NI	NI
% females with an income 20,000 — Sw.Cr.	7	NI	NI	NI	NI	NI
Contribution %	8	7	8	8	8	10

Note: Coefficients multiplied by 100. NI = variable not included.
Correlations marked with an asterisk significant at 5 % level.

	Factor 4, Work Place Area				
Population size	20	18	11	26	4
Mean income	2	21	NI	NI	NI
% aged 0—14	−18	−21	−18	28	−14
% aged 60—	13	19	20	15	NI
% females aged 15—	− 5	− 1	0	51*	6
% foreign nationality	0	− 4	0	NI	NI
Household size	−12	−20	−14	9	−15
% dwellings in one— and two family houses	− 7	−12	− 8	0	−13
% dwellings in municipal housing	− 3	− 3	− 9	6	− 8
% small dwellings	12	20	12	−12	13
% large dwellings	1	− 3	0	14	− 2
% old dwellings	26	28	23	−15	21
% households with children 0—17	−14	−21	−16	12	−16
% children with single working parents	11	6	13	1	17
% vacant dwellings	− 1	5	3	16	25
% work places	57*	60*	65*	31	70*
Industrial work places	73*	78*	81*	53*	76*
Commercial centre	83*	84*	83*	66*	81*
Distance from city centre	−18	−27	−20	2	−17
% overcrowded	13	10	6	−14	8
% blue—collar workers	4	3	4	NI	NI
% females with an income 20,000 — Sw.Cr.	0	NI	NI	NI	NI
Contribution %	5	10	10	8	9

Note: Coefficients multiplied by 100. NI = variable not included.
Correlations marked with an asterisk significant at 5 % level.

Multiple regression (R^2) of major defining variables of Factor I – Factor III (see Table 106 in Section 11.2.1) with offender and victim distribution

Variables in model	Dependent variable	Total city R^2
Household size, mean + Social security, % + Blue–collar workers, %	Offenders per 1,000 inhabi–tants	34
Household size, mean + Social security, % + Blue–collar workers	Young offenders (under 25 years) per young inhabi–tants (10—24 years)	26
Household size, mean + Social security, % + Blue–collar workers, %	Victims per 1,000 inhabi–tants	35

References

Alihan, M A (1961): Community and Ecological Studies. In: Theodorson (ed): Studies in Human Ecology. Row, Peterson and Company, New York.

Andersson, J E G (1984): Rånarna och deras offer. Exponeringens betydelse vid direkt-kontakt brott. Sociologiska institutionen, Stockholms universitet.

Andersson-Brolin, L (1984): Etnisk bostadssegregation. Byggforskningsrådet.

Arbell, G (1946): Manufakturer och industrier. In: P Humbla (ed): Gävle stads historia. Lantmännens tryckeri.

Aschaffenburg, G (1911): Brottet och dess bekämpande. Bonniers förlag.

Athens, L H (1980): Violent Criminal Acts and Actors. Routledge & Kegan Paul.

Aubert, V (1970): Socialt samspel. Almqvist & Wiksell, Stockholm.

Bagley, C (1965): Juvenile Delinquency in Exeter: an Ecological and Comparative Study. Urban Studies.

Baldwin, J (1975): British Areal Studies of Crime: an Assessment. British Journal of Criminology.

Baldwin & Bottoms (1976): The Urban Criminal. Tavistock Publications, London.

Baldwin & Xanthos (1981): Housing Policy and Crime in the British Public Sector. In: Brantingham & Brantingham.

Baron, R A (1977): Human Aggression. Plenum Press.

Bejerot, N (1975): Narkotikamissbruk och narkotikapolitik. Sober Förlag.

Bensing & Schroeder (1960): Homicide in an Urban Community. Springfield Thomas Books.

van den Berghe, P L (1974): Bringing Beasts Back. In: Toward a Biosocial Theory of Aggression. American Sociological Review.

Berkowitz, L (1962): Aggression: a Social Psychological Analysis. McGraw-Hill Book Company.

Berlind & Rundblad (1975): Arbetsmarknaden i Sverige. Esselte Studium.

Block, R (1976): Homicide in Chicago. A Nine-Year Study (1965–1973). The Journal of Criminal Law and Criminology.

Blomqvist et al. (1980): Arga katter får rivet skinn. Konsekvenser av knivvåldet i Stockholm. Läkartidningen nr 25.

Boggs, S L (1965): Urban Crime Patterns. American Sociological Review.

Bordua, D J (1958–59): Juvenile Delinquency and "Anomie": an Attempt at Replication. Social Problems.

Bottoms & Xanthos (1981): Housing Policy and Crime in the British Public Sector. In: Brantingham & Brantingham (eds): Environmental Criminology. Sage Publications.

Boyatzis, R E (1975): The Predisposition Towards Alcohol-Related Aggression in Men. Journal of Studies on Alcohol.

Braithwaite, J (1979): Inequality, Crime and Public Policy. Routledge and Kegan Paul.

Braithwaite, J (1981): The Myth of Social Class and Criminality Reconsidered. American Sociological Review.

Brantingham & Brantingham (1980): Residential Burglary and Urban Form. In: Bittner & Messinger (eds): Criminological Review Yearbook 1980. Sage Publications.

Brantingham & Brantingham (1981): Environmental Criminology. Sage Publications.

Brantingham & Brantingham (1981): Notes on the Geometry of Crime. In: Brantingham & Brantingham (1981). See above.

Brantingham & Brantingham (1981): The Dimensions of Crime. In: Brantingham & Brantingham (1981). See above.

Brantingham & Jeffery (1981): Crime, Space and Criminological Theory. In: Brantingham & Brantingham (1981). See above.

Brenner, C (1971): The Psychoanalytic Concept of Aggression. Int. J. Psycho-Anal.

Brodin & Oskarsson & Pettersson (1978): Kvinnomisshandel. Juridiska inst, Lunds universitet.

Brown & McCulloch & Hiscox (1972): Criminal Offences in an Urban Area and Their Associated Social Variables. British Journal of Criminology, Vol 12.

Buikhuisen & Jongman (1970): A Legalistic Classification of Juvenile Delinquents. British Journal of Criminology.

Bullock, H A (1955): Urban Homicide in Theory and Fact. The Journal of Criminal Law, Criminology and Police Science.

Burgess, E W (1925): The Growth of the City. In: Park & Burgess & McKenzie (eds): The City. The University of Chicago Press.

Burt, C (1944): The Young Delinquent. University of London Press, London.

Buss, A H (1963): Physical Aggression in Relation to Different Frustrations. Journal of Abnormal and Social Psychology.

Cahoon, D D (1972): A Behavioristic Analysis of Aggression. The Psychological Record.

298

Capone & Nichols jr (1976): Urban Structure and Criminal Mobility. American Behavioral Scientist.

Carlsson, G (1972): Samhällsmiljö och rumslig fördelning. In: SOU 1972:76.

Carlsson, G (1975): Kriminalitetsnivå och belastningsfördelningar. Brottsförebyggande rådet, utvecklingsenheten, PM 1975:1.

Carter & Hill (1978): Criminals' and Non-Criminals' Perception of Urban Crime. Criminology.

Carter & Hill (1979): The Criminal's Image of the City. Pergamon Press.

Castle & Gittus (1961): The Distribution of Social Defects in Liverpool. In: Theodorson (ed): Studies in Human Ecology. Row, Peterson and Company, New York.

Charpentier, A (no year): En undersökning av misshandelsbrottsligheten i Uppsala. Uppsala universitet.

Chilton, R J (1964): Continuity in Delinquency Area Research: a Comparison of Studies from Baltimore, Detroit and Indianapolis. American Sociological Review.

Christie, N (1975): Hvor tett et samfunn? Universitetsforlaget, Oslo.

Christie & Andenaes & Skirbeek (1965): A Study of Self-Reported Crime. Scandinavian Studies in Criminology.

Clarke, R V G & Mayhew, P (1980): Designing out Crime. Home Office Research Unit Publications, London.

Clinard, M B (1978): Cities with Little Crime. Cambridge University Press.

Cohen, A K (1955): Delinquent Boys. The Free Press, New York.

Cohen, A K (1973): Avvikande beteende. Wahlström & Widstrand, Stockholm.

Cohen & Felson (1979): Social Change and Crime Rate Trends: a Routine Activity Approach. American Sociological Review.

Connor, W D (1973): Criminal homicide, U.S.S.R./U.S.A.: Reflections on Soviet Data in a Comparative Framework. The Journal of Criminal Law and Criminology, Vol 64, nr I.

Curtis, L A (1974): Criminal Violence. Lexington Books, Massachusetts.

Curtis, L A (1974): Victim Precipation and Violent Crime. Social Problems, Vol 21, No 4.

Darwin, C (1968): The Origin of Species. Penguin Books.

Davies, J C (1970): Violence and Aggression: Innate or Not? Western Political Quarterly.

Deardorff et al. (1975): Situations Related to Drinking Alcohol. Journal of Studies on Alcohol.

Decker & Schior (1982): Urban Structure and Victimization. Lexington Books.

van Dijk & Vivanen (1978): Criminal Victimization in the Netherlands. The Ministry of Justice, The Hague.

Dobash & Dobash (1980): Violence against Wives. Open Books.

Doerner, W G (1978): The Deadly World of Johnny Reb. In: Inciardi & Pottieger (eds): Violent Crime. Sage Publications, Beverly Hills.

Dollard, et al. (1939): Frustration and Aggression. Yale University Press.

Doreian, P (1980): Linear Models with Spatially Distributed Data. Sociological Methods & Research.

Downes, D M (1957, 1958): The Delinquent Solution. Routledge & Kegan Paul.

Ds S 1982:2: En utvärdering av försöket med lördagsstängda systembutiker sommaren 1981.

Ds S 1984:8: Effekter av lördagsstängda systembutiker.

Duffla, D C (1976): Convenience Stores, Armed Robbery, and Physical Environment. American Behavioral Scientist.

Dunér & Haglund (1974): Tonårspojkar och brott. Utbildningsförlaget.

Dunn, C S (1976): The Patterns and Distribution of Assault Incident Characteristics Among Social Areas. Anyalytic Report 14. U.S. Dept. of Justice.

Durkheim, E (1968): Självmordet. Argos.

Elliott & Agetton (1980): Reconciling Race and Class Differences in Self-Reported and Official Estimates of Delinquency. American Sociological Review.

Elmer, M C (1933): Century-Old Ecological Studies in France. The American Journal of Sociology.

Elmhorn, K (1969): Faktisk brottslighet bland skolbarn. SOU 1969:1.

Erlanger, H S (1976): Is There a "Subculture of Violence" in the South? The Journal of Criminal Law and Criminology.

Felson & Steadman (1983): Situational Factors in Disputes Leading to Criminal Violence. Criminology.

Ferracuti & Newman (1974): Assaultive Offenses. In: Glaser, D (ed): Handbook of Criminology.

Firebaugh, G (1978): A Rule for Inferring Individual-Level Relationships from Aggregate Data. American Sociological Review, Vol 43.

Firey, W (1961): Sentiment and Symbolism as Ecological Variables. In: Theodorson (ed): Studies in Human Ecology. Row, Peterson and Company, New York.

Froom, E (1976): Den destruktiva människan. Natur & Kultur.

Gastil, R D (1971): Homicide and a Regional Culture of Violence. American Sociological Review.

Georges-Abeyie & Harries (1980): Crime. A Spatial Perspective. Colombia University Press, New York.

Gerle & Holmström (1968): Hustrumisshandel. Juridiska inst, Lunds universitet.

Gibbs, J J (1979): Crimes against Persons in Urban, Sub-Urban, and Rural Areas. U.S. Department of Justice. LEAA.

300

Goldstein, J H (1975): Aggression and Crimes of Violence. Oxford University Press.

Gordon, R A (1967): Issues in the Ecological Study of Delinquency. American Sociological Review.

Gorsuch, R L (1974): Factor Analysis. W.B., Sauders Company.

Grönholm, L (1960): The Ecology of Social Disorganization in Helsinki. Acta Sociologica.

Gustafsson & Kühlhorn (1980): Våldsbrottsutvecklingen i kriminalsociologisk belysning. In: Brottsutvecklingen 1980. BRÅ-rapport 1980:3.

Hackney, S (1979): Southern Violence. In: Graham & Gurr (eds): Violence in America. Sage Publications.

Hakim & Rengert (1981): Crime Spillover. Sage Publications.

Hammond, J L (1973): Two Sources of Error in Ecological Correlations. American Sociological Review.

Harries, K D (1974): The Geography of Crime and Justice. McGraw-Hill Book Company.

Hellspong & Löfgren (1977): Land och stad. Liber Läromedel, Lund.

Herbert, D (1972): Urban Geography. A Social Perspective. David & Charles, London.

Herbert, D T (1978): Social Deviance in the City: A Spatial Perspective. In: Herbert & Johnston (eds): Social Areas in Cities. John Wiley & Sons.

Hilgard et al. (1975): Introduction to Psychology. Harcourt Brace Jovanovich Inc.

Hindelang et al (1978): Victims of Personal Crime: An Empirical Foundation for a Theory of Personal Victimization. Ballinger Publishing Company.

Hindelang & Hirschi & Weis (1979): Correlates of Delinquency: The Illusion of Discrepancy between Self-Report and Official Measures. American Sociologcal Review.

Hindelang & Hirschi & Weis (1981): Measuring Delinquency. Sage Publications.

Hirschi, T (1969): Causes of Delinquency. University of California Press.

Hirschi & Selvin (1973): Principles of Survey Analysis. The Free Press.

Hirschi & Gottfredson (1983): Age and the Explanation of Crime. American Journal of Sociology.

Hoiberg & Cloyd (1971): Definition and Measurement of Continuous Variation in Ecological Analysis. American Sociological Review.

Hood & Sparks (1973): Kriminologi. Wahlström & Widstrand.

Hough & Clarke & Mayhews (1980): Introduction. In: Clarke & Mayhew (eds): Designing out Crime. Home Office Research Unit, London.

Janson, C-G (1953): Slutrapport för kriminologiska institutets undersökning av brottslighetens regionala fördelning. (Unpublished)

Janson, C-G (1971): A Preliminary Report on Swedish Urban Spatial Structure. Economic Geography, No 2. (Supplement)

Janson, C-G (1980): Factorial Social Ecology. American Sociological Review.

Janson, C-G (1982): Delinquency among Metropolitan Boys. Dept. of Sociology, University of Stockholm (Projekt Metropolitan rapport nr 17).

Janson, C-G (1984): Project Metropolitan. A Presentation and Progress Report. Department of Sociology, University of Stockholm.

Jeffery, C R (1977): Crime Prevention through Environmental Design. Sage Publications.

Jonassen, C T (1949): A Re-Evaluation and Critique of the Logic and Some Methods of Shaw and McKay. American Sociological Review.

Jonsson, G (1969): Det sociala arvet. Tidens förlag.

Karlström, T (1974): Gävle stadsbild. Westlund och söner.

Kim & Mueller (1978): Factor Analysis. Statistical Methods and Practical Issues. Sages University Paper 14.

Kleck, G (1982): On the Use of Self-Report Data to Determine the Class Distribution of Criminal and Delinquent Behavior. American Sociological Review.

Knutsson, J (1984): Våld mot personer under arbetet – speciellt tjänstemannavåldet. In: Kühlhorn et al.

Knutsson, J & Kühlhorn, E (1980): När checkbedrägerierna försvann. Brottsförebyggande rådet. Rapport 1980:4.

Koch, L (1966): Avdömd misshandel vid Stockholms rådhusrätt 1/1–30/6 1966. Kriminalvetenskapliga institutet, Stockholms universitet.

Kornhauser, R R (1978): Social Sources of Delinquency. University of Chicago Press, Chicago.

Kühlhorn, E (1976): Frihetsberövanden och polisen. Brottsförebyggande rådet. Rapport 1976:1.

Kühlhorn et al (1984): Den svenska våldsbrottsligheten. BRÅ Forskning 1984:1.

Kühlhorn, E (1984): Våldet i teoretisk belysning. In: Kühlhorn et al.

Kühlhorn, E & Svensson, B (1982): Crime Prevention. The National Council for Crime Prevention Sweden. Report No 9.

Labovitz, S (1972): Statistical Usage in Sociology. Sacred Cows and Ritual. Sociological Methods & Research.

Landau & Nathan (1983): Selecting Delinquents for Cautioning in the London Metropolitan Area. The British Journal of Criminology.

302

Lander, B (1954): Towards an Understanding of Juvenile Delinquency. Columbia University Press.

Lander, B (1968): Ecological Studies of Delinquency: a Rejoinder to Robert A Gordon. American Sociological Review.

Langbein & Lichtman (1978): Ecological Inference. Sage Publications.

Leiniö, T-L (1983): Invandrare som brottsoffer. In: Tham (ed): Utlänningarna och brottsligheten.

Lenke, L (1973): Den dolda våldsbrottsligheten i Stockholm – en sjukhusrevy. Nordisk tidskrift for kriminalvidenskab.

Lenke, L (1974): Våldsbrottsligheten i Stockholm. Institutionen för kriminologi, Stockholms universitet.

Lenke, L (1975): Våldsbrott och alkohol. Kriminalvetenskapliga inst, Stockholms universitet.

Lenke, L (1978): Risken för våldsbrott i Sverige. Institutionen för sociologi och kriminologi, Stockholms universitet.

Levin & Lindesmith (1937): English Ecology and Criminology of the Past Century. The Journal of Criminal Law and Criminology.

Lilienfeld & Lilienfeld (1980): Foundations of Epidemiology. Oxford University Press, New York.

Lindberg, G (1971): Urbana processer. Studier i social ekologi. CWK Gleerup Bokförlag, Lund.

Lofland, L H (1973): A World of Strangers. Basic Books, Inc., Publishers.

Loftin & Hill (1974): Regional Subculture and Homicide: an Examination of the Gastil-Hackney Thesis. American Sociological Review.

Lorenz, K (1974): Aggression. PAN Norstedts.

Lottier, S (1938): Distribution of Criminal Offenses in Sectional Regions. The Journal of Criminal Law and Criminology.

Lundsgaarde, H P (1977): Murder in Space City. Oxford University Press, New York.

Mannheim, H (1948): Juvenile Delinquency in an English Middletown. Kegan Paul, Trech, Trubner & Co Ltd, London.

Mayby, R I (1981): Police Practices and Crime Rates: a Case Study of a British City. In: Brantingham & Brantingham (reference, see above).

Mayhew, P (1975): Crime as Opportunity. Home Office Research Unit Study No 34.

Mays, J B (1963): Crime and the Social Structure. Faber and Faber Ltd, London.

McClintock, F H (1963): Crimes of Violence. Macmillan, London.

McClintock, F H (1974): Phenomenological and Contextual Analysis of Criminal Violence. In: Collected Studies in Criminological Research. Council of Europe.

McClintock, F H (1978): Criminological Aspects on Family Violence. In: Martin, J P (ed): Violence in the Family.

303

McIver, J P (1981): Criminal Mobility. In: Hakim & Rengert (eds): Crime Spillover. Sage Publications.

McKenzie, R D (1925): The Ecological Approach to the Study of the Human Community. In: Park & Burgess & KcKenzie: The City. The University of Chicago Press, Chicago.

Merry, S E (1981): Defensible Space Undefended. Urban Affairs Quarterly.

Merton, R K (1968): Social Theory and Social Structure. The Free Press, New York.

Messner, S F (1982): Poverty, Inequality, and the Urban Homicide Rate. Criminology.

Michelson, W (1976): Man and his Urban Environment. Addison-Wesley Publishing Company, London.

Morris, T (1958): The Criminal Area. Routledge & Kegan Paul, London.

Morris & Blom-Cooper (1964): A Calender of Murder. Michael Joseph, London.

Mowrer, E R (1938): The Isometric Map as a Technique of Social Research. The American Journal of Sociology.

Nelson, J F (1980): Alternative Measures of Crime. A Comparison of the Uniform Crime Reports and the National Crime Survey in Twenty-Six American Cities. In: Georges-Abeyiw & Harries (eds).

Newman, O (1972): Defensible Space. Architectural Press, London.

Olofsson, B (1971): Vad var det vi sa! Om kriminellt och konformt beteende bland skolpojkar. Utbildningsförlaget.

Overall & Klett (1972): Applied Multivariate Analysis. McGraw-Hill Book Company.

Pahl, R E (1975): Whose City? Penguin Books.

Park, R E (1925): The City: Suggestions for the Investigation of Human Behavior in Urban Environment. In: Park & Burgess & McKenzie: The City. The University of Chicago Press, Chicago.

Park, R E (1961): Human Ecology. In: Theodorson (ed): Studies in Human Ecology. Row, Peterson and Company, New York.

Persson, L G W (1972): Den dolda brottsligheten. Kriminalvetenskapliga inst, Stockholms universitet.

Persson, L G W (1975): Tillfället gör tjuven? Ett etiologiskt dilemma inom kriminologin. Nordisk tidskrift for kriminalvidenskab.

Persson, L G W (1976): Inbrottstjuvar i Stockholm. Svensk Juristtidning.

Persson, L G W (1977): Offer för tillgrepp, skadegörelser och våld. Svensk Juristtidning.

Persson, L G W (1977): Offer för tillgrepp, skadegörelser och våld – en redovisning av 1974 års offerundersökning. SCB Promemorior 1977:7.

304

Persson, L G W (1980): Hidden Criminality – Theoretical and Methodological Problems, Empirical Results. Dept. of Sociology, University of Stockholm.

Peterson et al. (1962): Stabilities of Deviance. A Study of Assaultive and Non-Assaultive Offenders. Journal of Criminal Law, Criminology and Police Science.

Phillips, P D (1980): Characteristics and Typology of the Journey to Crime. In: Georges-Abeyiw & Harries: Crime - a Spatial Perspective.

Pittman & Handy (1964): Patterns in Criminal Aggravated Assault. The Journal of Criminal Law, Criminology and Police Science.

Pittman & Handy (1968): Patterns of Criminal Homicide in Chicago. The Journal of Criminal Law, Criminology and Police Science, Vol 59, No 4.

Porkny, A D (1965): A Comparison of Homicides in Two Cities. The Journal of Criminal Law, Criminology and Police Science.

Porkny, A D (1965): Human Violence: a Comparison of Homicide, Aggravated Assault, Suicide and Attempted Suicide. The Journal of Criminal Law, Criminology and Police Science.

Prus, R C (1978): From Barrooms to Bedrooms: Towards a Theory of Interpersonal Violence. In: Gammon, M A B (ed): Violence in Canada.

Pyle, G F (1976): Spatial and Temporal Aspects of Crime in Cleveland, Ohio. American Behavioral Scientist.

Radzinowicz & King (1979): The Growth of Crime. Penguin Books.

Rhodes & Conly (1981): Crime and Mobility: an Empirical Study. In: Brantingham & Brantingham. See above.

Robinson, S M (1936): Can Delinquency be Measured? Colombia University Press, New York.

Robinson, W S (1950): Ecological Correlations and the Behavior of Individuals. American Sociological Review.

Roes & Nordström: Mord i Sverige 1957 och 1965. Kriminalvetenskapliga inst, Stockholms universitet.

Rojek & Erickson (1982): Delinquent Careers. Criminology.

Rosen & Turner (1967): An Evaluation of the Lander Approach to Ecology of Delinquency. Social Problems, Vol 15, No 2.

Sarnecki, J (1983): Fritid och brottslighet. BRÅ, forskningsenheten, rapport 1983:7.

SCB (1981): Offer för vålds- och egendomsbrott. Statistiska centralbyrån. Levnadsförhållanden 1978. Rapport nr 24.

SCB (1984): Tema invandrare. Statistiska centralbyrån. Levnadsförhållanden. Rapport nr 38.

Schlossman & Sedak (1983): The Chicago Area Project Revised. Crime & Delinquency.

Schmid, C F (1960): Urban Crime Areas. Part I. American Sociological Review.

Schmid, C F (1960): Urban Crime Areas. Part II. American Sociological Review.

Schuessler, K (1962): Components of Variation in City Crime Rates. Social Problems.

Shannon, L (1954): The Spatial Distribution of Criminal Offenses by States. The Journal of Criminal Law and Criminology.

Shaw, C R (1931): The Natural History of a Delinquent Career. The Univesity of Chicago Press.

Shaw & McKay (1949): Rejoinder. American Sociological Review.

Shaw & McKay (1969): Juvenile Delinquency and Urban Areas. The University of Chicago Press, Chicago.

Shelley, L (1980): The Geography of Soviet Criminality. American Sociological Review.

Shoham & Ben-David & Rahav: Interactions in Violence. Human Relations, Vol 27, No 5.

Skogan, W G (1977): The Changing Distribution of Big City Crime. Urban Affairs Quarterly.

Skogan, W G (1979): Crime in Contemporary America. In: Gram & Gurr (eds): Violence in America. Sage Publications, Beverly Hills.

Slatin, G T (1969): Ecological Analysis of Delinquency: Aggregation Effects. American Sociological Review, Vol 34, No 6.

Smith & Parker (1980): Type of Homicide and Variation in Regional Rates. Social Forces.

Somander, L (1979): Dödsfall till följd av våldsbrott i Sverige 1976. Kvinnor i brottssituationen. Universitetet i Linköping.

SOU 1976:72: Unga Lagöverträdare II. Familj, skola och samhälle i belysning av officiella data.

SOU 1977:88: Förtidspensionering.

Suikkila, J (1983): Några synpunkter på alkoholbruk och brottslighet bland ungdomar i Sverige och Finland. In: Tham, H (ed): Utlänningarna och brottsligheten.

Svensson & Danielsson (1978): Lägenhetsbråk. Kriminalvetenskapliga inst, Stockholms universitet.

Sveri, K (1960): Kriminalitet og alder. Almqvist & Wiksell.

Sveri, B (1980): Utlänningars brottslighet. Kriminalvetenskapliga inst, Stockholms universitet.

Taylor & Gottfredson & Brower (1980): The Defensibility of Defensible Space. In: Hirschi & Gottfredson (eds): Understanding Crime. Sage Publications.

Tham, H (1979): Brottslighet och levnadsnivå. Liber förlag.

Thornberry & Farnworth (1982): Social Correlates of Criminal Involvement: Further Evidence on the Relationship between Social Status and Criminal Behavior. American Sociological Review.

Timms, D W G (1971): The Urban Mosaic. Cambridge University Press.

Tittle & Villemez & Smith (1978): The Myth of Social Class and Criminality. American Sociological Review.

Trost & Lewin (1978): Att sambo och gifta sig. SOU 1978:55.

Thålin, M (1984): Fritid och rekreation. In: Erikson & Åberg (eds): Välfärd i förändring.

USK (1984): Stockholmarnas levnadsförhållanden. 1. Områdesvisa jämförelser. Utredningsrapport 1984:3.

Walker et al. (1967): Repeated Violence. Criminal Law Review.

Walldén, M (1975): Individers aktivitetsmönster. Del 3. Tidsanvändning. Byggforskningen, R10:1975.

Walldén, M (1981): Bostadssegregation-socioekonomi-arbetsplatsläge. Rapport R111:1981. Byggforskningsrådet, Stockholm.

Walldén & Modig (1981): Boendesegregation – underlag för diskussion om framtida forskning. Rapport G18:1981. Byggforskningsrådet, Stockholm.

Wallis & Maliphant (1967): Delinquent Areas in the Count of London. British Journal of Criminology.

Watkins, C K (1975): Social Control. Longman.

Weber, M (1966): The City. The Free Press, New York.

Werner, B (1964): Den ekologiska fördelningen av tillgrepp och tillgreppsbrottslingar i Malmö. Nordisk Tidskrift for Kriminalvidenskab.

Werner, B (1971): Socialgruppsfördelning vid självdeklarerad brottslighet. Nordisk Tidskrift for Kriminalvidenskab.

West & Farrington (1977): The Delinquent Way of Life. Heinemann.

Wikström, P-O (1980): Våldsbrott i Gävle. Kriminalvetenskapliga inst, Stockholms universitet.

Wikström, P-O (1981a): Våldsbrottslighetens rumsliga fördelning i Stockholm. Allmän kriminologi, Stockholms universitet.

Wikström, P-O (1981b): Misstänkta och offer för våldsbrott. Allmän kriminologi, Stockholms universitet.

Wikström, P-O (1982): Brottsligheten i stadsmiljön. En litteraturstudie. Kriminalvetenskapliga inst, Stockholms universitet.

Wikström, P-O (1983a): Kan misshandel förebyggas? BRÅ-apropå nr 2.

Wikström, P-O (1983b): Social klass och brottslighet. BRÅ-apropå nr 3.

Wikström, P-O (1983c): Grannskap och brottslingskoncentration. BRÅ-apropå nr 6.

Wikström, P-O (1984): Brott och brottsmobilitet. BRÅ-apropå nr 1.

Wikström, P-O (1985a): Storstadskriminalitet. Brottsförebyggande rådet. (Forthcoming)

Wikström, P-O (1985b): Patterns of Criminality in a Birth Cohort. Project Metropolitan Research Report. (Forthcoming)

Wilson, S (1980): Vandalism and "Defensible Space" on London Housing Estates. In: Clarke & Mayhew (eds): Designing out Crime. Home Office Research Unit Publications.

Wolfgang, M (1958): Patterns in Criminal Homicide. University of Philadelphia, Philadelphia.

Wolfgang et al. (1972): Delinquency in a Birth Cohort. The University of Chicago Press.

Wolfgang & Ferracuti (1982): The Subculture of Violence. Sage Publications.

Voss & Hepburn (1968): Patterns in Criminal Homicide in Chicago. The Journal of Criminal Law, Criminology and Police Science.

Yablonsky, L (1968): The Delinquent Gang as a Near-Group. In: Rubington & Weinberg (eds): Deviance.

Zorbaugh, H W (1961): The Natural Areas of the City. In: Theodorson (ed): Studies in Human Ecology. Row, Peterson and Company, New York.

Åkerström, M (1983): Crooks and Squares. Studentlitteratur. Lunds universitet.

Reports published in English by the NCCP

No 1   Non-Institutional Treatment – a preliminary evaluation of the Sundsvall experiment

No 2   General Deterrence
A conference on current research and standpoints June 2–4, 1975

No 3   Labeling Theory
– a critical examination

No 4   Deprivation of Freedom and the Police – an evaluation of the temporary custody act

No 5   A New Penal System
Ideas and Proposals

No 6   Police and the Social Order –
Contemporary Research Perspectives

No 7   Non-Institutional Treatment and Rehabilitation
An evaluation of a Swedish correctional experiment. Shortened version

No 8   Computer Techonology and Computer Crime

No 9   Crime Prevention

No 10   Drug Criminality and Drug Abuse in Sweden 1969 – 1981

No 11   Current Swedish Legislation on Narcotics and Psychotropic Substances

No 12   Crime and Criminal Policy in Sweden

No 13   The Swedish Penal Code

No 14   Operation Identification – a way to prevent burglaries?